# AMC'S BEST DAY HIKES IN
# THE BERKSHIRES

Four-season Guide to 50 of the Best Trails
in Western Massachusetts

RENÉ LAUBACH

Appalachian Mountain Club Books
Boston, Massachusetts

The AMC is a non-profit organization and sales of AMC books fund our mission of protecting the Northeast outdoors. If you appreciate our efforts and would like to make a donation to the AMC, contact us at Appalachian Mountain Club, 5 Joy Street, Boston, MA 02108.

http://www.outdoors.org/publications/books/

Front cover photograph © Nancie Battaglia
Back cover photographs: left and right © Eliot Cohen, middle © Michael P. Gadomski
All interior photographs © René Laubach
Maps by Ken Dumas

Distributed by The Globe Pequot Press, Guilford, Conn.

**Library of Congress Cataloging-in-Publication Data**
Laubach, René.
   AMC's best day hikes in the Berkshires: four-season guide to 50 of the best trails in Western Massachusetts / René Laubach.
      p. cm.
   Includes index.
   ISBN 978-1-934028-21-6 (alk. paper)
   1. Hiking—Massachusetts—Berkshire Hills—Guidebooks. 2. Walking—Massachusetts—Berkshire Hills—Guidebooks. 3. Berkshire Hills (Mass.)—Guidebooks. I. Appalachian Mountain Club. II. Title. III. Title: Best day hikes in the Berkshires.

   GV199.42.M42B474 2009
   796.5109744'1—dc22

                              2008045420

The paper used in this publication meets the minimum requirements of the American National Standard for Information Sciences-Permanence of Paper for Printed Library Materials, ANSI Z39.48-1984. ∞

Outdoor recreation activities by their very nature are potentially hazardous. This book is not a substitute for good personal judgment and training in outdoor skills. Due to changes in conditions, use of the information in this book is at the sole risk of the user. The author and the Appalachian Mountain Club assume no liability for accidents happening to, or injuries sustained by, readers who engage in the activities described in this book.

Printed in the United States of America.
Printed on paper that contains 30 percent post-consumer recycled fiber, using soy-based inks.

10 9 8 7 6 5 4 3 2 1                    09 10 11 12 13 14 15 16

This book is dedicated to my good friend Don Reid.

And to all those who have worked so diligently to conserve, protect, and steward the Berkshire environment for today and for the future.

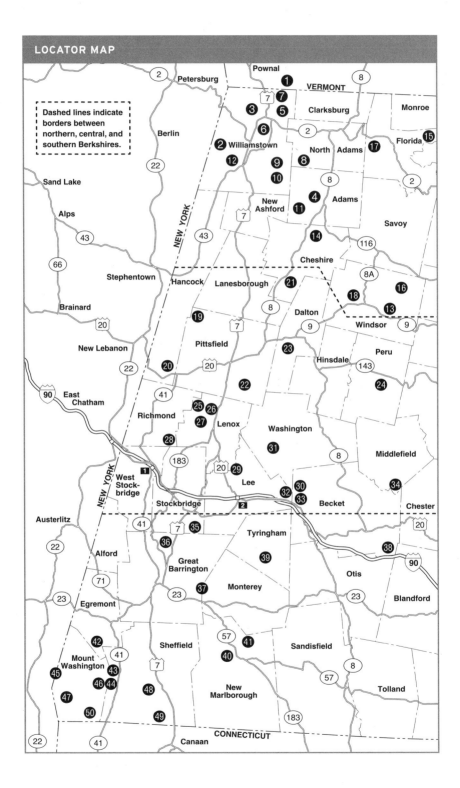

## LOCATOR MAP

Dashed lines indicate borders between northern, central, and southern Berkshires.

# CONTENTS

## SECTION 1: NORTHERN BERKSHIRES

## NATURE ESSAYS

# AT-A-GLANCE TRIP PLANNER

| # | Trip | Page | Location (Town) | Rating | Distance and Elevation Gain |
|---|------|------|-----------------|--------|------------------------------|
| | **NORTHERN BERKSHIRES** | | | | |
| 1 | The Dome | 2 | Pownal, VT | Moderate-Difficult | 5.2 mi, 1,715 ft |
| 2 | Berlin Mountain | 6 | Williamstown; Berlin, NY | Difficult | 4.7 mi, 1,545 ft |
| 3 | Hopkins Memorial Forest and Taconic Crest Trail | 13 | Williamstown; Petersburg, NY; Pownal, VT | Difficult | 10.4 mi, 1,650 ft |
| 4 | Mount Greylock State Reservation, East Side–Cheshire Harbor/Gould Trails | 18 | Adams | Difficult | 6.6 mi, 1,930 ft |
| 5 | Pine Cobble and East Mountain | 23 | Williamstown, Clarksburg | Moderate-Difficult | 4.2 mi, 1,340 ft |
| 6 | Stone Hill | 27 | Williamstown | Easy | 2.3 mi, 350 ft |
| 7 | Mountain Meadow Preserve | 32 | Williamstown | Moderate | 4.0 mi, 470 ft |
| 8 | Mount Greylock and Ragged Mountain | 37 | North Adams, Adams | Difficult | 8.8 mi, 2,140 ft |
| 9 | Greylock Range Circuit | 42 | Williamstown, Adams, North Adams | Difficult | 12.7 mi, 2,390 ft |
| 10 | Hopper Trail to Mount Greylock Summit | 48 | Williamstown, Adams | Difficult | 8.5 mi, 2,390 ft |

| Estimated Time | Fee | Good for Kids | Dogs Allowed | X-C Skiing | Snow-Shoeing | Trip Highlights |
|---|---|---|---|---|---|---|
| 3.5 hrs | | | 🐕 | | 📍📍 | scenic summit, boggy wetlands |
| 3–3.5 hrs | | | 🐕 | | 📍📍 | views from summit |
| 6 hrs | | | 🐕 | | 📍📍 | Taconic ridgeline vistas |
| 4.5–5 hrs | | | 🐕 | | 📍📍 | state's highest summit |
| 2.5–3 hrs | | | 🐕 | | 📍📍 | stunning views |
| 1.5 hrs | | 🚶 | 🐕 | 🎿 | 📍📍 | pastoral views, massive hardwoods |
| 2.5 hrs | | 🚶 | 🐕 | | 📍📍 | wildflower meadow and panoramic views |
| 5–6 hrs | | | 🐕 | 🎿 | 📍📍 | magnificent view of Greylock's east face |
| 8 hrs | | | 🐕 | | | four summits, the best vista in Massachusetts |
| 6 hrs | | | 🐕 | | 📍📍 | a scenic route to boreal forest and Greylock summit |

| Estimated Time | Fee | Good for Kids | Dogs Allowed | X-C Skiing | Snow-Shoeing | Trip Highlights |
|---|---|---|---|---|---|---|
| 6-7 hrs | | | ✓ | | ✓ | a flower-filled meadow with wonderful views, boreal bog |
| 2 hrs | | ✓ | ✓ | ✓ | ✓ | meadows with bucolic mountain vistas |
| 3-4 hrs | $ | ✓ | ✓ | ✓ | ✓ | mixed high-elevation woodlands |
| 4.5 hrs | | ✓ | ✓ | ✓ | ✓ | scenic lakeside, Hoosic River wetlands |
| 4 hrs | | | ✓ | | ✓ | old growth and roaring brook |
| 2 hrs | $ | ✓ | ✓ | ✓ | ✓ | a gushing torrent in a box, fairyland forest |
| 1.5-2 hrs | | ✓ | ✓ | | ✓ | fabulous views, migrating hawks in fall |
| 2-2.5 hrs | | ✓ | ✓ | ✓ | ✓ | unusual winter bird visitors, evergreen groves |
| 4-4.5 hrs | $ | | ✓ | | ✓ | a trifecta of water attractions |
| 3-4 hrs | | ✓ | ✓ | | ✓ | a sojourn back in time |
| 3.5 hrs | | ✓ | ✓ | ✓ | ✓ | wildlife-rich wetlands |
| 1.5 hrs | $ | ✓ | | ✓ | ✓ | excellent birding |
| 3.5 hrs | | ✓ | ✓ | ✓ | ✓ | attractive northern hardwoods, evergreen stands, views of Greylock |

| Estimated Time | Fee | Good for Kids | Dogs Allowed | X-C Skiing | Snow-Shoeing | Trip Highlights |
|---|---|---|---|---|---|---|
| 2 hrs | | ✓ | ✓ | ✓ | ✓ | wild woodlands |
| 1 hr | $ | ✓ | | | ✓ | an active and easily observed beaver colony |
| 2 hrs | $ | | | | ✓ | fine summit views |
| 2.5–3 hrs | | ✓ | ✓ | ✓ | ✓ | interesting local history, splendid views |
| 1.5–2 hrs | | ✓ | ✓ | ✓ | ✓ | attractive woodland and a pleasing lookout |
| 2.5 hrs | | | ✓ | | ✓ | a cascading brook and massive trees |
| 4 hrs | | ✓ | ✓ | | ✓ | serene pond ringed by mountain laurel |
| 2 hrs | | ✓ | ✓ | | ✓ | intimate experience with a freshwater marsh |
| 1.5 hrs | | ✓ | ✓ | ✓ | ✓ | truck-sized glacial boulders |
| 2 hrs | | ✓ | ✓ | | ✓ | serene and scenic Upper Goose Pond |
| 2–3 hrs | | ✓ | ✓ | ✓ | ✓ | massive keystone arch bridges spanning the wild Westfield River |
| | | | | | | |
| 1.5 hrs | | ✓ | ✓ | | ✓ | magical rocky cleft shaded by ancient evergreens |
| 2 hrs | | | ✓ | | | picturesque summit of jagged quartzite boulders with wonderful views |

| Estimated Time | Fee | Good for Kids | Dogs Allowed | X-C Skiing | Snow-Shoeing | Trip Highlights |
|---|---|---|---|---|---|---|
| 1.5–2 hrs | | ✓ | ✓ | | ✓ | scenic pond and splendid long views |
| 1.5–2 hrs | | ✓ | ✓ | ✓ | ✓ | Former granite quarry artifacts |
| 1.5 hrs | | ✓ | ✓ | ✓ | ✓ | bucolic pastures, lovely views |
| 1.5 hrs | | ✓ | ✓ | ✓ | ✓ | towering trees and remnants of early colonial settlement |
| 1 hr | | ✓ | ✓ | ✓ | ✓ | pleasant loop through nice mountain laurel display |
| 1.5 hrs | | ✓ | ✓ | ✓ | ✓ | scenic meadows, views of mountain ridges |
| 4.5 hrs | | | ✓ | | ✓ | spectacular views from the southern Taconics |
| 2.5–3 hrs | | | ✓ | | ✓ | Guilder Pond laurel bloom, picturesque mountain summit |
| 1.5 hrs | | | ✓ | | ✓ | most spectacular waterfall in Massachusetts |
| 4 hrs | | | ✓ | | ✓ | wonderful series of waterfalls, fabulous ridge-top views |
| 3–3.5 hrs | | ✓ | ✓ | | ✓ | an open summit with tri-state vistas |
| 1.5 hrs | $ | ✓ | | ✓ | ✓ | rolling hay meadows with magnificent vistas |
| 2–2.5 hrs | $ | ✓ | | | ✓ | biologically rich, panoramic view |
| 3–3.5 hrs | | | ✓ | | | a charming chasm with roaring brook, stunning mountaintop views |

# INTRODUCTION

**WALKING IS NATURAL. MOST OF US DO IT EASILY, AND WITH LITTLE THOUGHT.**
Yet there is a distinct difference between merely placing one foot in front of the
other and hiking. Walking is merely locomotion; it is how we get from point
A to point B (although increasingly less so at this moment in history). Hiking
is walking with a purpose; it generally implies walking on a dirt path through
a natural or naturalized environment. For me, as for many others, hiking is
exercise, therapy, meditation, discovery, education, and joy. The end point,
be it a lofty summit, an enchanting waterfall, a particularly massive tree, or a
cascading brook, draws me to the trailhead. Yet it is the soothing rhythm of
placing one foot in front of the other and in essence being one with nature that
makes it so rewarding.

After living in the Berkshires and working in the environmental field for
nearly 25 years, I thought I knew the area well. In working on this project, I
was surprised to learn that there were many wonderful places and trails I had
little or no knowledge of. This project has therefore enabled me to stretch my
legs, as it were, and embark on a pilgrimage of discovery. A significant number
of hikes included in this guide were admittedly new to me, and I am grateful
for having had the opportunity to experience them. It is truly amazing how
many exceptionally beautiful and biologically rich properties there are.

The Berkshires are for the most part rather settled, so it may surprise some to learn that there remain wild, untamed pockets of woodland and wetland where one can feel far from it all. Yet there is enough of a veneer of civilization even in the wildest locations to give one comfort. So in some ways the Berkshires offer the hiker the best of two worlds. One world provides security, and the other provides the adventure and connection to nature that we all need. I hope you enjoy these excursions as much as I have.

I ask but one thing of you: Please do your part to protect these very special places. We are the beneficiaries of these gifts from those who came before us. These were people who took the long view. Let us join them in ensuring that these places remain for future generations to enjoy and learn from as well.

# ACKNOWLEDGMENTS

**THANK YOU TO HEATHER STEPHENSON,** publisher of *AMC Outdoors* and AMC Books, for considering me for this project. I've also enjoyed working with Dan Eisner, editor for AMC Books, whose patience and flexibility have been greatly appreciated. Thanks also to production manager Athena Lakri. Working with the AMC is always a pleasure.

There are many individuals in the Berkshires from whom I have learned much over the years. I thank Thomas F. Tyning, Bernard Drew, Pamela Weatherbee, Joseph Strauch, and Edward Kirby for their tutelage. I have drawn from their expertise in various subjects and am grateful to them. A debt of gratitude is also owed to area colleagues and friends for alerting me to hiking destinations that I had not previously been aware of.

A significant number of individuals from nonprofit conservation organizations and state government agencies reviewed drafts of narratives for hikes on properties under their management or for which they have particular knowledge. Collectively they constructively pointed out both errors of commission and omission. This group of reviewers included Tad Ames, President, Berkshire Natural Resources Council; Henry W. Art, Director of the Williams College Center for Environmental Studies; Si Balch, Director of Forest Stewardship, New England Forestry Foundation; Rebecca Barnes, West Region Trail Coordinator, Massachusetts Department of Conservation and Recreation

(DCR); Jim Caffrey, Manager, Notchview Reservation; Tammis Coffin, Education & Outreach Coordinator, Berkshires Region, The Trustees of Reservations (TTOR); Sean Cowhig, The Trustees of Reservations; Leslie Reed-Evans, Executive Director of Williamstown Rural Lands Foundation; Alec Gillman, Visitor Services Supervisor, Mount Greylock State Reservation; Tony Gola, Western District Game Biologist, Massachusetts Division of Fisheries and Wildlife; Drew Jones, Manager, Hopkins Memorial Forest; Scott Lewis, Director, Williams Outing Club; Steve McMahon, Western Region Director, The Trustees of Reservations; Robert S. Mellace, West Region Director, DCR; David Pierce, Friends of the Keystone Arches; Nicholas M. Ratcliffe, U.S. Geological Service; Ole Retlev, Innkeeper, Field Farm Reservation; Hilary Russell, formerly of Berkshire School; Ann C. Smith, Secretary, Becket Land Trust; Jim Wells, Berkshire County Representative, Appalachian Mountain Club; Rene Wendell, Manager, Bartholomew's Cobble Reservation; and Ruth Wheeler, Member, Kennedy Park Committee. Although I am very grateful to all these folks for their time and efforts, any errors that remain are my sole responsibility.

My companion on many of these hikes throughout the years has been my wife, Christyna M. Laubach. Chris's assistance and encouragement has made this journey that much more enjoyable. I remain indebted to her.

Finally, this book would not have been possible were it not for all the hardworking people who construct and maintain the wonderful system of trails that we are so fortunate to have in the Berkshires. Thank you!

—René Laubach

# HOW TO USE THIS BOOK

**YOU MAY WISH TO BEGIN BY REFERRING TO THE** At-a-Glance Trip Planner. Then be sure to review the trip description before you lace up your boots. Each excursion includes the basics—location, rating, distance, elevation gain, approximate time, and pertinent maps. Ratings are based on the author's perceptions and experience, and are therefore subjective. You may rate the hike easier or more difficult than I did. Likewise, approximate time is relative. Here it is based on an average walking pace of 1.5 to 2.0 miles per hour. That does not include time for long breaks, although brief water stops and the like are factored in. It is generally a good idea to allow extra time in case you become lost or suffer injury. While no one plans to get lost or injured, give yourself some breathing room. And remember the old axiom, "A group moves only as fast as its slowest member."

The trip's elevation gain refers to *simple* elevation gain—the difference between the hike's lowest and highest points. *Total* elevation gain, in contrast, is a cumulative accounting of every dip and rise along a route. A hike's total elevation gain is often greater than the simple elevation gain.

A hike summary follows the basics and is intended to give you a snapshot of the excursion, stressing the outstanding natural or cultural features to look forward to.

The Directions section steers you to the trailhead from a major intersection in the area. Some hikes include directions from more than one compass point, but in general a road atlas is necessary to reach the starting point for the driving directions, especially if you are new to the area or otherwise unfamiliar with it.

The heart of each entry is the Trail Description—references to trail locations, signage, and landmarks to keep you on the right path. Interwoven with the route-finding information in this narrative are tidbits about the fascinating flora, fauna, and human history of the area, and a little geology. I've tried to draw attention to landmarks, objects, and phenomena that beg examination and invite discovery. You could cover the distances faster than what is proposed in this guide, but slow down a bit and smell the azaleas. The journey, after all, is as important as the destination.

Use the book's trail maps as a guide, but be sure to bring along more detailed topographical maps, available from outdoor outfitters and in some instances the Internet, especially for longer, elevation-rich excursions. The Appalachian Mountain Club publishes a trail map that includes the northern Berkshires and southwestern Massachusetts. You will find many of the trails covered in this book on those maps. And don't leave home without a compass. Map and compass go hand in hand.

Each trip ends with a More Information section about the property that you will be exploring, including access times and fees, if any; the property's rules and regulations; and contact information for the organizations and agencies that own and/or maintain the lands and trails on which you will be walking.

In the end, the main reason for this guide is my ardent wish that you enjoy and appreciate these special places and take steps to ensure their continued healthy existence. So please go out and explore!

# TRIP PLANNING AND SAFETY

**AN OUNCE OF PREVENTION IS WORTH A POUND OF CURE**—an old adage to be sure, but so true. Although there is no actual wilderness in the Berkshires, there are remote locations miles from the nearest paved and well-traveled road. So there are a few very important items you should have with you each time you set out. You may want to keep these in your daypack so that you are always ready to go. The following are the basics:

- First-aid kit
- Compass and map (and the knowledge to use them in conjunction)
- Extra clothing (in case of unexpected inclement weather)
- Pocketknife or multitool
- Flashlight or headlamp (in case you are caught out after dark)
- Whistle (for use in emergencies)
- Waterproof matches (coated with wax and kept in a jar)
- Water (two liters per person per day)
- High-energy food bars or other nutritious munchies
- This guide

You may also want to bring a cell phone, although there is a debate about that. Realize that you will be unable to receive a sufficiently strong signal in many areas due to the distance from the nearest tower as well as irregularities in the terrain. Important: Do not depend on the phone. Although cell phones have saved people in serious trouble, they may also lull people into a false sense of security. I myself carry a cell phone, but I don't use it on the trail; in fact I keep it turned off. Given its small size and weight, I regard it as just another item that may help ensure my safety and well-being at some point, but I set out assuming that it will not work.

If you can enjoy the outdoors with a fellow hiker, do so. If you must hike alone or prefer to do so, as many do, be sure to write a note or leave word with someone regarding your destination and expected time of return.

Most important, dress appropriately. I swear by synthetic apparel. Such clothing dries much faster than cotton if you've been unlucky enough to be caught in a downpour. Cotton clothing also wicks heat away from your body, making you more prone to hypothermia. Dress for the conditions, and bring gear for inclement weather.

Speaking of weather, check the forecast in advance of your trip. If you are planning a ridge or summit hike, especially in summer, get an early start so as to be off the ridgeline before the often-predictable afternoon thunderstorms build up.

Slippery rocks and roots are major safety hazards; watch your footing. Your footwear should be sturdy, and the soles should have good traction. In rough terrain, you may want to consider shoes that cover and protect your ankles.

Wild animals should not be a cause for alarm. The population of bears in the region has grown steadily, but these are retiring creatures that want as little to do with you as you want with them, so simply give them wide berth if you are fortunate enough to actually see one during your hike. Invariably they will smell or hear you long before you ever see them.

A number of much smaller creatures cause discomfort or annoyance; these include blackflies in May, deerflies in June and July, and mosquitoes during most of the warm months. On all but the hottest days I prefer wearing long sleeves, long pants, and a cap rather than applying insect repellent, but sometimes a repellent is the only relief. While the aforementioned insects are mostly an annoyance, deer ticks, or more properly black-legged ticks, may transmit serious diseases, including the now well-known Lyme disease. Stay on the trail, tuck your pants into your socks, apply repellent, and do a tick check after each hike. And wearing light-colored clothing makes it easier to spot a tick crawling up your pant leg or on your sleeve.

Finally, be sure to use sunscreen. Harmful ultraviolet rays can cause damage even on overcast days.

# LEAVE NO TRACE

**THE APPALACHIAN MOUNTAIN CLUB** is a national educational partner of Leave No Trace, a nonprofit organization dedicated to promoting and inspiring responsible outdoor recreation through education, research, and partnerships. The Leave No Trace Pro-  gram seeks to develop wildland ethics—ways in which people think and act in the outdoors to minimize their impacts on the areas they visit and to protect our natural resources for future enjoyment. Leave No Trace unites four federal land management agencies—the U.S. Forest Service, National Park Service, Bureau of Land Management, and U.S. Fish and Wildlife Service—with manufacturers, outdoor retailers, user groups, educators, organizations such as the AMC and the National Outdoor Leadership School (NOLS), and individuals.

The Leave No Trace ethic is guided by these seven principles:

- Plan ahead and prepare
- Travel and camp on durable surfaces
- Dispose of waste properly
- Leave what you find
- Minimize campfire impacts
- Respect wildlife
- Be considerate of other visitors

The AMC has joined NOLS—a recognized leader in wilderness education and a founding partner of Leave No Trace—as a national provider of the Leave No Trace Master Educator course. The AMC offers this five-day course, designed especially for outdoor professionals and land managers, as well as the shorter two-day Leave No Trace Trainer course, at locations throughout the Northeast.

For Leave No Trace information and materials, contact Leave No Trace Center for Outdoor Ethics, P.O. Box 997, Boulder, CO 80306; toll free: 800-332-4100, or locally, 303-442-8222; fax: 303-442-8217; www.lnt.org.

# 1

# NORTHERN BERKSHIRES

**THE NORTHERN BERKSHIRES COMPRISE SOME OF THE HIGHEST** and most remote lands in the county. The area boasts the only true boreal forest in Massachusetts, the only summits above 3,000 feet elevation, craggy outcrops yielding splendid vistas, and sphagnum-filled fairy-tale bog lands. Eighteen of the excursions in this guide are located in this section. Mount Greylock State Reservation is the centerpiece and includes a sizable stretch of the Appalachian Trail as well as miles of blue-blazed side trails. This section beckons the hiker with many fine trails ranging in difficulty from easy to rugged.

Hikes located in this northern section include the Hopkins Memorial Forest, along the spine of the Taconic Range (Trip 3); Berlin Mountain, along the border with New York (Trip 2); the trail-rich Greylock Range, boasting the state's loftiest peak (Trips 4, 8, 9, and 10); Spruce Hill, in the Hoosac Range east of the marble valley (Trip 17); and the southernmost extension of Vermont's Green Mountains, including The Dome (Trip 1) and Pine Cobble and East Mountain (Trip 5). This section contains the longest, most arduous hikes, but also one of universal access—a northern portion of the Ashuwillticook Rail Trail (Trip 14)—and a stroll through bucolic Field Farm (Trip 12).

## TRIP 1
## THE DOME

**Location:** Pownal, VT
**Rating:** Moderate–Difficult
**Distance:** 5.2 miles
**Elevation Gain:** 1,715 feet
**Estimated Time:** 3.5 hours
**Maps:** AMC Massachusetts Trail Map #1: A3; USGS North Adams; USGS Pownal, VT

**Quite unlike any other mountaintop in the area, The Dome's rounded quartzite summit, boggy wetlands, and spruce-fir forest are tantalizingly reminiscent of northern New England or Canada.**

### DIRECTIONS
From the intersection of Routes 7 and 2 at the rotary in Williamstown, follow Route 7 north for 1.5 miles to Sand Springs Road. Turn right onto Sand Springs and follow it for approximately 0.2 mile, bearing left at the three-way intersection. After driving 0.25 mile more, you will reach White Oaks Road. Bear left and drive 1.1 miles to a wide gravel pull-off on the right approximately 0.3 mile north of the Massachusetts–Vermont border (where the pavement ends). There is space for approximately six vehicles on the right, where the sign reads Dome Trail Parking.

### TRAIL DESCRIPTION
Following an old roadway that bears right, go past a sign for Dome Trail on a tree with a rectangular red blaze and step over a cable. The rocky road leads easily and steadily uphill under sugar maple, ash, several species of birches, and towering white pines. After oaks appear, enter a small clearing filled with goldenrod, a few black-eyed Susans, and Saint-John's-wort, whose starry yellow flowers appear in summer. You'll soon reach an old road on the right blocked by earth. American beech sprouts form a thick sapling layer below the oaks and sugar maples, and a rock wall runs adjacent to the old road. You'll encounter a number of detours or reroutes made by all-terrain vehicles along the trail.

As the slope steepens somewhat, bear left in an arc past wood betony plants and twining hog peanut, a legume with three leaflets that looks a bit like poison ivy. Level out and continue past another blocked road. The trail narrows to a

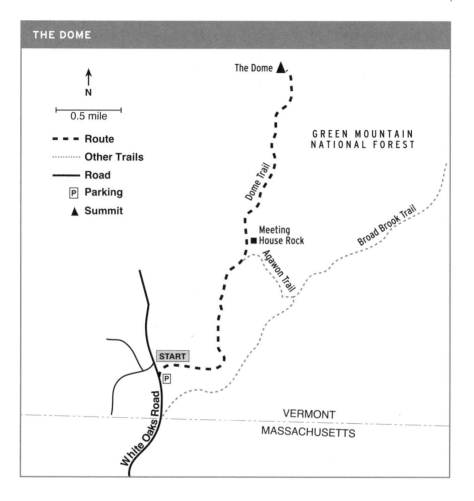

THE DOME

The Dome ▲

↑
N

|—— 0.5 mile ——|

- - - Route

·········· Other Trails

—— Road

P Parking

▲ Summit

GREEN MOUNTAIN
NATIONAL FOREST

Dome Trail

Broad Brook Trail

Meeting
House Rock

Agawon Trail

START

P

White Oaks Road

VERMONT

MASSACHUSETTS

single rocky track lined with quartzite bedrock and ascends gently. Chunks of milky white quartz also protrude. Water and other impurities color the otherwise clear quartz. In summer, listen for the hauntingly beautiful flutelike song of Vermont's state bird, the hermit thrush. It is a fairly common breeder along the route from here on. Note the dead American chestnut sprouts killed back by the blight when they attain about 5 inches in diameter. But live root sprouts with long, toothed leaves remain as an identifier. This forest is markedly drier than what you began walking through and what lies ahead. Knee-high sassafras saplings, with mitten-shaped leaves, lowbush blueberry, huckleberry, mountain azalea, and bracken fern all hint at the dry, acidic nature of the soils under the oaks of this young forest.

The path becomes rutted, climbs moderately, and soon gets rougher. Quartzite bedrock, fractured at sharp angles, paves the treadway. Oaks are varied as

**Meeting House Rock, a monolithic quartzite boulder, marks the halfway point en route to the summit of the Dome.**

well as numerous. Besides red and white oaks (white oaks have rounded lobes), chestnut oak (with wavy leaf margins) is also present on this sunny south-facing slope. This is indeed a wood with southern affinities. The thin soil is ocher—high in limonite, a low-grade iron ore. After walking 1.2 miles, you will find the yellow-blazed Agawon Trail, which joins from the right. It is a steep downhill trail that serves as a 0.7-mile-long connector to Broad Brook Trail, which in turn leads north to the Appalachian Trail or south back to very near where you parked. Note, however, that this 1.3-miles-longer route requires fording a substantial, high-flow brook without the aid of a bridge or stones.

Bear left and continue on the Dome Trail past a monolithic and rounded light gray quartzite boulder known as Meeting House Rock halfway to the summit. When you reach another reroute, remain on the older path. Berry bushes, azaleas, some low sheep laurel, shadbush or juneberry, bilberry, and viburnum form a dense vegetative cover. Tiny cow-wheat plants with lance-shaped leaves and light yellow blossoms, as well as wintergreen and trailing arbutus, line the path through these fairly dry and open oak/red maple woods. After the grade eases, note the first small red spruce and then hobblebush shrubs, with big heart-shaped, paired leaves thriving under a taller deciduous canopy.

Arrive at a major intersection where a long-abandoned truck lies just ahead. Dome Trail, 1.7 miles from the trailhead here, turns right and continues to follow red blazes. The road splits again almost immediately. Continue straight on the main dirt road. At another junction, head straight uphill rather than level and to the left. A luxuriant layer of yellow-green hay-scented ferns graces the level woodland floor—the first in a series of benches interspersed between steeper climbs. This northern hardwood forest is very different from what you recently walked through. Yellow birches, American beeches (many succumbing to beech bark disease), black cherries (note the black scaly bark likened by some to burnt potato chips), and red maples shade thicket-producing hobblebushes.

Some decaying logs are entirely encased in a thick mat of mosses that serve as nurseries for yellow birch seedlings. Patches of sphagnum moss fill wet spots trailside, and a small plant with shiny dark green leaves—called goldthread because of its orange roots—thrives in cool, moist woodland such as this. Walk on stones through a low boggy area colonized by cinnamon fern and red spruces. Hobblebushes produce doilies of showy white blossoms in May in this sunlit space. Climb easily, bearing left. Stride over tilted quartzite bedrock on an increasing gradient. A jutting, benchlike outcrop is a fine spot for a rest. Canada mayflower and clintonia bloom in spring along the margins. The sweet perfume of balsam fir fills the air—reason enough for me to make the effort.

Begin a steep climb over a treadway cushioned by conifer needle duff. Tiny dogwoods of the heights—bunchberries—enliven the walk. As you zigzag around and over the crest of a ledge outcrop, you enter the true boreal forest zone—a fairy-tale forest of closely spaced pole-sized red spruce and balsam fir. The trail corridor permits light to reach the ground along a thin ribbon, and here lowbush blueberries find a niche. Little grows in the stifling shade of the evergreens. Soggy, boggy spots are interspersed between the erosion-resistant quartzite outcrops. Silvery green reindeer lichen is brittle when desiccated, but it softens right up after a soaking rain. You will see it where you level out in a bedrock opening surrounded by 20- to 25-foot-high spruces. It's easy to imagine that you are standing in northern New England or perhaps even on the Canadian Shield.

Various hardy shrubs and small trees ring the summit of the Dome, at 2,748 feet above sea level. Mountain holly (with small elliptical, waxy leaves), huckleberry, and a few versatile red maples (at home in swamps or dry earth) maintain a hardscrabble existence. The red blazes end on the rounded dome summit at 2.6 miles from the trailhead; no trail has been cut farther into the forest. This rock is light gray and stained attractively with rusty hues. A tenacious little fir has colonized one crevice. Nearby, a section of rock has cleaved, creating a shallow basin that fills with rainwater and serves as bird-bath and watering hole.

Six-inch-long dark-eyed juncos—gray-and-white members of the sparrow family—trill from spruce tops in summer but nest on the ground, while yellow-rumped warblers and golden-crowned kinglets also call the boreal zone home. I was excited to find a pile of winter moose droppings just a few feet into the vegetation on a July visit (it doesn't take much to excite me). If luck or good planning rewards you, you may arrive on a clear day and enjoy the limited views of Pine Cobble due south, with the Greylock Range beyond and the Taconic Range to the southwest. The spruces are rapidly diminishing the viewshed, but no matter—this is a unique and gorgeous summit even without any views at all. You'll want to spend some quality time up here. When you are ready to start back, retrace your steps down the mountain, being sure to turn left at the old truck.

## MORE INFORMATION

Trail open dawn to dusk. Access is free. Green Mountain National Forest, 231 North Main Street, Rutland, VT 05701; 802-747-6700; http://www.fs.fed.us/r9/forests/greenmountain/htm/greenmountain/g_home.htm. The trail is maintained by the Williams Outing Club, 39 Chapin Hall Drive, Williamstown, MA 01267; 413-597-2317; http://wso.williams.edu/orgs/woc/.

## TRIP 2
## BERLIN MOUNTAIN

**Location:** Williamstown; Berlin, NY
**Rating:** Difficult
**Distance:** 4.7 miles
**Elevation Gain:** 1,545 feet
**Estimated Time:** 3.0–3.5 hours
**Maps:** AMC Massachusetts Trail Map #1: C1; USGS Berlin, NY

**Views of Mount Greylock from Berlin Mountain's flat summit are particularly pleasing, and an enchanting little waterfall adds to your enjoyment at the end of the hike.**

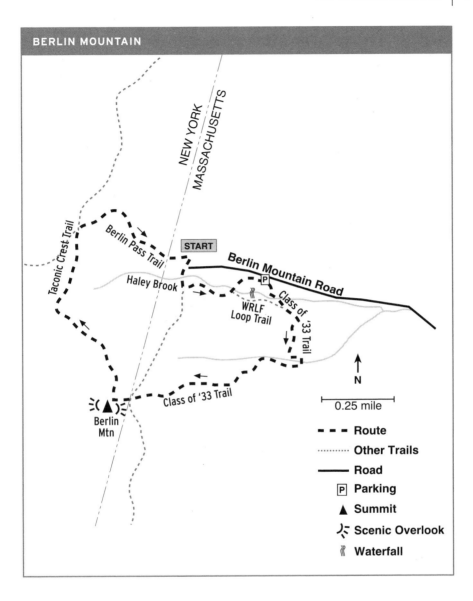

**BERLIN MOUNTAIN**

## DIRECTIONS

Traveling north on Route 7 heading toward Williamstown, watch for the intersection south of Williamstown Center. Turning left (leaving Route 7), take Route 2 west for 0.3 mile to Torrey Woods Road on the left. Follow Torrey Woods Road (where the pavement ends, it becomes Berlin Mountain Road after approximately 0.5 mile) for 2.1 miles to a small gravel parking area on the left with space for three or four vehicles.

## TRAIL DESCRIPTION

A wooden sign at the parking area reads "Class of '33 Trail and WRLF Loop Trail 100 Yards East." Williams College Outing Club students cut the sign in 1933, and WRLF stands for Williamstown Rural Lands Foundation. Walk back down the gravel road that you just drove in on for approximately 300 feet and look for a different sign on a large oak tree on the right. Enter an attractive forest of white and yellow birches, red spruce, red maple, and striped maple, following blue blazes and descending easily. The trees in this forest are mostly young. Oaks and American beech soon join in. As the downhill walking becomes steeper, you'll hear the soothing sounds of Haley Brook, a clear, fast-flowing stream that, according to an interpretive sign, is home to native brook trout and the rare Appalachian brook crayfish.

Step across it on stones and look up to your right where water descends over mossy bedrock—a pretty spot. Advance under northern hardwoods. At a Y intersection, take either fork, as the paths soon rejoin, and arrive at a signed intersection. Turn left to remain on the initially level Class of '33 Trail. (The WRLF Loop Trail turns right.) The abundance of pole-sized timber indicates fairly recent harvesting, and the remnants of former logging roads are still visible. An old yellow birch that avoided the saw holds forth on the left. Soon the grade increases as you follow a trenchlike former skid road under the deciduous canopy, with scattered hemlocks and spruces. Some of the hemlocks are considerably older than the hardwoods—beech, birch, and oak. Most of the beeches suffer from the bark disease that is killing beech trees throughout the region.

For a change of pace, bear left and drop down rather abruptly. Watch and listen for the antics of hyperactive red squirrels in this mixed forest. As you level out among mature yellow birches, note the overturned privy ruins on the left—the Williams College Outing Club Berlin Cabin once stood here. A hemlock and a yellow birch, intertwined, represent a curiosity on the right. Turn sharply right at the sign and follow along the contour under hemlocks for a short, sloping descent to a nameless brook that has an exposed bedrock of jutting phyllite. Use caution when crossing on the slick, wet stones, and give the stinging nettles wide berth.

The next mile or so represents one of the most challenging ascents of any hike covered in this guide. An almost relentless series of steep climbs is moderated only slightly by an occasional less exhausting grade, permitting you to catch your breath. I began to wonder if the concept of switchbacks was unknown to the builders of this trail! When you stop, note that the upslope to your left has more mature timber than that below you to the right. Plenty of

**Near the conclusion of the hike, Haley Brook plunges some 30 feet into a crystal pool.**

neotropical migrant birds feel right at home on this eastern face of the Tacon-ics, including the 5.5-inch-long, black-and-yellow Canada warbler. Others include the black-throated green warbler, the ovenbird, and the rose-breasted grosbeak.

At one point you'll detour around a fallen hemlock. Once you see the root-ball, it's easy to envision how heavy rain and high winds might have separated its shallow root network from the bedrock. The sunny gap enables shade-intolerant species to gain a foothold. Hay-scented ferns have colonized other light gaps. The trail continues to be well blazed with blue through dense northern hardwoods as you finally reach the junction on the right with the old Williams College Ski Trail at the border with New York State. This trail is not maintained and even steeper than the one you just ascended, so it is not recommended for a return. Bear left and traverse a lush hay-scented fern glade just below the mostly flat open summit of Berlin Mountain, at 2,818 feet eleva-tion and 2 miles from the trailhead.

The views of the Greylock Range, only 7 miles to the southeast, are splen-did, but summit trees are growing taller and vistas are limited more now than in the past. Red spruces ring the circular open area where a fire tower once stood. Crumbling concrete footings are all that remain. A very large eastern garter snake, appearing as though it had just had a meal, took refuge in the crevice between the blocks during a July visit to its home. Sunshine has encouraged raspberry, bilberry, and lowbush blueberry to proliferate, offering tasty nourishment to birds and mammals, including humans.

The return route follows the Taconic Crest Trail (TCT)—blazed by a white diamond within a blue square, as well as by round blue plastic discs in New York—to Berlin Pass. It is obvious that this trail is heavily utilized by all-terrain vehicles. Follow the wide, rocky track downhill to the right, passing through numerous lovely fern glades. White or paper birch trees look especially attractive in this setting of yellow-green ferns. The wide path, steep at times and filled with lots of loose stones, is eroded to phyllite bedrock by wheeled vehicles. As a result, side trails have been created. Juneberry or shadbush trees are among the members of the low-stature ridgeline forest, producing lovely white flowers in April, before their leaves emerge.

After hiking the undulating wooded crest for 1.2 miles, you'll arrive at a four-way intersection in a shrubby depression or saddle called Berlin Pass. The TCT continues straight, toward Petersburg Pass, but you'll need to turn right onto the somewhat hidden, unmarked, unblazed Berlin Pass Trail. Opposite this trail, the old Boston-to-Albany Post Road descends to Berlin, N.Y. The treadway of the Berlin Pass Trail is rutted and damp in spots, but wide and easy to follow. There are excellent examples of the wafer-thin, layered phyllite bedrock in the trail. This rock began as clay deposits, rich in mica, in a shallow sea, and was then metamorphosed by great heat and pressure into a rock intermediate between shale and schist.

The dry south-facing slope to your left sports lowbush blueberries, mountain azaleas, and a little snapdragon family member with the intriguing name of cow-wheat, which bears modest yellow trumpet-like flowers in summer. It draws its nourishment from the roots of oaks. And as you proceed down the rocky trail, oaks indeed become more common. Haircap moss meanwhile softens the margins. Finally, bear right in an arc and emerge into a graveled clearing where the trail meets Berlin Mountain Road. Still visible on the slope across the way are the runs of the old Williams College Ski Area, built in 1960.

You could turn left and walk down the road 0.4 mile to your vehicle, but more fun awaits. Instead, turn right; follow the gravel to its end, and turn left to head down a grassy track toward the base of the ski slope. Note the small sign on the right for the Williamstown Rural Lands Foundation (WRLF) foot trail, but turn left onto the loop trail. An interpretive panel illuminates the interesting history of the college ski area's development. Haley Brook flows through a large culvert and down a ravine on your left. A canopy of maples, ashes, birches, and beeches shades striped maples and patches of delicate maidenhair fern. Blue cohosh, forming solid stands, and wild leek are profligate on this moist, nutrient-rich slope. Twin leaves that have an unmistakable onion fragrance wither completely away by the time the leek's globes of white flowers emerge in summer.

At the intersection turn left, amble down to the stream, and cross it on stones. The trail is marked by blue diamond WRLF blazes. Ascend short steep slopes via rock steps through deciduous woodland. Just before a wooden bridge, turn right onto a side trail that leads steadily and then more steeply down, past a beech snag pitted with big pileated woodpecker excavations, to a small viewing platform constructed of recycled plastic lumber. The waterfall is enchanting and consists of cascades and a horsetail falls (the water remains in contact with the rock, fanning out into a horsetail configuration) for a total drop of at least 30 feet. This vantage point is screened somewhat by young woody growth, so late fall would provide better views. Be sure to appreciate the auditory aspect of this experience as well. After returning to the main trail, turn right and cross the wooden span. Berlin Mountain Road and your vehicle are just a short distance ahead.

## MORE INFORMATION

There are no restroom facilities or potable water along this route. Property crossed by this route is owned by the Williamstown Rural Lands Foundation, the town of Williamstown, Williams College, the New York Department of Environmental Conservation, and private owners. The Taconic Crest Trail is maintained by the Taconic Hiking Club, 39 Campagna Drive, Albany, NY 12205. Class of '33 and Berlin Pass trails are maintained by the Williams College Outing Club, 1004 Baxter Hall, Williamstown, MA 01267; 413-597-2317; http://wso.williams.edu/orgs/woc/. The WRLF Loop Trail is maintained by the Williamstown Rural Lands Foundation, 671 Cold Spring Road, Williamstown, MA 01267; 413-458-2494; http://www.wrlf.org/berlin.html. New York Department of Environmental Conservation, Division of Lands and Forests, 50 Wolf Road, Albany, NY 12233; 518-457-2475; http://www.dec.ny.gov.

## CAT O' TALL TALES

At the peril of leaping, figuratively at least, from the tangible to the mysterious, consider the controversy surrounding the presence, real or imagined, of mountain lions in the Berkshires. Sighting reports surface regularly, though hard proof—a body or a bona fide photograph—is still lacking. But the possibility exists that these big cats once again roam the region. Although not having the good fortune to observe one myself, I know folks who are convinced they have done so. Some reports are doubtless simple cases of mistaken identity; some may even be hoaxes. Yet as someone who has observed more than a few bobcats, I can't imagine anyone mistaking one for the other.

A colleague of mine who takes a no-nonsense, scientific approach to nature spotted one crossing a road in front of him as he rounded a curve on his bicycle while coasting down a hill at Quabbin Reservoir. And scat found at a predator-killed deer carcass from the same "accidental wilderness" tested positive for mountain-lion DNA in 1997. The Quabbin, in central Massachusetts, is only 40 miles east as the crow flies.

Mountain lion, cougar, puma, panther, or catamount—this fabled creature has many names. Local place names (such as the Catamount Ski Area) hark back to a time when catamounts did indeed inhabit western Massachusetts. The last one shot in the wild in the commonwealth (in Hampshire County) was way back in 1858, when the extent of forested landscape was significantly less than it is today. The mounted form of that mountain lion now resides at the Massachusetts Audubon's Arcadia Wildlife Sanctuary in Easthampton.

Scanning published distribution maps reveals the nearest population of the predator to be no closer than the Florida Everglades, although verified reports do exist from elsewhere along the eastern seaboard. The catamount's chief prey item is deer. Certainly a large and thriving regional deer population would provide ample sustenance to support at least a few animals. And black bear and moose have reclaimed much of their former range in southern New England.

If indeed a wild population exists, and that is yet unproven, the question of origin remains. Some claim that escaped pets are the genesis of local cougar sightings. That may indeed be correct, but could there be more to it than that? Until there is tangible proof in the form of a corpse or irrefutable photographic evidence, the very existence of this mysterious feline will remain tantalizingly in doubt.

## TRIP 3
## HOPKINS MEMORIAL FOREST
## AND TACONIC CREST TRAIL

**Location:** Williamstown; Petersburg, NY; Pownal, VT
**Rating:** Difficult
**Distance:** 10.4 miles
**Elevation Gain:** 1,650 feet
**Estimated Time:** 6.0 hours
**Maps:** AMC Massachusetts Trail Map #1: B1; USGS North Adams and
Berlin, NY; trail map available online

**This excursion features monumental hardwood trees, babbling
brooks, thrilling vistas, and a cool geologic curiosity called the
Snow Hole.**

## DIRECTIONS

From the intersection of Routes 7 and 2 at the rotary in Williamstown, follow
Route 7 north for a short distance to Bulkley Street on the left. Follow Bulkley
Street for 0.75 mile to the gravel Northwest Hill Road on the right and follow
it for 0.1 mile, bearing left onto the gravel entrance drive for Hopkins Memorial Forest (at the carved wooden sign). Park in the small gravel lot on the left,
which has room for about eight vehicles.

## TRAIL DESCRIPTION

Amble up the gravel drive between apple trees and small fields, where blue-
and-white tree swallows nest in boxes provided for cavity-nesting birds. The
Rosenburg Visitor Center, an impressive frame building that was once a carriage house, serves as the Hopkins Memorial Forest headquarters. Excellent
trail maps are available at the attractive kiosk, which features a posted trail
map and historical information. Bear right past Buxton Garden, filled with a
riot of color in summer, onto a gravel carriage road. The former Moon Farm
barn, relocated, stands on the left.

Tread beneath a canopy of sugar maple, black locust, and white ash, passing by the Williams College Outing Club cabin. A bit beyond stands a maple
sugar shed. An adjacent large field hosts the forest's weather station. Numerous research projects are under way at any one time on the property's 2,600
acres, and visitors are asked not to interfere with research plots. After you

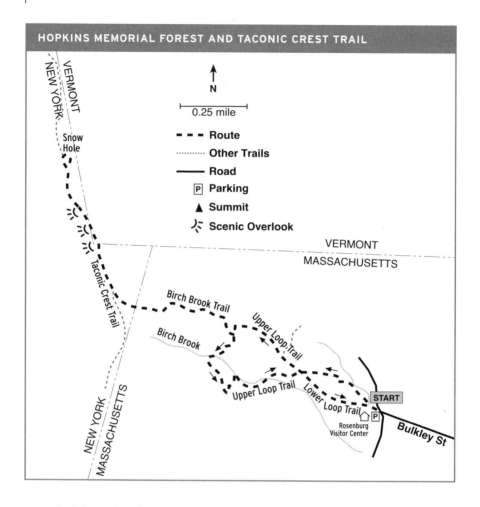

**HOPKINS MEMORIAL FOREST AND TACONIC CREST TRAIL**

VERMONT
NEW YORK

Snow
Hole

N

0.25 mile

- - - Route
.......... Other Trails
———— Road
P  Parking
▲  Summit
☀  Scenic Overlook

VERMONT
MASSACHUSETTS

Taconic Crest Trail

Birch Brook Trail

Birch Brook

Upper Loop Trail

Upper Loop Trail

Lower Loop Trail

START

P

Rosenburg
Visitor Center

Bulkley St

NEW YORK
MASSACHUSETTS

pass the Nature Trail intersection on the left, Ford Glen Brook reveals itself 60 feet below to your right. The forest's character changes after the road bears left, with the addition of black birch, beech, oaks, and hop hornbeam—easy to identify by its flaky tan bark.

As you bear right, a canopy walkway is partially visible. It enables scientists to gain access to a world usually hidden from human eyes. Soon gigantic oaks tower above; it is 40 feet to their first branches. As you continue your pleasant stroll, beech and yellow and black birches increase in an obviously younger forest. Starflower and Canada mayflower bloom here in spring, while lowbush blueberry, prince's pine, shining club moss, and cedar club moss spread largely by runners in the acidic soil. During an early July visit I was thrilled to see a gorgeous male scarlet tanager nervously descend twice to feed a tidbit to its fledgling. Watch for pink lady's slipper orchids in June just before the four-way intersection outfitted with benches.

Turn onto the rightmost fork for Upper Loop Trail. On your ramble to Birch Brook, ignore several side paths. As you proceed, a forest of red maple changes to one dominated by oak. Tiny lowbush blueberry shrubs thrive in the acid soil beneath the oaks. Notice that a significant number of oaks have more than one trunk, a sure sign that these woods were logged. By the way, don't mistake the dabs of yellow paint on trees for blazes, as these demarcate forest study plots. At the North Branch of Birch Brook, bear right onto blue-blazed Birch Brook Trail. From here, you'll walk 1.5 miles up to meet the Taconic Crest Trail.

So far it's been an easy stroll, but now the real hiking begins. Stride across a fallen stone wall indicating former pasturing. Dragging out logs produced the rutted skid road on the left. Bear right, away from the flow and past knee- to waist-high blueberries. The abundant chipmunks and numerous other creatures, large and small, seek out their vitamin-rich fruit. The grade of this old wood road increases under mixed northern hardwoods and oaks. On a more moderate slope, notice the dying paper birches—pioneering trees that followed the ax and were later shaded out by species whose seeds required less sunlight to germinate. About two-thirds of the way to the ridge, you'll cross into New York State.

Log steps help you ascend the eastern slope past glades of yellow-green ferns—most notably hay-scented or boulder fern. This prolific species characteristically forms solid stands. Hopkins Forest researchers are trying to determine whether it secretes a substance that inhibits the growth of competing species. Finally, you'll reach the well-trodden and undulating Taconic Crest Trail (TCT). The TCT is blazed by a white diamond within a blue square for 35 miles along the spine of the Taconic Range. From the intersection it is 1.6 miles north to the Snow Hole. Turn right under northern hardwoods that now include yellow birch. Up here the forest is reduced in height but with a thick sapling layer—especially American beech, a prolific sprouter.

At a Y intersection in a lovely waist-high fern glade, continue straight ahead. Shortly after the trail leaves Hopkins Memorial Forest property and passes onto New York State Forest land, you'll arrive at the first of three shrubby clearings where scenic vistas abound. Gaze out upon row after row of verdant rolling hills running toward the western horizon. Close at hand, shiny-leaved bilberry shrubs thrive in the sunny gap, as do a few red spruces. Bilberries and less common huckleberries fill a second clearing offering additional views, but the third is the best of all.

Back in the forest you can't help but notice the many beech trees with black bark lesions. Most are inflicted with beech bark disease—a death sentence. About ten minutes after leaving the third clearing you'll reach the first of two red-blazed side trails on the right. These are the ends of a short loop leading to a geological and meteorological wonder—the Snow Hole.

Continue to the second red-blazed path; turn right past a splendid patch of shining club moss, and walk downhill about 250 feet to the entrance on the right. Old graffiti—some dating to 1865—is carved into the relatively soft phyllite bedrock near the entrance. You will want to descend into the crevice to explore it from within, but watch your footing, as the rock may be slick. Immediately you'll feel a radical drop in temperature, especially during the summer months—a sort of nature's icebox. Mosses, wood sorrel, and ferns soften the tilted, wafer-thin layers of phyllite, while yellow birches clutch the rim. It feels a bit as though you're walking into a giant terrarium. The promise of the Snow Hole held true for me on a steamy July 4 visit, as a small pile of dirty snow and ice remained within.

When ready to continue, you can walk back the way you came in or continue on the short loop; both lead back to the TCT. Be sure to turn left when you join the main trail, and watch for the easy-to-miss Birch Brook Trail on the left to retrace your steps downhill to the junction with Upper Loop Trail at the bridge over the brook. Turn right to cross the brook on a wooden bridge. This woodland contains all four common birch species—white, gray, black, and yellow—all separable by unique bark true to their names. Soon you'll reach Middle Branch of Birch Brook, lumpy with mossy stones, and cross it via another wooden bridge. Descend easily on a wide path.

Bear left in an arc to drop down close to the South Branch of Birch Brook—the third tributary. Shade-casting hemlocks—some sizable—populate the slope. In summer, shade-tolerant woodland butterflies like the northern pearly-eye may make an appearance, although they may be difficult to locate when they alight. This eye-spotted species rarely visits flowers, preferring to sip tree sap and other fluids. Soon you'll arrive again at Middle Branch, crossing on a wooden bridge. The old roadway continues brookside under oaks, beeches, birches, and maples. The soothing sound of the flow may lull you to sleep at this stage of the hike.

Gaze into the depths of clear pools to spot native brook trout. This attractive stream has cut its way through a phyllite bedrock layer cake. A significant number of monumental oaks populate this woodland—a 3.5-foot-diameter individual stands on the right. Cross a bridge over the North Branch built to

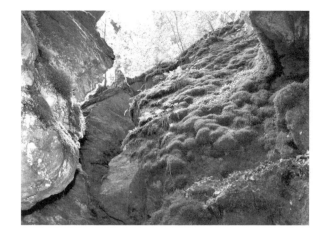

Mosses have colonized the cool, damp walls of the bedrock cleft known as the Snow Hole.

accommodate vehicles and climb easily back to the four-way intersection with benches. Turn right to walk back on the south side of Lower Loop Trail along the dividing line between two watersheds—Ford Glen Brook and Birch Brook.

Pass through more fern glades, where an interpretive panel describes the possible chemical warfare waged by hay-scented fern against its competitors. Another informs that club mosses are more common in earth once pastured. You'll enjoy seeing all four local and aptly named species—prince's pine, shining club moss, cedar club moss, and staghorn club moss—during this hike. Although capable of reproducing via spores, slow-growing club mosses rely mostly on cloning themselves. Pass a dark stand of Norway spruces planted by the U.S. Forest Service, which operated the forest from 1935 to 1968.

Nearby an ancient oak with rotting heartwood seems right out of a Winnie the Pooh tale as you amble downhill. Soon exotic plants along the margins presage your return to the Rosenburg Center, the cheerful bubbling song of house wrens, and your vehicle beyond.

## MORE INFORMATION

Open daily dawn to dusk, year-round. Access is free. Public restrooms and drinking water are available at the Rosenburg Center; hours: 7 A.M. to 6 P.M. All pets must be leashed. Hunting is prohibited except deer hunting by special permit in the Massachusetts portion of the property. All vehicles, including mountain bikes, are prohibited. Collection of fauna and flora is prohibited; do not disturb research sites. Hopkins Forest Manager, Center for Environmental Studies, Williams College, P.O. Box 632, Williamstown, MA 01267; 413-597-2346; http://www.williams.edu/ces/hopkins.htm.

## TRIP 4
## MOUNT GREYLOCK STATE RESERVATION, EAST SIDE–CHESHIRE HARBOR/GOULD TRAILS

**Location:** Adams
**Rating:** Difficult
**Distance:** 6.6 miles
**Elevation Gain:** 1,930 feet
**Estimated Time:** 4.5–5.0 hours
**Maps:** AMC Massachusetts Trail Map #1: E4; USGS Cheshire, North Adams; trail map available online, at DCR regional office

**This is the shortest route up the state's highest peak, with significant elevation gain, but anyone in reasonably good physical condition should be able to complete the hike.**

### DIRECTIONS

From the south: From the Allendale Shopping Center in Pittsfield, drive north on Route 8 for 9.1 miles into Cheshire and turn left onto Fred Mason Road. Follow it north for 2.8 miles (it becomes West Road after approximately 1 mile) to West Mountain Road on the left. Turn left and follow West Mountain Road for 1.6 miles, past parking for Gould Trail to the Cheshire Harbor trailhead.

From the north: Take Route 8 south to Adams and turn right at the statue of President McKinley onto Maple Street. Follow Maple Street for 0.9 mile and turn right onto West Mountain Road. Follow it 1.6 miles to the trailhead.

### TRAIL DESCRIPTION

Park in the gravel lot at the end of road at an elevation of 1,560 feet. Follow the gravel roadway to your right (northwest); it leads through a field. The mountain's summit, complete with the Veterans War Memorial Tower, is visible briefly through a gap in the treeline as you make your way past a small sign on the left reading "Old Adams Rd. & Cheshire Harbor Tr." From the map kiosk at the woodland edge, walk past a metal gate and follow the old rocky roadbed gradually up along stone walls and under a canopy of sugar and red maples, black and gray birches, red spruce, and hemlock. Green-trunked striped maple and American beech populate the understory. Hay-scented, New York, and spinulose wood ferns border the road, as do the shiny paired leaves

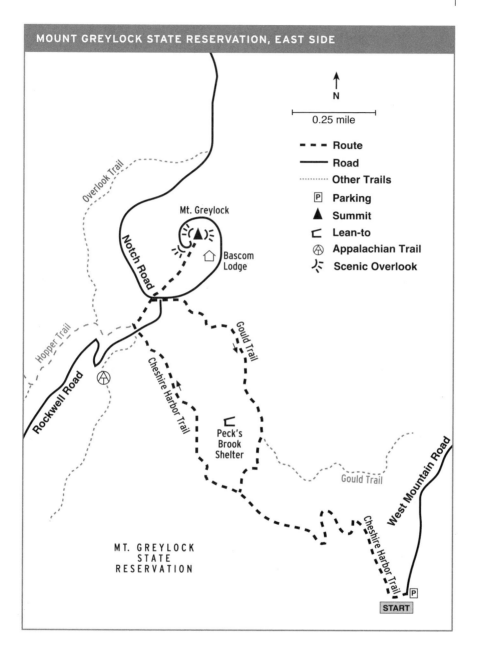

of partridgeberry (watch for bright red fruits in fall). Bits of rusty barbed wire imbedded in trees prove that livestock once pastured here.

Cutting gently across the slope's contour lines, you soon cross some inter-mittent brook beds. Then, as you curve sharply left, a sign on the right reads

"To Gould Tr." A major split in the roadway occurs here, but the paths rejoin 50 yards farther up. Several switchbacks lead you up the slope, where you'll note the first balsam firs of the hike. Very shortly you'll reach an intersection with Old Adams Road on the left, but continue straight on the Cheshire Harbor Trail. The heart-shaped paired leaves of waist-high hobblebushes produce kaleidoscopic color in autumn. They also provide nest sites for black-throated blue warblers that construct their nests low to the ground among their branches. The path becomes even rockier, and you'll step over ledge outcrops of metamorphic schist. When the sun shines, mica crystals in the schist sparkle at your feet. You'll reach a sign for the Peck's Brook Loop on the right (you will return via this loop later), but continue straight uphill for now. The triangular seed capsules of a patch of sessile-leaved bellwort are notable on the right in autumn. A large, shaggy, three-trunked red maple stands on the left where the surface roots of beech lace the trail.

The path now leads up through woods of beech and yellow birch. Although some trees are sizable, this forest is generally young. Beeches sprout from roots and form clones of smooth, gray-barked trees that are all the same organism. To your left, a 4-foot-long quartz boulder perched on schist will catch your eye. Mountain maple saplings have taken root among the boulders. Distinguish the mountain maple's leaves, which porcupines are fond of, by their sawtooth edges. The sound of flowing water and the sweet aroma of balsam fir are evident as you reach Peck's Brook. Beware of possible loose and missing boards as you cross the brook on a wide bridge.

On the far side, the path splits, but it soon rejoins as it ascends. You'll reach an outcrop of schist/quartz on the right at Rockwell Road. The southbound Appalachian Trail (AT) is on the left just before the pavement. But instead, cross the road (note the sign on a tree indicating that this is the way to the summit) and follow the AT north over wooden stairs amid a heavenly balsam fragrance. The AT here is single-file as it weaves through stunted spruce, yellow birch, and mountain ash, and over bog bridges to reach an intersection with the blue-blazed Hopper Trail on the left. Turn right to continue over more bog bridges toward the summit.

You'll be walking through a magical boreal forest zone in the company of spruce and fir trees that generally grow above 2,600 feet elevation in only a handful of locations in Massachusetts. The zone's climate is equivalent to that of interior Canada. Upper reaches of the mountain are often fog-shrouded, and the condensing moisture is acidic enough, along with shallow soil and a harsh temperature, to negatively affect the growth of woody vegetation. Soon you'll reach a scenic pond that supplies water to the summit lodge. In summer,

**The 93-foot-tall granite Veterans War Memorial Tower, from which five states may be visible, tops the highest point in Massachusetts.**

dragonflies zip about, seeking prey and patrolling territories. The communication tower on the summit is easily visible from here.

Follow briefly along the shore to reach Rockwell Road again. Turn left; walk about 100 feet, past the intersection with Notch Road, and catch the AT on the left side of Rockwell Road. Follow the signature white blazes up over a rocky path to reach an asphalt parking area adjacent to the antenna tower. Composting toilets are located here. From this point, it is only a few hundred feet across the roadway to the 93-foot-high memorial tower on the summit. Attractively rustic Bascom Lodge—where drinking water, flush toilets, meals, and overnight accommodations will be available when it reopens—stands to the right. On a clear day you'll want to explore the summit (3,491 feet) and take in the expansive views.

When you're ready to begin your descent, retrace your steps to the composting toilets and continue south on the AT (beware of wet or loose rocks), soon reaching Rockwell Road. To return on a different path, using a portion of the Gould Trail, look for the trailhead on the left at a small gravel parking area opposite the intersection with Notch Road. Initially narrow and steep, Gould Trail soon levels off under maple, beech, striped maple, and hobblebush. Pass through a stand of yellow birch and balsam fir—I never tire of the fragrance! Raspberry canes flourish in the light gaps. At a junction with an overgrown trail, bear left to continue descending. Sugar maples predominate in the now deciduous woodland. Cross a couple of intermittent streambeds. There is much spruce regeneration on the fairly steep slope, and then the trail widens to become a rocky roadway.

One mile after leaving the summit, a short side trail on the right crosses the brook to Peck's Brook Shelter. The lean-to shelter, nestled on the hillside above the tumbling brook, is well worth the 3-minute walk. Upon your return to the main trail, turn right and level out under hardwoods. At a "blocked" intersection, bear right as the sign directs and reach a signed intersection with the Peck's Brook Loop. The left fork leads down to West Mountain Road, but turn right toward the Cheshire Harbor Trail. The path is quite level as you tread past prince's pine, shining club moss, and the wildflowers clintonia and wild sarsaparilla. Leaf fall enhances your ability to discern the sound of flowing water and glimpse a forested ridge to your right. Bear right and proceed toward the sound. A few fairly steep switchbacks deposit you at the exceedingly rocky brook. Follow Peck's Brook downstream briefly through a lovely narrow ravine. Clear pools provide abodes for brook trout and spring salamanders in this idyllic spot.

Be vigilant for a trail on your right that crosses the brook and ascends the far slope. This angular trail is easily missed! The blue blazes are very difficult to see from the east side of the stream. The trail leads steeply up the slope on short switchbacks. Continue through another hobblebush thicket to the intersection with the Cheshire Harbor Trail. You passed this point earlier near the beginning of the hike. Turn left to follow it back to the intersection with Old Adams Road on the right. From here it is 1 mile back to your vehicle. Continue straight, and after the series of switchbacks you'll reach the parking area.

## MORE INFORMATION

Mount Greylock State Reservation is managed by the Massachusetts Department of Conservation and Recreation. Regional headquarters: 740 South Street, Pittsfield, MA 01201; 413-442-8928; http://www.mass.gov/dcr/parks/mtGreylock/. Carry-in, carry-out rules apply. *Roads leading to the summit were under construction during 2007 and 2008 and were rescheduled to reopen in 2009.*

## TRIP 5
## PINE COBBLE AND EAST MOUNTAIN

**Location:** Williamstown, Clarksburg
**Rating:** Moderate–Difficult
**Distance:** 4.2 miles
**Elevation Gain:** 1,340 feet
**Estimated Time:** 2.5–3.0 hours
**Maps:** AMC Massachusetts Trail Map #1: B3, USGS North Adams

**This out-and-back hike takes you up the sunny slope of East Mountain to a quartzite- and pitch-pine-studded summit and some of the most stunning views in the region.**

### DIRECTIONS
From the intersection of Routes 7 and 2 at the rotary in Williamstown, follow Route 2 east for 0.6 mile to the Cole Avenue traffic light. Turn left on Cole Avenue and travel for 0.8 mile (crossing the Hoosic River en route), and turn right onto North Hoosac Road. Drive for 0.4 mile to Pine Cobble Road on the left, and follow Pine Cobble Road for 0.1 mile to a gravel parking area on the left with space for six or seven vehicles. A sign urges hikers to take valuables with them and to lock their cars.

### TRAIL DESCRIPTION
From the parking area cross Pine Cobble Road diagonally and walk uphill for about 100 feet to the signed trailhead on the right. The path initially parallels the road and passes a wooden sign erected by the Williams Outing Club that indicates this blue-blazed trail leads 1.6 miles to Pine Cobble summit, 2.1 miles to the Appalachian Trail junction, and 3.4 miles to the Vermont border. Shortly turn left into oak woodland. White and red oaks predominate, but black cherry, red maple, American beech, black birch, ironwood, tulip tree, and hop hornbeam all add diversity. Distinguish white oak by its flaky light gray bark. Rounded quartzite boulders litter the trail.

Striped maple appears as a member of the understory as you climb gently, while the deep green leaves of wintergreen appear as a pleasing ground cover. After passing through a tangle of ropy grapevines, bear left into woodland dominated by big, rough-barked black locusts. This area has a disturbed,

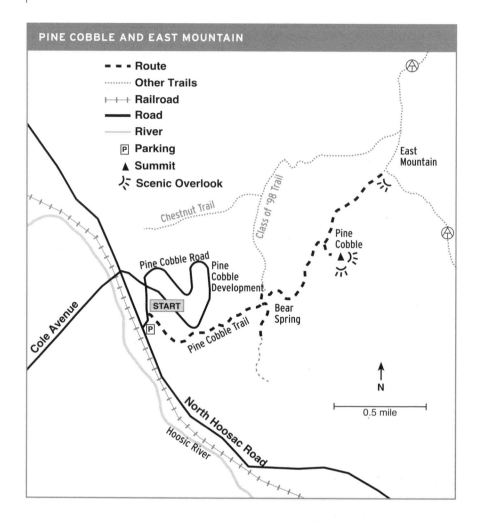

**PINE COBBLE AND EAST MOUNTAIN**

- - - Route
......... Other Trails
⊦—⊦ Railroad
━━ Road
——— River
Ⓟ Parking
▲ Summit
⋇ Scenic Overlook

Chestnut Trail

Class of '98 Trail

East Mountain

Pine Cobble Road

Pine Cobble Development

Pine Cobble ▲⋇

START

Ⓟ

Pine Cobble Trail

Bear Spring

Cole Avenue

North Hoosac Road

Hoosic River

N

0.5 mile

unkempt appearance. Invasive species, like these locusts, often colonize disturbed sites. As you pass near a number of homes in Williams College's Pine Cobble Development, chestnut oak appears, along with smooth-skinned black birch, and multitrunked witch hazel.

The trail steepens, and lowbush blueberry thrives in the acidic soil under the tannin-rich oaks. Gray squirrels scamper about in search of buried acorns and perky gray tufted titmice call sweetly from the trees. After the path turns, gray birches join the mix. The level bench you are on is thought to be the ancient shoreline of glacial Lake Bascom. Its waters were once 500 feet deep! Two-foot-high sheep laurel, another indicator of acid soil, first shows up near here, becoming abundant later. It is said to be poisonous to livestock. After another quarter mile, watch for a side trail on the right that leads about 300 feet toward a dark green wall of eastern hemlocks and the modest Bear Spring.

Bear Spring, at the base of a resistant cliff, is the only surface water on this south-facing slope. The cooler microclimate here fosters sapling yellow birch and striped maple, both northern hardwood species. Ferns are more noticeable too, including common polypody on quartzite boulders. Return to the main trail and continue uphill past luxuriant growths of shiny-leaved wintergreen to a signpost at the 0.8-mile mark, where the Class of '98 Trail heads left. Continue straight, among abundant sheep laurel that shows off deep pink blossoms in June. These nutrient-poor soils host a variety of other heath family species including blueberries, huckleberry, and the Massachusetts state flower—trailing arbutus, or mayflower. Its leaves have a sandy texture, while its delicate spring flowers are pale pink.

Notice that as you've gained elevation, the stature of the oaks and other hardwoods has decreased while the shrub layer has thickened. Chestnut oak, with wavy-margined leaves and deeply furrowed trunks, are now far more common. The trail steepens again as you reach a sign surrounded by a mat of moss proclaiming "Welcome to Pine Cobble, a unique natural area owned by the Williams Rural Lands Foundation and maintained for hiking and enjoyment of nature." Soon you'll pass through a small boulder field of gray, angular hunks of quartzite. At 1.1 miles you'll reach a blocked side trail on the right; bear left.

Sassafras trees, which do well in sandy soils, become common. Their leaves have one, two, or three lobes and emit a spicy aroma when crushed. Continue the steady climb amid white birches, young red maples, and chestnut oaks. Marvel at the wooden bowl formed by a triple-stemmed oak that collects and holds rainwater. Soon you'll arrive at a signpost indicating that the Pine Cobble summit is 0.1 mile to the right. Follow the side trail to a number of excellent vista points. A fine view of Williamstown is yours from a perch atop rounded quartzite cobbles on the right. Beyond is the spine of the northern Taconics, with Berlin Mountain (see Trip 2) the most prominent feature. From the Pine Cobble summit, at an elevation of 1,893 feet and a bit higher, enjoy a wonderful view to the east of nestled North Adams. Due south 6 miles is the summit of Mount Greylock, complete with the Veterans War Memorial Tower.

The smooth gray stone beneath your feet is Cheshire quartzite. Five hundred and fifty million years ago it was beach sand. The pure silica of this rock type was once the raw ingredient in Sandwich glass. Some broken rock faces show a reddish tinge of iron. When ready, return to the main trail and turn

**The inquisitive, social, and hardy black-capped chickadee—the state bird of Massachusetts—adds a note of cheer to almost any hike.**

right to continue another 0.5 mile to the Appalachian Trail junction. After mostly level walking through oaks, gray birch, red maple, witch hazel, sheep laurel and wintergreen, there is a moderate climb. A small blue metal diamond affixed to a tree delineates the Clarksburg State Forest boundary. Watch for a metal anchor point in the rock that once helped support a fire tower. Level out through a shrubby growth of birches, and leave the forest for an open rocky promontory. The trail is marked with rock cairns and blue blazes on stones.

Turn around occasionally to take in the stunning views that only improve as you climb higher. This boulder field, amid picturesque pitch pines, is the perfect place to enjoy a snack and the Taconic panorama. The pitch pines are mostly 10–12 feet tall. Taller, longer-needled white pines are also present. Even a few red spruces stand among the light gray quartzite slabs, while the rocks are decorated with tight-clinging gray-green lichens. Follow the rock-strewn treadway to its junction with the Appalachian Trail at 2.1 miles (elevation 2,050 feet), marked by a signpost on the summit of East Mountain. A mountain azalea shrub stands to the left. One April, I found a collection of 1-inch-diameter winter moose pellets among the rocks. If you are so inclined, turn left and walk another 1.3 miles (one way) to the Vermont border. When ready, retrace your route to return to your vehicle.

## MORE INFORMATION

Open daily, year-round; no fees. There are no restroom facilities. The Pine Cobble Trail traverses lands owned by Williams College, Williamstown Rural Lands Foundation (WRLF), 671 Cold Spring Road, Williamstown, MA 01267, http://www.wrlf.org/pinecobble.html; the Massachusetts Department of Conservation and Recreation, Berkshire Region headquarters, 740 South Street, Pittsfield, MA 01210; 413-442-8928; and private owners. The trail is maintained by the WRLF and members of the Williams Outing Club, 39 Chapin Hall Drive, Williamstown, MA 01267; 413-597-2317.

## TRIP 6
## STONE HILL

**Location:** Williamstown
**Rating:** Easy
**Distance:** 2.3 miles
**Elevation Gain:** 350 feet
**Estimated Time:** 1.5 hours
**Maps:** AMC Massachusetts Trail Map #1: C2, USGS North Adams

**This trip features stunning pastoral vistas of Williamstown, the Taconics, and the Green Mountains, along with massive hardwoods and evergreens and an iconic stone bench; it's a great family excursion.**

## DIRECTIONS

From the intersection of Routes 7 and 2 at the rotary in Williamstown, turn onto South Street (a right turn if arriving from the south) and follow it for 0.4 mile to the entrance drive for the Sterling and Francine Clark Art Institute on the right. Follow the drive as it bears left and then right to the large paved west-side parking lot at the back of the museum complex. The trailhead is at the near (southeast) corner of the lot.

## TRAIL DESCRIPTION

Mammoth twin oaks create an informal but majestic portal to the recently revamped museum trail system. Twin headstones at the burial place of the former property owner's pets and a handsome cedar bridge with balusters will

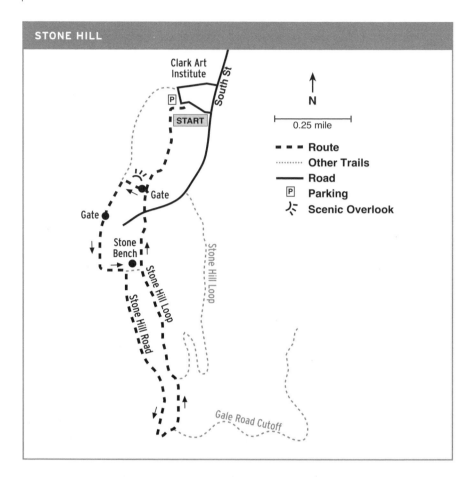

also help you locate the trailhead. A stylized trail map on an elegant bronze marker stands near the footbridge. It does not, however, illustrate the most southerly portion of the trail system. Maps of the Stone Hill trails are available at the information desk in the main courtyard of the Manton Center.

After crossing two lovely cedar bridges you'll be walking initially on Nan Path, surfaced with fine crushed stone. The trail bears left at a split-rail fence bordering a pasture and leads up through maples, ashes, oaks, and hemlocks, over boardwalk sections and by benches to a four-way intersection. Turn right at a sign for Woodland Trail and leave the crushed stone behind. Follow the white-diamond blazes easily up past a thicket of invasive Japanese barberry to another four-way intersection. Turn right and follow wood-chipped Pasture Trail under northern hardwoods to a barbed-wire fence and wooden gate.

Pass through the gate, being sure to close it behind you, as dairy cattle frequent the meadow you are about to traverse. Follow the wide mowed path

**A stone bench occupies the site where Williams College professor George Moritz Wahl once enjoyed sunsets.**

through a bucolic meadow. You'll have to avoid the odd cow patty, but that's what makes it bucolic! The views to the right (north) are idyllic. Especially prominent on the horizon is the rounded mound of The Dome (Trip 1) just across the border in Vermont. You'll also have a bird's-eye view of the Clark Art Institute and the various town and Williams College spires that poke above the trees. Beyond them, the Green Mountains form a lovely backdrop.

In addition to eastern bluebirds, savannah sparrows, eastern kingbirds, and bobolinks, other pasture-dwellers include curious black-and-white dairy cattle. The not-altogether-unpleasant smell of manure reminds you of where you are as you gaze on scattered and picturesque clumps of white birch, ash, maple, and cherry that enhance the scene. And it is a scene truly worth painting. A sinewy ironwood tree on the right has been used as a rubbing post by the stock. After cresting the hill, turn left and stroll to the pasture's southern treeline. Butterflies are small but very watchable wildlife. Two common meadow species are the dark brown wood nymphs with blue-and-yellow eyespots, and tiny orange-and-black pearl crescents.

Trees near the crest shade a glacial souvenir—a large gneiss boulder banded with milky white quartz. The treeline on the right exhibits a clear browse line.

At the Y split, bear right and walk toward another wooden gate. Again, be sure to close the gate behind you. The white-blazed trail enters a mixed forest of hardwoods and hemlocks. Soon you'll skirt a hillside meadow and pass through a gap in a line of large marble boulders strategically placed to prevent entry by cars and trucks. Beyond them the spacious roadway is shaded by maples, ashes, black cherries, and hemlocks. Bear left at an enormous ancient white ash with spreading arms. Soon you'll arrive at a mowed clearing; continue into the forest beyond it.

An iconic stone bench with a quartzite back stands just inside the forest at a major intersection with Stone Hill Road. It was erected by the townspeople to memorialize George Moritz Wahl, a Williams College German professor unfairly treated during World War I. This location, once graced by long views, was apparently a favorite site of contemplation for him. Turn right on this wide gravel colonial-era thoroughfare, once the chief north-south artery in the county. A tough quartzite ledge runs parallel with the road, which is bounded by oaks and hemlocks—some of them impressively large. The oaks too are gargantuan. A few are 4 feet or more in diameter. A tree-sized limb has separated from one oak and is hung up high above the path. Brilliant scarlet tanagers hunt for caterpillars high in the oak canopy in summer.

Chunks of quartzite have calved off and tumbled down toward the level path, which is popular with joggers and cyclists as well as walkers. The erosion-resistant outcrop is what gave Stone Hill its name. Bearing witness to former logging are some moldering old stumps that foster the growth of colorful fungi in damp summers. As you approach the yellow-blazed Gale Road Cutoff on the left, remnants of wire protrude from the trees; sugar maples come to dominate with abundant sapling growth below. Turn east and move through a gap in a low rock wall on a pleasant woodland path under the leafy cover of beech, black birch, maple, and oak. Look in these rich woods for rattlesnake ferns, which have a single, finely cut triangular blade and a spore-bearing fertile frond above the blade.

Soon you'll bear sharply left and then left again where logs block an old wood road. The yellow-blazed path turns right immediately toward Gale Road, but continue straight (north), through the rather open hardwood forest on the western side of Stone Hill Loop. Small outcrops here and there are dark and finely layered. These are phyllite (a metamorphosed clay) rather than quartzite. Oaks increase again as you climb gently on a serpentine path into a distinctly drier forest than the one you recently passed through. Lowbush blueberries thrive in the acid soils that result from the decay of tannin-rich oak leaves. Walk through a gap in a stone wall composed mostly of phyllite slabs.

Knee-high huckleberries, whose dark blue fruits are tasty in late summer, flourish near the top of Stone Hill along this unblazed but easy-to-follow path. In summer, the sweet flutelike music of the wood thrush fills the air (listen for its characteristic *ee-o-lay* phrases).

Begin an easy downhill walk amid young beech trees to a light gap opened by toppled hemlocks. Black (a.k.a. sweet) birch saplings have colonized the clearing. Beyond this the trail is wider, passing another forest giant—a red oak, this one showing off a long-healed lightning-strike scar. There are formidable eastern hemlocks here too. The return becomes somewhat steeper and rockier, levels out briefly, and then descends again into a light gap in the canopy created by a fallen oak. The treadway becomes eroded and takes on the appearance of an old skid road just before you reach a gravel road that provides access to the town's buried water tank. At the intersection on your left in midsummer, pink Herb Robert, a geranium relative, flowers. When not blooming, its lacy leaves may fool you into thinking it is a fern.

Cross the sunny roadway. A sign ahead reads Clark Trail. Follow the white-diamond-blazed Woodland Trail easily downhill under red maples. Reach the chipped path to your left, but continue straight, following the white blazes to the crushed-stone pathway. Bear left and retrace your steps over Nan Path back to the parking area and your vehicle.

## MORE INFORMATION

Parking lots, trails, and picnic tables are open to the public during daylight hours, year-round. Access to these facilities is free. Museum gallery hours: July and August, daily, 10 A.M. to 5 P.M.; September through June, Tuesday through Sunday, 10 A.M. to 5 P.M. Closed Mondays, except Monday holidays. Closed Thanksgiving, Christmas, and New Year's Day. Museum admission: Free November through May; $12.50 June through October; children 18 and under and full-time students with ID free. Sterling and Francine Clark Art Institute, 225 South Street, Williamstown, MA 01267; 413-458-2303; http://www.clarkart.edu.

## TRIP 7
## MOUNTAIN MEADOW PRESERVE

**Location:** Williamstown
**Rating:** Moderate
**Distance:** 4.0 miles
**Elevation Gain:** 470 feet
**Estimated Time:** 2.5 hours
**Maps:** AMC Massachusetts Trail Map #1: B2, USGS North Adams; trail map available online

**The Greylock Range and the Taconics are a stunning backdrop to a meadow that in summer is filled with colorful wildflowers and butterflies.**

### DIRECTIONS

From the intersection of Routes 7 and 2 at the rotary in Williamstown, follow Route 7 north for 1.7 miles, crossing the Hoosic River along the way. Turn right onto Mason Street and follow it 0.1 mile to where it terminates at a gravel parking area. The lot accommodates approximately ten vehicles.

### TRAIL DESCRIPTION

A kiosk complete with large trail map stands just beyond the far end of the parking area; small trail maps may be available here. The 176-acre property was a gift from Pamela Weatherbee in 1998. Follow the mowed path across a field of goldenrod, yellow hawkweed, and robin plantain, bordered by copious amounts of autumn olive as well as apple trees, honeysuckle, and dogwood. Autumn olive, now considered an invasive exotic, was planted to control erosion. Its yellowish blossoms fill the air with a sweet perfume in late spring, and plump, fuzzy bumblebees clamber over its flowers, pollinating them in the process. The trail rises into a strip of woodland and then enters another small field. Quaking aspen and cottonwoods line the left perimeter. As the trail steepens, white pines and young white ashes with compound leaves appear.

Turn right at the trail split to follow the mowed path along the margin of a large, attractive meadow, the preserve's namesake. At this low end of the hillside meadow various field flowers add dashes of color from late spring to fall. The path bears left and climbs the modest slope. Paired nest boxes attract iridescent blue-and-white tree swallows and blue, rusty, and white eastern

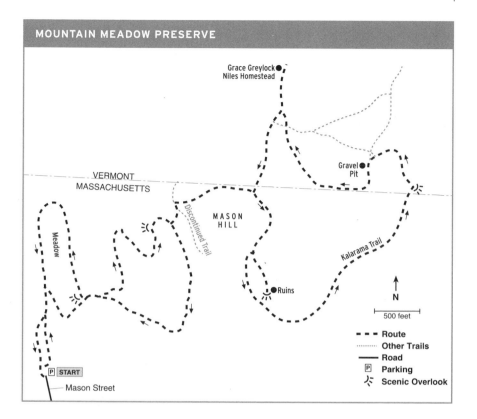

**MOUNTAIN MEADOW PRESERVE**

bluebirds. The two species often compete for such nest sites. The wonderful panoramic vista of the Greylock Range to the right is without doubt the highlight of this hike. Glance over your shoulder and be treated to another excellent view of rolling verdant ridges. This 20-acre grassland habitat is alive with a bountiful array of butterflies in summer. The little wood satyr, a small brown species with a row of black bull's-eye spots, is abundant in late spring.

Turn right to enter the forest and cross a tiny stream on a short boardwalk. Note the yellow blazes painted on tree trunks. At the trail junction, turn left toward the summit. White pines, and below them witch hazel and striped maple, predominate. Oaks are present too. A low wall of water-tumbled quartzite stones lies on the left. Your climb on a narrow trail becomes steeper and passes a spreading white oak with three trunks. Note that the leaves of the white oak have rounded lobes, unlike the bristly lobes of red and black oaks. Their acorns are also sweet and mature in the fall of their first year, unlike the two years required for red and black oaks. The trail climbs the slope with the aid of switchbacks. The last 200 yards or so is at quite a sharp angle. Wild geraniums bloom pink in late spring along the path. Due to encroaching trees, only

Sweeping vistas of Mount Greylock and the Taconics constitute the backdrop of a 20-acre, flower-filled meadow.

a limited view is possible from the summit at 1,120 feet. An interesting small tree here is a multitrunked hop hornbeam, a tree with thin, light brown, shredding bark. Its wood is extremely hard and durable.

Continue straight, and soon you'll descend to an intersection on the left with a signed trail that leads to the preserve's Vermont parking area. Turn left and descend past low maple-leaved viburnum shrubs under a canopy of oaks and red maples. At a junction with a wood road, bear left onto the roadway, then almost immediately right at the preserve's boundary. Mature red pines, characterized by scaly pinkish bark, were probably planted along the road, which skirts Mason Hill, during the Great Depression. Enjoy treading on a nice wide path that virtually parallels the Vermont state line for a brief time. You'll soon reach a cabled road and then wend around a cable and a green metal gate to reach a T intersection with another wood road. Turn right to explore the ruins of Mausert's Camp.

During damp conditions in late spring and summer, be alert for red efts traversing the road. The red eft, the terrestrial stage of the aquatic red-spotted newt, spends between 2 and 7 years roaming woodlands before returning to ponds as a breeding adult. The fiery orange skin warns potential predators that red efts are poisonous when eaten. Saplings, pole-sized trees, and decaying stumps speak of relatively recent logging here. Watch on the left for a luxuriant patch of wild geraniums in late spring. Bear left at the intersection with the Kalarama Trail; you'll return here shortly. Ahead stands a stone chimney at the end of a clearing. A second fireplace sits on the opposite side. The camp was destroyed by fire in the 1970s. The views of Mount Greylock are partially obscured by woody vegetation. Indigo buntings nest along the edge of the clearing.

Retrace your steps to the intersection with the relatively new Kalarama Trail (not currently shown on the preserve website map) and turn left onto it. Descend on this old roadway cut into the hill contour; on the left you'll see an old borrow pit later used as a dumpsite. Black birches and oaks with lowbush blueberries below dot the rising slope. A couple of beech trees on the right show faint black scars of having been climbed by bears, which relish beechnuts. Cross a pile of quartzite cobbles gathered during field clearing and marvel at the huge twin-trunked oak on the right that exhibits the scars of four strands of barbed wire. A bit of poison ivy borders the path before it bisects a handsome patch of spinulose wood fern.

Look for a lovely cluster of delicate maidenhair fern on the left where the trail climbs again. The wire-thin ebony stems and fan-shaped fronds make the maidenhair the loveliest of all ferns. When you reach a junction on the right with a narrow trail, leave the road and follow the woodland path. A couple of dogwood trees sport large white four-petaled blossoms in spring at this intersection. But young white birches are generally more noticeable near the trail. A few signs of former habitation—metal artifacts—dot the hillside on the left before you descend into a shallow hemlock ravine cut by a modest rocky brook. Beyond the brook crossing, a yellow marker on the right indicates the boundary of Williamstown conservation land. A massive white pine towers behind it.

Bear left and climb past the nearly 5-foot-tall bracken ferns to an intersection with another wood road at the end of Kalarama Trail. A sign on the right marks East Vista, the former view now lost to lush tree growth. You are now in Vermont. Turn left instead and follow the old road, cut into the slope, toward the gravel pit. When you reach the sunny clearing at a signed intersection, bear left through the former gravel pit, where gravel was removed for road and railroad-bed construction in the 1950s and '60s. Sun-loving white pines and quaking aspens colonized the edge of the pit, now carpeted by grass. Reenter the woodland of oaks and a variety of birches on a gravelly track. You'll pass through a small gravel pit and by the remnants of a stone wall on the left before emerging into an attractive small meadow where bluebirds nest in the boxes put up for them. Follow the mowed path across the meadow.

At a T intersection, turn right for a brief walk to the old stone-and-cement foundation of the Grace Greylock Niles Homestead on the left and then retrace your steps to the intersection. Continue straight ahead this time and arrive back at the intersection with the trail on the left leading to Mausert's Camp. Turn right to retrace your steps back to Massachusetts along the base of Mason Hill and climb back to the intersection below the summit. Rather than return to the summit, however, turn left to descend moderately steeply under a canopy of oaks. Note the flaky light gray bark of the white oaks. White pines soon become more numerous above a sapling layer of maple, beech, and birch. The pileated woodpecker excavations in one pine ooze sticky pitch that protects the wound from insect attack. Listen for the sweet, languid trill of 5.5-inch-long pine warblers high in the trees.

The path continues steadily downhill, steeply at times; bear right to level out in the closely spaced pine groves. Stay to the right at the intersection that leads to the big meadow and turn right again on the mowed path to explore the north end of the field. Here you have a second chance to admire the stunning views and perhaps observe tawny-coated white-tailed deer in summer, as well as more butterflies. A rusty hayrack sits idly along the path. Follow the woodland margin around the field and then enter the woods briefly. Some 10-inch-diameter ironwood trees (big for this species) may catch your eye. Musclewood is an apt alternate moniker for the species, given their sinewy gray trunks. When you reach the trail intersection, stay straight to return to your vehicle.

## MORE INFORMATION

Open daily sunrise to sunset, year-round. Free access; on-site donation is welcome from nonmembers. Dogs permitted, but must be on a leash at all times. Mountain biking, horseback riding, motorized vehicles, hunting, and firearms are not permitted. The Trustees of Reservations, Western Regional Office, The Mission House, P.O. Box 792, 1 Sergeant Street, Stockbridge, MA 01262-0792; 413-298-3239, ext. 3000; westregion@ttor.org; http://www.thetrustees.org.

## TRIP 8
## MOUNT GREYLOCK AND RAGGED
## MOUNTAIN VIA THE BELLOWS PIPE TRAIL

**Location:** North Adams, Adams
**Rating:** Difficult
**Distance:** 8.8 miles
**Elevation Gain:** 2,140 feet
**Estimated Time:** 5.0–6.0 hours
**Maps:** AMC Massachusetts Trail Map #1: D4, USGS North Adams;
trail map available online

**Fabulous spring wildflowers grace the route followed by Henry
David Thoreau 170 years ago. A side path leads to Ragged Mountain and a magnificent view of Greylock's east face.**

### DIRECTIONS
From Route 8 south (State Street) in North Adams, travel 1.1 miles to West
Main Street. Follow West Main Street for 0.6 mile and turn left on Woodlawn
Avenue. Drive 0.7 mile and bear left onto Notch Road. From the sharp left
turn at the Mount Williams Reservoir, drive 1 mile to a point where Notch
Road turns sharply right. Continue straight into a small gravel lot with room
for about six vehicles.

### TRAIL DESCRIPTION
A map is posted at the trailhead, where trail maps may be available as well. To
begin, stride easily up an old gravel road under an inviting canopy of sugar
maples. Planted Norway spruces stand darkly on the left. This initial portion
of the route passes through North Adams Watershed land. Some impressive
red oaks and white ashes border the raised roadbed that likely follows a road
initially built by pioneering farmer Jeremiah Wilbur in the late 1700s. The surface of Notch Reservoir sparkles on sunny days through the trees down to your
left. The road soon crosses a feeder stream confined to a culvert. In all, there
are around twenty water crossings (some merely a trickle) in the first 2 miles
or so, but none pose a problem for the hiker. Wildflowers such as wild ginger,
foamflower, false Solomon's seal, and jack-in-the-pulpit grace the verge.

On the left you'll pass an old cellar hole, evidence of former agricultural activity here. Three mills once bordered Notch Brook down to the left. Old trees

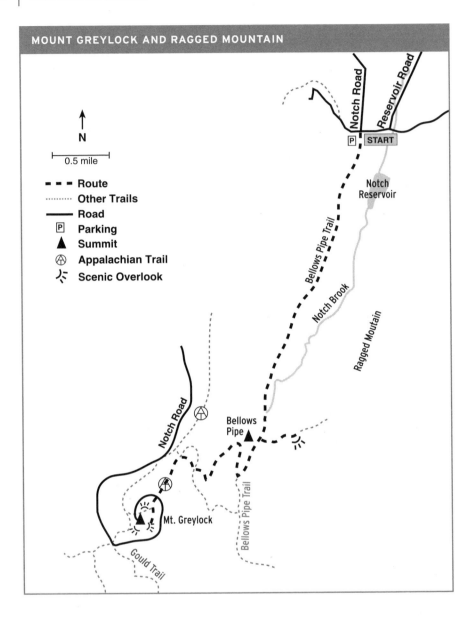

**MOUNT GREYLOCK AND RAGGED MOUNTAIN**

N

0.5 mile

- - - Route
......... Other Trails
——— Road
P  Parking
▲  Summit
Ⓐ  Appalachian Trail
ⳅ  Scenic Overlook

Notch Road

Reservoir Road

P  START

Notch Reservoir

Bellows Pipe Trail

Notch Brook

Ragged Moutain

Notch Road

Bellows Pipe ▲

Mt. Greylock ▲

Bellows Pipe Trail

Gould Trail

now border the roadway's left flank. Iconoclastic naturalist and transcendentalist Henry David Thoreau tramped this route toward the summit of Greylock in July 1844. Of it he wrote, "My route lay up a long and spacious valley called the Bellows, because the winds rush up or down it with violence in storms, sloping up to the very clouds between the principal range and a lower mountain." That lower mountain is Ragged Mountain. Trees now hem in Thoreau's "spacious valley." In his day the landscape was virtually devoid of trees and the half-pipe shape of the Bellows would have been much more noticeable.

One late May day, I watched a little orange, black, and white Blackburnian warbler gathering tiny branchlets in her bill from a small spruce near the road. Unfortunately, I wasn't able to follow her to where she was constructing her nest, no doubt high in a conifer. After a time, the path steepens and becomes rockier. Some of the feeder streams have carved out small ravines. In spring the lacy leaves and white, heart-shaped flowers of squirrel corn are exceedingly common. This lovely plant is the original version of the cultivated plant bleeding heart. False Solomon's seal is also very numerous among the ashes, maples, and birches. With the continued ascent, trees characteristic of northern hardwood forest soon appear—American beech and yellow birch, with striped maple in the understory. Wildflowers—among them mitrewort (named for the traditional bishop's headdress), clintonia, and wild sarsaparilla—grow lush in these rich woods, blooming in spring.

The tongue-shaped leaves of trout lily (a.k.a. adder's-tongue) blanket the steep slopes. In spring, sections of the trail may be wet. More wildflowers—Solomon's seal, rose twisted stalk, Indian cucumber-root, violets of various hues, and Canada mayflower—are a delight to the eye. The state forest boundary is marked by blue blazes. The path soon becomes narrower and more eroded. You'll notice that wildflowers that have begun to set seed in the valley, such as red trillium, are still in full bloom at this elevation. You've literally followed spring up the mountain. The trail splits briefly after you cross a flowing stream and turns sharply left. Apparently, a mill once stood at the head of the brook. Do not follow eroded path.

Note that the trees are of shorter stature here due to the harsher growing conditions. There is another temporary trail split (stay left). Spring beauty, with five delicate pink-veined whitish petals, blooms in profusion from here on. As the slope moderates, young deciduous growth is evident. Planted spruces and red pines are also in evidence as you reach the 0.5-mile-long side trail to Ragged Mountain South Peak on the left—well worth the extra walk. Turn to follow a narrow woodland path under Norway spruces. The undulating trail reaches a stone wall and turns left to parallel it for a short stretch. This wall once bordered sheep pasture. Bear left and commence climbing quite steeply through semi-open birch, beech, and maple woods. Shiny fragments of schist litter the path.

You'll reach a schist ledge on the right perhaps 12 to 15 feet high. Stunted trees, mountain ash, and azaleas convey the effects of elevation. Watch for the

**Pink-veined spring beauty is an ephemeral wildflower that must blossom before trees leaf out and shade it.**

sharp turn to the right that takes you up the steep and rocky trail via switchbacks, as it's easy to miss. After the second switchback, an attention-getting view of Mount Greylock's east face presents itself. Notice the flaky brown rock tripe (a type of lichen) attached to the outcrop a bit farther. Watch for a tiny side path on the right that leads a few feet to an open lowbush-blueberry-filled ledge where a truly stunning view of the Greylock massif awaits—wow! You are only about 150 yards from the wooded southern summit of Ragged Mountain, at 2,528 feet. Ahead lies the Hoosic River valley.

Retrace your steps to the Bellows Pipe Trail and turn left on the fairly level old road. Yellow birch, with brassy and peeling bark, predominates. You'll reach an intersection, where you'll turn right to leave the Bellows Pipe and ascend moderately. From here, it is 1 mile to the Appalachian Trail (AT) on a rockier path via the lean-to shelter on the right. Continue past it. A privy stands a few hundred feet farther on the same side. In spring watch for small, native white butterflies—West Virginia white and mustard white—nectaring on violets. The trail alternately steepens and levels out. Soon the angle becomes more serious and you'll find yourself stopping to catch your breath. In May white-blooming hobblebush brightens this slope traversed by switchbacks.

Among the stunted elephant-gray beeches and rock outcrops, the golden stars and glossy leaves of trout lilies glorify the hillside in spring, along with abundant spring beauties and red trilliums. At the Y trail intersection with the AT, take the left fork (actually more or less straight ahead). One glorious day near the end of May, I was treated on these heights to the most magnificent wildflower spectacle I have ever witnessed in the region. Shortly you'll arrive at intersections with the Thunderbolt Trail (the pioneering downhill ski trail) on the left and a short trail leading to Notch Road on the right, but continue straight ahead and ever uphill on the white-blazed AT. The treadway is rocky but firm, and the sweet spicy aroma of balsam fir fills the mountain air.

The beacon on the top of the Veterans War Memorial Tower soon comes into view ahead, appearing as a huge crystal sphere. This 93-foot high granite structure was built in 1932 to honor casualties of war. Stone and then railroad-tie steps lead you up to Rockwell Road. Cross it and climb the last angular section over ledge to the restored Thunderbolt Shelter on the right. Follow a paved path to skirt the summit parking area and find yourself among 15- to 20-foot-tall pyramidal balsams and to the granite Veterans War Memorial Tower on the commonwealth's highest summit, at 3,491 feet. A web of summit paths, with the tower at their center, leads to various lookout points that offer views northeast to New Hampshire's Mount Monadnock and many other points 60 miles or more distant. At the attractively rustic Bascom Lodge, water, restrooms, meals, and trail merchandise will be available when it reopens. The Civilian Conservation Corps constructed the lodge in the 1930s. Note that hikers are asked to fill water bottles from a spigot around the back of the building, rather than from the drinking fountain inside.

The plaintive, whistled *Old Sam Peabody, Peabody, Peabody* of white-throated sparrows is emblematic of this bit of boreal forest. Yellow-rumped warblers and dark-eyed juncos (sparrows that are slate gray above and snowy white below) also breed at these heights. When ready to return, walk back to the Thunderbolt Shelter and the AT, and begin the descent along the same route.

## MORE INFORMATION

Open sunrise until dusk, year-round. Access is free. The tower is open 9 A.M. to 5 P.M. daily from Memorial Day to Columbus Day, weekends only mid- to late May. Bascom Lodge was closed at press time. Mount Greylock State Reservation, Rockwell Road, Lanesborough, MA 01237; 413-499-4262 or 413-499-4263; http://www.mass.gov/dcr/parks/mtGreylock/.

## TRIP 9
## GREYLOCK RANGE CIRCUIT

**Location:** Williamstown, Adams, North Adams
**Rating:** Difficult
**Distance:** 12.7 miles
**Elevation Gain:** 2,390 feet
**Estimated Time:** 8.0 hours
**Maps:** AMC Massachusetts Trail Map #1: D4, USGS North Adams; trail map available online

**Four summits, including the state's highest peak, and arguably the most sensational panoramic vista in the entire commonwealth. The most exhilarating hiking the Berkshires has to offer!**

### DIRECTIONS
From the intersection of Routes 7 and 43 (a.k.a. Five Corners), travel north on Route 7 for 1.3 miles to Scott Hill Road on the right. Follow Scott Hill Road for 0.25 mile and bear left onto Route 43. Follow Route 43 for 0.9 mile to Mount Hope Park on the right. Turn right and cross the Green River on Hopper Road and drive for 2.1 miles (bearing left at Potter Road) to a large gravel parking area on the right at Haley Farm.

### TRAIL DESCRIPTION
From the parking area, at elevation 1,100 feet, follow the cobbled farm road overhung by sugar maples, past two gates and between stone walls to the Haley Farm Trail junction on the right; you'll be returning via that trail. A panoramic view of the steep, three-sided valley known as the Hopper—because of its resemblance to a grain hopper—is laid out beyond the hayfield. For now, continue past the Hopper Trail intersection on your right and descend gently on blue-blazed Money Brook Trail, where a dense stand of jewelweed blooms in midsummer. Unlike the predominantly orange jewelweed blossoms in this area, these are lemon yellow. Traverse the grassy low-impact camping area via a mowed path that skirts Hopper Brook at the boundary of the Hopper Natural Area. Bear left to cross the clear brook by way of a fine wooden footbridge, and begin an easy uphill walk along the opposite bank.

A recent reroute, where the raging brook had undercut the trail, winds up along the hillside to rejoin the trail where the fast-flowing brook bends

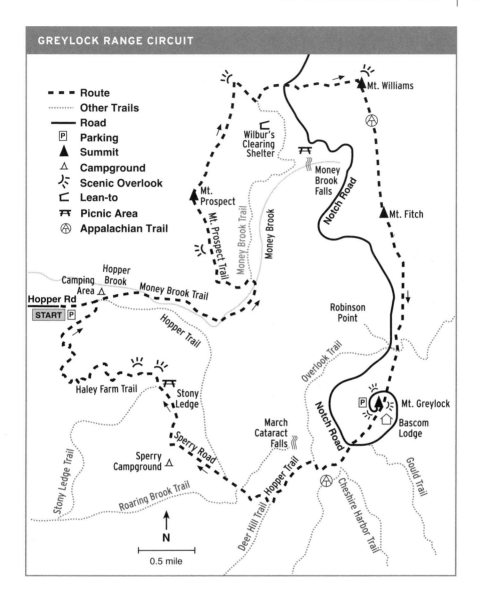

**GREYLOCK RANGE CIRCUIT**

Route
Other Trails
Road
Ⓟ Parking
▲ Summit
△ Campground
⚞ Scenic Overlook
⊏ Lean-to
🛱 Picnic Area
Ⓐ Appalachian Trail

Mt. Williams

Wilbur's
Clearing
Shelter

Money
Brook
Falls

Mt.
Prospect

Mt. Fitch

Notch Road

Money Brook Trail

Money Brook

Mt. Prospect Trail

Hopper
Camping Brook
Area △

Money Brook Trail

Hopper Rd
START Ⓟ

Hopper Trail

Robinson
Point

Haley Farm Trail

Stony
Ledge

Sperry Road

March
Cataract
Falls

Overlook Trail

Notch Road

Mt. Greylock

Bascom
Lodge

Stony Ledge Trail

Sperry
Campground △

Roaring Brook Trail

Deer Hill Trail

Hopper Trail

Cheshire Harbor Trail

Gould Trail

N

0.5 mile

right. You are walking along the southern flank of Mount Prospect, with the
brook accelerating between boulders. Sugar maple, white ash, black and yellow
birches, beech, and oak shield the path. The eroding force of water is evident at another bend in the flow. Soon after a stone-lined cellar hole on the
right, you'll reach a wooden footbridge across cascading Hopper Brook. At
a Y intersection, turn left to remain on spacious Money Brook Trail. At this
point you're now paralleling Money Brook, a tributary of Hopper Brook, upstream. Magnificent eastern hemlocks rise from the steep slopes as you cross

an energetic feeder stream on stones. Money Brook presents a lovely scene as it gushes through the ravine. A wider feeder brook flowing down through the Hopper requires a traverse on rocks; use caution. This is practice for a final crossing of Money Brook via stones a short distance farther.

Commence ascent of the rocky Mount Prospect Trail. The path turns left at a signed junction and narrows. It becomes very steep and winds along a virtual talus slope of schist, requiring some use of hands to negotiate. Caution is called for, especially when the rocks are wet. Soon you bear right under oaks to climb the prominent spine of Mount Prospect. Blueberries and huckleberries both offer the hiker sweet morsels in midsummer. Know huckleberry by its rough leaves. The challenging climb is interrupted now and again by more moderate sections, but the overall theme is relentlessly upward. Red maple, shad, and mountain azalea join the oaks on this dry, south-facing slope. You'll reach a vista point on the left where you'll be treated to wonderful long views of the Taconic Range and the Haley Farm close at hand as a reward. Some moderate uphill stretches remain until the wooded high point, where a rock cairn marks the 2,690-foot summit.

An easy-to-moderate descent leads through ferns; under yellow birches, maples, beeches, and a few red spruces; and over gneiss bedrock, taking turns leveling out and dropping. One mile beyond the cairn and after passing by darkened stands of young spruces, you'll emerge onto bedrock offering fabulous vistas of the northern Taconics and Vermont's Green Mountains beyond. Turn sharply right here to follow the white-blazed Appalachian Trail (AT) south over a needle-cushioned treadway down a spruce-covered east slope. Beneath the spruces thrives a sapling layer of beech and striped maple as well as maturing birches. Meet Money Brook Trail in a squishy light gap. A sign notes that Wilbur's Clearing Shelter is but 0.25 mile down the trail. Instead turn right and traipse over bog bridges through a damp spruce stand. On an early-August excursion, I came across an industrious AMC teen work group busy installing new bog bridges.

Bear right to cross Rockwell Road, rebuilt in 2007–2008, and begin your ascent of Mount Williams. Mature spruces are reproducing well here. Later, hobblebush and beech form a dense understory. The ascent becomes more challenging as you climb rocky "steps." But switchbacks make climbing the west slope of Williams very manageable. After leveling off in a low-stature wood, the AT bears left to reach the 2,951-foot summit of Mount Williams, named for Ephraim Williams Jr., whose estate posthumously helped found nearby Williams College. Limited views to the northeast are very nice and invite a welcome respite. Pin cherries with long-tipped leaves are among the

**Snowshoe or varying hares molt from brown to white to blend into the winter whiteness and evade bobcats.**

bordering woody growth. When ready to resume walking, be sure to turn left. The contorted bedrock along the initially level path shows the effects of the tremendous heat and pressure created by continental collision hundreds of millions of years ago.

A steeper and rockier downhill leads to Bernard Farm Trail junction on the left, but remain on the AT and begin a mostly easy climb to Mount Fitch. You will probably detect the aroma of balsam firs before you actually see them. Soon they become numerous. You will most likely have crested the 3,110-foot summit of Mount Fitch and dropped slightly in elevation again before you realize that you passed over it; at least that is always the case for me. The roughly 3 miles of trail between Williams and Bellows Pipe Trail wend through woodland that is pleasant but unremarkable, due no doubt to the anticipation of reaching the state's highest point. More than a mile beyond Mount Fitch, the Bellows Pipe Trail (Trip 8) goes left. It's only another 100 yards to the precipitously steep Thunderbolt Trail, one of the Northeast's pioneering downhill ski runs, on the left. Opposite the Thunderbolt, a side path leads to Notch Road and Robinson Point, but continue up on the AT, which in May is alive with wildflowers.

Blackberry canes fill a linear gap through which the trail passes on its somewhat rocky ascent past low beech, birch, and cherry trees. If it's not obscured by clouds or fog, you'll have your first glimpse of the globe atop the Veterans War Memorial Tower here. Finally, tread up stone and then railroad ties to paved Notch Road. Looking back yields a spectacular panorama that includes the rocky spine of Ragged Mountain and the Hoosic River valley. Cross the asphalted road and climb over bony outcrops to arrive shortly at the renovated Thunderbolt Shelter. The summit, topped by the granite tower, rises just a short distance ahead. A web of trails encircles the summit, which is enlivened by the clear, plaintive whistles (*Old Sam Peabody, Peabody, Peabody*) of white-throated sparrows in summer.

For fabulous views eastward, turn left at the Y split. A universal access path leads to an overlook where all promontories are identified on a granite tableau. Bascom Lodge, a real gem, was built in 1937 by the Civilian Conservation Corps but was closed at press time. When ready to depart, pick up the AT beyond the tower (where a unique roadside bronze relief map of the Greylock Range is situated) and cross the road. Stroll through bluish conical firs and cross the paved road again near the lofty radio antenna, where three toilets are situated. The AT descends steeply over rock amid red spruce and firs. When you reach the paved road, turn right, walk 100 feet, and reenter the woods on the right. A brief descent brings you via bog bridges to a scenic little boreal pond—the lodge water supply and headwater for Hopper Brook—where dragonflies zip about and green frogs gulp. At the Y split, leave the AT and stay right on blue-blazed Hopper Trail toward Sperry Road. Bear right at paved Rockwell Road and descend on a wide rocky path, turning left at the junction with Overlook Trail on the right.

The grade is moderate as you contour down the slope under a canopy of beech and birch trees with red spruces mixing in. After leveling out and passing by a shielded spring on the right, turn right to follow Hopper Trail down more steeply under a leafy canopy and along an unnamed brook to the gravel Sperry Road. Turn right and stroll down through the campground shaded by lofty spruces, passing junctions for a number of other trails, including Hopper Trail on the right. But remain on the roadway, passing the toilet facilities. The road begins to climb, easily at first then moderately, through mixed forest. During one visit here I was able to approach a dining snowshoe hare within 15 feet before it bounded away. The road loops at the end to Stony Ledge (elevation 2,560 feet), where in my opinion the most breathtaking vista in the state awaits.

What a scene—directly across the 1,500-foot-deep chasm of the Hopper, and 1,000 feet higher, is Greylock. From left to right, an expansive view encompasses all the peaks you scaled today—Prospect, Williams, Fitch, and Greylock. Wow! Picnic tables invite a long pause. Hopper Brook is audible, and the voices of thrushes spiral up from the extensive forest below. When ready to continue, find the Stony Ledge Group Site sign at the trailhead on the far side of the gravel turnaround. At the Y split, follow the sign left for the Stony Ledge and Haley Farm trails past an outhouse on the left and the brown picnic shelter on the right on a blue-blazed path. The drop is fairly steep amid hardwoods and spruce to the junction with blue-blazed Haley Farm Trail, where you turn right. Luxuriant spinulose wood ferns form a dense layer beneath the forest canopy, and mossy boulders make for very attractive woodland.

A final splendid vista, this one north toward Williamstown and the Greens, is yours at the end of a short path on the right. Haley Farm Trail descends the now oak-covered slope quite steeply, using switchbacks through two small bowls, and continues through a forest of well-spaced large oaks beneath which new growth seeks the sun. This forest shows signs of selective logging. Farther down, oaks give way to sugar maples, which do best in nutrient-rich soils. You'll reach level ground at last among birches and arrive at the hayfield you gazed across hours ago at the start of your hike. Mount Prospect looms ahead. Stroll through the meadow to the soothing trill of crickets in late summer. Turn left on the old road toward the parking area to end a rewarding day.

## MORE INFORMATION

Open daily, year-round. Access by foot is free of charge. Toilet facilities are located at the trailhead, the campground on Sperry Road, and the Stony Ledge Group Site, along Stony Ledge Trail. Carry-in, carry-out rules apply. Mount Greylock State Reservation is managed by Massachusetts Department of Conservation and Recreation. Regional headquarters: 740 South Street, Pittsfield, MA 01201; 413-442-8928; http://www.mass.gov/dcr/parks/mtGreylock/.

## TRIP 10
## HOPPER TRAIL TO MOUNT GREYLOCK SUMMIT

**Location:** Williamstown, Adams
**Rating:** Difficult
**Distance:** 8.5 miles
**Elevation Gain:** 2,390 feet
**Estimated Time:** 6.0 hours
**Maps:** AMC Massachusetts Trail Map #1: D4, USGS North Adams;
trail map available online

**From pastoral Haley Farm, you'll hike through lush woodlands to the Appalachian Trail and the state's only true boreal forest—arguably the most scenic route to the summit.**

### DIRECTIONS
From the intersection of Routes 7 and 43 (a.k.a. Five Corners), travel north on Route 7 for 1.3 miles to Scott Hill Road on the right. Follow Scott Hill Road for 0.25 mile and bear left on Route 43. Follow Route 43 for 0.9 mile to Mount Hope Park on the right. Turn right and cross the Green River on Hopper Road and drive for 2.1 miles (bearing left at Potter Road) to a large gravel parking area on the right at Haley Farm.

### TRAIL DESCRIPTION
A trail map is posted at the kiosk; copies may be available here as well. On weekends a Department of Conservation and Recreation employee may be on hand to answer questions. A chemical toilet is situated to the right. A wonderful view of the valley—nicknamed the Hopper because of its resemblance to a grain hopper—greets you from the very beginning. Follow the farm road past machinery, livestock, hayfields, and pastures of the functioning Haley Farm— a bucolic setting for a trailhead, to be sure. The angular mound of Mount Prospect rises off to your left. Shortly, you'll pass a sign with regulations and a brown metal barway. The cobbled roadway is lined by stone walls and overarching sugar maples. Blue blazes mark the route.

When you reach Haley Farm Trail on the right, step out into the edge of the hay meadow for a fabulous view of the Hopper, then continue straight on Hopper Trail. A bit farther, Hopper Brook Loop Trail leads off to the left. Continue straight to the Hopper Trail intersection and bear right on a narrow

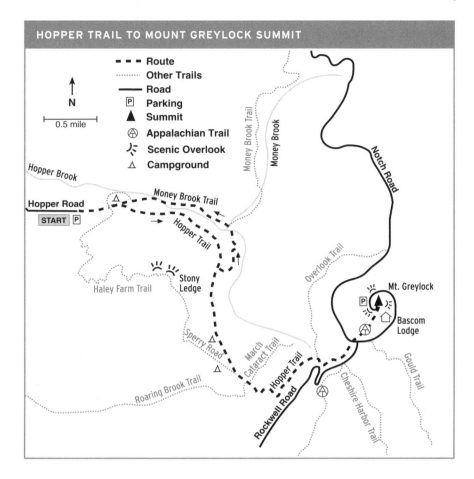

path up through prickly Japanese barberry, multiflora rose (which blooms in June), and honeysuckle shrubs—all invasive exotics characteristic of human disturbance. Before long, you'll enter a more attractive maple and white birch woodland and traverse bog bridges across seepages. Hopper Brook is audible. If wearing shorts, give wide berth to the stinging nettles lining the path. A steeper climb over a rocky path begins soon after you enter the Hopper—a 1,600-acre National Natural Landmark.

You'll reach the cutoff trail to Money Brook Trail on the left. You'll be taking this trail upon your return, but continue uphill now. Shiny schist with a high mica content litters the trail through sugar maple, white ash, and American beech woodland. Work your way up a grade that reaches 35 degrees in places. Yellow birch, another northern hardwood forest indicator, becomes quite numerous. When stopping to catch your breath, take a moment to appreciate the abundant bird life in this forest. Male black-throated blue warblers, black-throated green

**Gore Pond, the state's highest water body, hosts green frogs, dragonflies, and damselflies during Greylock's brief summer.**

warblers, ovenbirds, American redstarts, red-eyed vireos, and hermit thrushes sound off to attract mates and announce their claims to nesting territories.

Alternately level out and climb under sugar maples with an understory of sapling beeches, striped maple, and hobblebush. Sharp-needled red spruce becomes a dominant species as you approach the campground on Sperry Road at elevation 2,400 feet and 2.4 miles from the trailhead. The road was named for W. H. Sperry, the Greylock Reservation commissioner in 1900. Turn left at the gravel road (a chemical toilet is located along the road in the other direction) and pass another gravel road on the right that leads to Roaring Brook Trail, Circular Trail, and Deer Hill Trail Shelter. Slate-gray-and-white dark-eyed juncos trill sweetly from the tall spruces but nest on the ground. Opposite the check-in station is the path to March Cataract Trail. A wayside panel relates the history of the Civilian Conservation Corps (CCC), which at its zenith employed 100,000 men in 68 Massachusetts camps. Crews of 200 men, rotating every six months, were based here between 1933 and 1941. We continue to benefit from their fine work some 75 years on.

Bear right and follow the road over two gushing high-gradient streams—the first bounces over schist steps. About 100 yards past the check-in station, turn left to continue on Hopper Trail. Native stone steps indicate the route up through mixed woods of beech, birch, and spruce to a T intersection with

Deer Hill Trail—an old roadway. Turn left, on a gentle grade, past the source of a spring below to the left. Striped maple and hobblebush (with paired, heart-shaped leaves) are abundant. Five-and-one-quarter-inch black-throated blue warblers construct cup nests among the latter's pliable branches. You'll cross a few small flowages and maneuver over bedrock outcrops that are often slick underfoot. The evocative aroma of balsam should already be apparent.

In some spots the layered bedrock serves as a handy staircase. At the junction with Overlook Trail on your left, turn sharply right and continue uphill on rocky Hopper Trail. Soon you'll reach Rockwell Road, which ascends the mountain from the visitor center in Lanesborough, but the path bears left away from the asphalt. This and the other access roads were reconstructed during 2007–2008. Before reaching Rockwell Road again, turn left to follow the signed path to the Appalachian Trail (AT). The narrow path climbs into the balsam fir zone—part of the very circumspect boreal forest in this state. Here, at 3,000 feet above sea level, among the stunted yellow birches and firs, blackpoll warblers breed. This small black-capped, black-and-white bird is abundant in the vast boreal forests of Canada but virtually restricted to upper Greylock in Massachusetts. Its sibilant, vibrating notes are insect-like.

Very soon you'll merge with the white-blazed AT and continue straight ahead following a line of bog bridges to a serene pond where dragonflies dart about in search of insect prey and green frogs gulp like plucked banjo strings. I always linger at this lovely spot. You will see a small pump house on the right. If clouds do not obscure the summit, the 200-foot-tall radio tower with a 70-foot-tall TV antenna visible across the pond indicates that the summit is but a few hundred vertical feet away. The trail follows the shoreline briefly, leads up over a staircase ledge, and meets Rockwell Road near its junction with Notch Road (leading to North Adams and Route 2) on the left. Turn left and walk about 100 feet (past the intersection) to pick up the AT again on the left.

Your final ascent is through low-stature beech, yellow birch, mountain ash, and young balsams. Luxuriate in the sweet smell of balsam fir. The soil is thin at this elevation, and the growing season very short. Some trees show signs of stress, from both the harsh climate and acid deposition. Cloud droplets contain an elevated level of atmospheric pollutants—sulfuric acid among them. Although the trail traverses exposed bedrock, clintonia manages to thrive in pockets of soil. Its yellow flowers transform into china-blue berries that have given the plant its other moniker—blue-bead lily.

Finally, step out onto pavement near the summit garage. Chemical toilets are situated on the right, opposite the TV tower. In winter chunks of wind-blown ice from the structure can be hazardous to anyone below. Handsomely rustic Bascom Lodge, constructed during 1933–1938 mostly by the CCC, stands a short distance to the right. Here, restroom facilities, meals, accommodations, and some supplies will be available when it reopens. John Bascom was an original member of the Greylock Commission.

Walk straight, cross the access road, and continue on the AT through clumps of firs. A bronze relief model of the Greylock Range invites examination just after you cross the roadway again at the entrance to the summit parking area. Ahead rises the Veterans War Memorial Tower. Contrary to the belief that it was originally meant for the Charles River Basin, this tower was designed specifically for this summit. You can ascend the 93-foot-high granite tower, erected in 1932, via a spiral metal staircase. From a paved path on the other side of the tower, enjoy excellent views north, east, and south, including the bare summit of Mount Monadnock in New Hampshire. Bronze plaques interpret key landmarks. Listen for the signature plaintive whistle of the white-throated sparrow—*Old Sam Peabody, Peabody, Peabody*—at these heights.

After enjoying the refreshing air of the summit, retrace your steps all the way back down the mountain to the blue-blazed Money Brook Cutoff Trail on the right, which you passed on your ascent. Turn right and amble downhill fairly sharply under a canopy of sugar maples and ashes. Sharp-lobed hepatica (one of the earliest bloomers in April), red trillium, baneberry, jack-in-the-pulpit, mitrewort, and foamflower make this a fine wildflower trail in spring. Luxuriant growths of delicate maidenhair fern add to its charms in summer. Red oaks appear as you descend toward rushing Bacon Brook. The trail turns left at a flat spot under hemlocks. Pass large oaks and descend to Bacon Brook, but first cross a feeder stream on stones.

Turn left, walk 60 feet, and turn right to cross Bacon Brook on a fine wooden bridge. Bear left on a level path to Money Brook Trail. Follow the trail (signed Hopper Road) left and then right over a bouncy wooden bridge. At the T intersection on the far side, turn left (notice the big, columnar white ash on the bank), following Money Brook and blue blazes briefly downstream to Money Brook's confluence on the left with Bacon Brook. The merged streams flow west together as Hopper Brook. An old cellar hole on the left is all that remains of a former farmstead. Red-flowering raspberry thrives in a seepage area and blooms in late June. This old wood route carries you along an easy downhill adjacent to Hopper Brook (on Money Brook Trail), tumbling and cascading over stones—a pleasing finale to this mountain excursion.

The erosive force of flowing water is evident where the stream has cut deeply into the bank. Reach and cross another nice wooden span over the brook. Rumbling bass sounds, akin to distant thunder, emanate from rocks

## OLD-GROWTH CHAMPIONS

The recognized guru of old-growth forest in Massachusetts is an amiable, soft-spoken former Tennessean named Robert Leverett. Leverett has, more than once, bushwhacked up and down just about every rugged hillside that could possibly hide ancient trees. To be sure, almost all old-growth stands occur on steep, virtually inaccessible slopes that defy logging. Finding them has been a career-long challenge and a labor of love for Leverett, who is executive director of the Eastern Native Tree Society and president and cofounder of Friends of the Mohawk Trail State Forest, where many of the ancient ones reside.

In Massachusetts a mere 1,100 acres of designated old-growth forest remain out of a statewide forested expanse of 3 million acres. The two largest stands are only 200 acres each. Most are far smaller, some hardly bigger than a rural backyard. To be considered old growth, a stand must cover at least 5 acres and hold at least eight trees per acre that are a minimum 150 years old. It's not a high threshold to meet, one would think, but in Massachusetts, which was 75 percent deforested by the mid-1800s, even meeting those standards is not an easy proposition.

The largest Berkshire stand is within the Hopper, a federally designated 1,600-acre National Natural Landmark on the western flanks of the Greylock Range. Those 115 acres, and another 60 within Mount Greylock State Reservation, still hold 200-year-old red spruce. Six parcels totaling almost 100 acres remain in southwestern Berkshire County, within the Mount Washington and Mount Everett State Forests, including Mount Everett (Trip 44), Bash Bish Falls (Trip 45), Mount Race (Trip 46), Alander Mountain (Trip 47), Sages Ravine and Bear Mountain (Trip 50). Additionally, several stands of 20 acres or more exist in Monroe State Forest, including Dunbar Brook (Trip 15).

But old-growth forest is much more than old trees sporting eye-popping statistics. An old-growth stand is a climax forest type; by definition, that means it is self-perpetuating. In order for that to occur, the old trees must be regenerating themselves. Otherwise, the entire stand would eventually succumb to old age. Trees have natural life spans. For eastern hemlock that is about 600 years, for red spruce about 400. In addition to trees of every age class, old-growth forests host myriad other species. There is nothing like standing in the dim light beneath 150-foot-high old-growth giants listening to the ascending flutelike notes of a Swainson's thrush.

being jostled against each other by the swift current. Soon you'll pass through a couple of small grassy clearings where low-impact camping is permitted. There is an outhouse on the left. Reenter the woods and walk gradually up, soon rejoining Hopper Trail on the left, and straight back to your vehicle.

## MORE INFORMATION

The reservation is open sunrise until dusk, daily, year-round. Access for hikers is free. The Veterans War Memorial Tower is open 9 A.M. to 5 P.M. daily from Memorial Day to Columbus Day, weekends only mid- to late May. Bascom Lodge was closed at press time. Dogs must be on a 10-foot-maximum leash and must be attended at all times; owners must have proof of a current rabies vaccination and must clean up after their pet. Mount Greylock State Reservation, Rockwell Road, Lanesborough, MA 01237; 413-499-4262 or 413-499-4263; http://www.mass.gov/dcr/parks/mtGreylock/.

## TRIP 11
## SADDLE BALL MOUNTAIN

**Location:** Adams, Cheshire, New Ashford, Williamstown
**Rating:** Difficult
**Distance:** 10.4 miles
**Elevation Gain:** 1,675 feet
**Estimated Time:** 6.0–7.0 hours
**Maps:** AMC Massachusetts Trail Map #1: E4, USGS Cheshire, North Adams; trail map available online at the Mount Greylock State Reservation website

**This hike allows you to delight in a flower-filled hillside meadow offering incredible views and a damp boreal forest atop Saddle Ball Mountain, where sphagnum moss carpets the ground.**

## DIRECTIONS

From the south: From the Allendale Shopping Center in Pittsfield, drive north on Route 8 for 9.1 miles into Cheshire and turn left onto Fred Mason Road. Follow it north for 2.8 miles (it becomes West Road after approximately 1 mile) to West Mountain Road on the left. Turn left and follow West Mountain Road for 1.6 miles, past parking for Gould Trail to the Cheshire Harbor trailhead.

From the north: Take Route 8 south to Adams and turn right at the statue of President McKinley onto Maple Street. Follow Maple Street for 0.9 mile, and turn right onto West Mountain Road. Follow it for 1.6 miles to the trailhead.

## TRAIL DESCRIPTION

Park in the gravel lot at road's end, at an elevation of 1,560 feet. Follow the gravel roadway to your right (northwest) that leads into a meadow. Mount Greylock's summit looms above a gap in the treeline as you make your way past a small sign reading "Old Adams Rd. & Cheshire Harbor Tr." There is a map kiosk at the woodland edge. Just before a metal forest gate, a sign on the left reads "Old Adams Road to Cheshire Harbor Trail." A short path cuts off the corner of the rutted road. Bear right and follow the rocky roadbed up along stone walls in a forest of sugar and red maples, black and gray birches, young red spruce, and hemlock. Green-trunked striped maple and American beech fill the understory. Hay-scented, New York, and spinulose wood fern border the road. Bits of rusty barbed wire imbedded in trees hint that livestock once grazed on what was once a grassy hill.

Cutting gently across the slope's contour lines, you'll soon stride across intermittent brook beds. As you curve sharply left, a sign on the right reads "To Gould Tr." There is a major split in the roadway here, but the paths quickly rejoin. Several switchbacks lead up the slope, where you'll find the first balsam firs. Ancient steel culverts held together with rivets are artifacts of a bygone age. At the 1.0-mile mark, you'll reach Old Adams Road on the left. Turn left onto this predominantly level route as it contours along the lower slopes of Saddle Ball Mountain. These rich woods are fertile grounds for wildflowers, including Indian cucumber-root, sessile-leaved bellwort, Canada mayflower, red trillium, and clintonia (a.k.a. blue-bead lily).

Stream crossings are an enjoyable feature of this trail. In short order, you'll find a wooden vehicle bridge crossing an unnamed tributary of Bassett Brook. The brook wends through a small rocky ravine, producing nice little cascades en route. Some of the cobbles that paved the early road remain. Northern hardwood forest has reclaimed these slopes. One yellow birch reaches up four trunks. Hobblebush shrubs, along with spindly goosefoot (striped) maple saplings, dominate the understory, while hay-scented ferns soften the road shoulders. Arcing through a deeply cut bank brings you to a hemlock ravine offering a glimpse of a staircase of gushing cataracts—another Bassett Brook headwater. On the left, a small vernal pool hosts wood frogs and salamanders that play out an ages-old breeding ritual in early spring. Cross another wide vehicle bridge, and relish a small horsetail falls a few feet upstream.

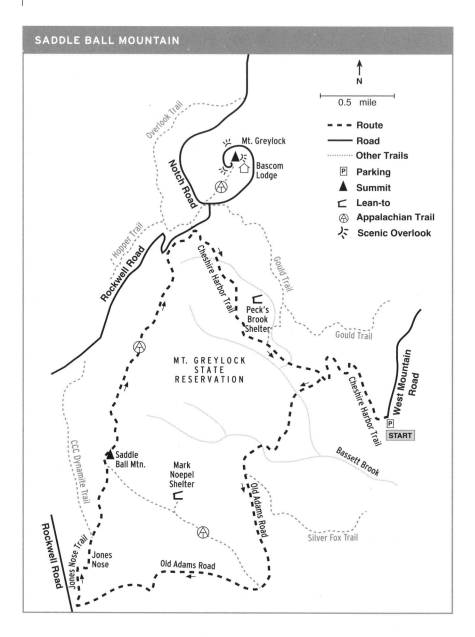

**SADDLE BALL MOUNTAIN**

N

0.5 mile

- - - Route
——— Road
·········· Other Trails
P Parking
▲ Summit
⊏ Lean-to
Ⓐ Appalachian Trail
⅄ Scenic Overlook

Overlook Trail

Mt. Greylock

Bascom Lodge

Notch Road

Hopper Trail

Rockwell Road

Cheshire Harbor Trail

Gould Trail

Peck's Brook Shelter

Gould Trail

West Mountain Road

MT. GREYLOCK STATE RESERVATION

Cheshire Harbor Trail

P
START

Bassett Brook

CCC Dynamite Trail

Saddle Ball Mtn.

Mark Noepel Shelter

Old Adams Road

Silver Fox Trail

Rockwell Road

Jones Nose Trail

Jones Nose

Old Adams Road

Enjoy the easy grade. The trail soon junctions with Silver Fox Trail, but remain on wider Old Adams Road. Trees with multiple trunks, along with pole-sized and sapling growth, belie former logging. A third brook crossing, the final Bassett Brook feeder stream, lacks the drama of the previous two. Vehicles have gouged muddy swales in the road, which winds through forest dominated by beeches and other hardwoods. Near the intersection with Red

Gate Trail on the left, red spruce become more numerous—first 6- to 15-foot-tall trees, then mature ones with boles 2 feet across. Continue straight ahead 100 more feet to cross the Appalachian Trail. Dense spruces create a refreshing microclimate. Old Adams Road continues through mixed woods and skirts a green, plush schist boulder as it heads easily downhill.

A tight-skinned beech on the right exhibits the claw marks of a black bear that scaled the tree years ago for the tasty nuts. Remnants of old stone construction lie on the left. The old cellar holes are soon joined by a stone wall bounding a former sheep pasture. A mewing and squealing mother grouse distracted me from my contemplation of the ruins before she took leave in a blur of wings. Some seemingly fresh bear scat filled with raspberry seeds also got my attention. After you pass another yellow birch with multiple spreading trunks, the descent steepens on a rougher track. Cross the modest headwaters of Kitchen Brook on another wooden bridge, and arrive at a T intersection. Turn right on Old Adams Road and continue upward over protruding thinly layered phyllite rock toward Jones Nose.

Here the roadway is cut deeply into the earth. At another old road junction, a sign informs that it is but 0.5 mile to Jones Nose parking. The descent now turns gradual. A few oaks, the first of the day, mingle with beech, birch, maple, and spruce. Lush undergrowth characterizes this young spacious forest. But soon forest gives way to a shrubby clearing of chokecherry, meadowsweet, steeplebush, and birch. A grassy path runs through this early growth, where indigo buntings and common yellowthroats reside in summer. The trail splits where the snowmobile route bears left. Detour around a metal gate and emerge into the open at gravel Jones Nose trailhead parking lot along paved Rockwell Road.

Pick up the Jones Nose trail on the right before the kiosk, which has a large topographical map of the reservation. The blue-blazed route leads up a sharply sloping meadow resplendent with blooming shrubs in midsummer. In late July and early August the hillside is ablaze as fireweed, steeplebush, and meadowsweet all add splashes of pink to the angular hillside, which is said to resemble the profile of a man who once farmed this area. Fireweed, as you might imagine, colonizes burned sites; its spike of orchid-like flowers are candy for the eyes. Steeplebush is also well named, since this shrub's tiny magenta blossoms form a spire; it's also called hardhack. Meadowsweet, which is related to steeplebush, has pale pink frothy flowers that attract bees and beetles alike.

Chokecherry (with blood-red fruits), goldenrod, and yellow Saint-John's-wort also enliven the slope in midsummer. And scrumptious lowbush blueberries may be reason enough to make the climb then. As you tread the

**Shrubland nesting birds favor the meadowsweet-filled slope of Jones Nose at Saddle Ball Mountain's southern end.**

narrow grassy path, glance over your shoulder to take in the ever expanding view to the south and west. The Taconic Range forms the border between Massachusetts and New York. As the ascent becomes tougher following a dip, a switchback leads up over stone steps into sapling mountain maples and over bedrock outcrops. A moist opening holds the odd white blossoms of turtle-head in midsummer. This plant's leaves comprise the sole diet of the colorful Baltimore checkerspot butterfly caterpillar. The big, coarse fern with bronzy green fronds is Goldie's fern. Hobblebush too is abundant under trees that reach greater heights.

At a Y intersection with CCC Dynamite Trail, take the right fork to the Appalachian Trail (AT) 0.5 mile distant. The climb increases again as you near the summit of Saddle Ball, and hermit thrushes play their magic flutes in summer. An outcrop on the right is a veritable rock garden of mosses, ferns, tree seedlings, and flowers. Enjoy the sunshine from a small bedrock clearing bounded by spruce, mountain ash, and birch. A side path on the left beckons you to a view of the Catskills; you won't be disappointed. From the ledge, enjoy views of the central Berkshire lakes, Lenox Mountain, and the distant Catskills. Back on the main trail, you'll soon bear right at the blue paint blaze for a detour. Watch your footing over rocks and roots under wet conditions. The narrow footpath goes serpentine, rocky, and undulating as you enter the boreal zone of redolent balsam fir just before the signed AT junction. Four-inch golden-crowned kinglets glean tiny insects from the foliage.

The AT leads north over the level wooded summit of 3,247 feet. Among the most abundant wildflowers along the trail is clintonia (a.k.a. blue-bead lily); in midsummer clusters of porcelain-blue fruits top its flower stalks. The spongy ground forms a great seedbed for balsam fir, as evidenced by all the young ones. The trail alternately rises and falls, crossing a small brook whose flow is stained root-beer brown by tannins. The erect stems of shining club moss poke up from runners like emerald bottlebrushes in luxuriant patches. Milky quartz rocks pop up here and there. At this elevation fog, cloud droplets, and rain produce near temperate rainforest conditions. The result—boulders covered with mossy mats from which toadstools emerge to create a scene from a Brothers Grimm fairy tale. Sphagnum moss, which contains dead cells that hold moisture, carpets the forest floor. Ghostly white Indian pipes rising from the mossy mat lack chlorophyll and so must obtain nourishment from other plants. Thin boardwalks called bog bridges lead through this cool, acidic wetland, past ground-hugging bunchberries adorned with clusters of scarlet berries in midsummer—a magical scene.

On clear days you can catch a glimpse of the Greylock summit to your right just before the AT arrival at the S curve on Rockwell Road—a reliable site for nesting blackpoll warblers, found in the commonwealth only on upper Greylock. Turn right on the AT to reenter the woodland. This forest is pre-dominantly deciduous—featuring beech—and the trail alternates level spots with steep climbs and descents, soon arriving at Cheshire Harbor Trail on the right at Rockwell Road. Turn right for the final 3-mile leg of the hike on this wide cobbled path under a canopy of northern hardwoods. Your descent will be moderate to steep over a well-worn trail that thousands take from Adams to the summit each Columbus Day.

Peck's Brook Loop Trail intersects on the left approximately halfway down. You'll level off amid copious hobblebush and then descend in earnest. At the familiar intersection with Old Adams Road on the right, continue straight on Cheshire Harbor trail, retracing your steps 1 mile to the parking area along West Mountain Road.

## MORE INFORMATION

Open daily, year-round. Access by foot is free of charge. There are no toilet facilities along the route. Carry-in, carry-out rules apply. Mount Greylock State Reservation, Rockwell Road, Lanesborough, MA 01237; 413-499-4262 or 499-4263; http://www.mass.gov/dcr/parks/mtGreylock/.

## POOL PARTY

In many ways, vernal pools are oddities. They're called pools, but they usually dry up by midsummer. They're referred to as "vernal" because the breeding frenzy they host happens in early spring, sometimes while snow still coats the ground. As ephemeral as they are, vernal pools are absolutely vital to a group of creatures able to reproduce nowhere else. These creatures are mole salamanders, wood frogs, and fairy shrimp. None can exist without these fleeting woodland water bodies.

Mole salamanders are a group of species that spend the bulk of their lives beneath the leaf litter. When they do emerge during the first early spring rains, when temperatures are about 40 degrees (late March or early April in the Berkshires), they head cross-country, straight for depressions flush with snowmelt and vernal moisture. The pools must contain leaves, sticks, and other woodland detritus that forms the basic energy source for the minute creatures that provide food for the salamander and wood frog larvae.

The mating ritual of spotted and Jefferson salamanders is really something to behold as the animals writhe and twirl in love's embrace. He drops packets of sperm that she picks up with her cloaca. She will then lay a fist-sized mass of gelatinous eggs that are attached to twigs beneath the surface. The eggs hatch into gilled salamander tadpoles and must reach sufficient size to survive on dry land before the pool disappears under the blazing summer sun.

But why rely on such undependable water sources? Well, because vernal pools don't contain fish. Fish eat salamander (and wood frog) eggs and larvae. Only the toxic red-spotted newt of local beaver ponds is able to coexist with the finned tribe. Other salamander species breed in brooks, bogs, or other locations out of the reach of fish. So it is only the large yellow-polka-dotted spotted salamander and the less common blue-flecked Jefferson's salamander that put all their eggs in one basket, so to speak.

If you have the opportunity to get out during what biologists call "big night," when the bulk of salamander movement to vernal pools occurs, wear your rain slicker, take a flashlight, and prepare to be amazed by the spectacle of dozens of mole salamanders and wood frogs, driven by age-old instincts, crossing highways and country lanes en route to breeding pools they may have visited each spring for 10 or 15 years. It's a sight you won't soon forget.

## TRIP 12
## FIELD FARM RESERVATION

**Location:** Williamstown
**Rating:** Easy
**Distance:** 2.9 miles
**Elevation Gain:** 120 feet
**Estimated Time:** 2.0 hours
**Maps:** AMC Massachusetts Trail Map #1: D2, USGS Berlin; trail map
available online

**Lying in the valley between the Greylock Range and the Taconics,
this loop leads through towering hardwoods, over marble ledges,
and along subterranean "caves."**

### DIRECTIONS
Coming from the south, at the intersection of Routes 7 and 43 in Williamstown (a.k.a. Five Corners), turn left onto Route 43 for less than 100 feet before
turning right onto Sloan Road. Follow Sloan Road for 1.1 miles to the signed
entrance drive for Field Farm on the right. Drive 0.1 mile to the small gravel
parking lot adjacent to the trailhead and maintenance garage/nature center.

### TRAIL DESCRIPTION
After studying the kiosk where trail maps are available, turn onto Pond Trail
and follow the yellow blazes through shrubby growth that includes invasive exotic buckthorn. On a January visit, I saw a flock of crested, tan cedar waxwings
gobbling down the blue-black berries. I watched as two birds comically passed
a berry back and forth between them several times—bill to bill—characteristic
courtship behavior in this lovely species.

Soon you'll reach a spring-fed pond adjacent to the former guesthouse,
called the Folly, built in 1965. The building is not occupied, but a large beaver
lodge resting along the shore near it certainly is. Turn right to follow along
the pond shore past a cattail marsh where muskrats—smaller cousins of the
beaver—reside. When the water level is high, you'll tiptoe over the waterlogged beaver dam and outflow before finding firmer footing beyond.

When you arrive at the North and South Trails intersection, turn right
and walk among young woody growth draped with vines—including poison
ivy—and then left to follow North Trail as it briefly approaches Sloan Road.

Big-tooth aspen, black cherry, white ash, and white pine stand tall, while old apple trees drop fruits for white-tailed deer. In winter, ruffed grouse snack on fruit-tree buds. You'll reach a large hayfield where North Trail turns right and skirts the edge. Pass through a hedgerow gap on the right, turn left, and continue in a northerly direction, paralleling the hedgerow where brush piles indicate recent cutting.

Gaze left to admire the Taconic Range, including Berlin Mountain (Trip 2). Pass through a gap in the barbed-wire fence and enter another old apple orchard. At the field's far end, follow Oak Loop as it jogs off to the right into a forest of cherry, white birch, ash, and sugar maple. Smaller sinewy ironwood and flaky hop hornbeam trees comprise the understory. After crossing a couple of rivulets and another fence gap, the path enters a stand of straight, tall hardwoods. This is the haunt of the crow-sized pileated woodpecker. Look for its big rectangular excavations in carpenter-ant-infested trees and listen for its wild laughing call.

Soon you'll descend wooden steps to cross a bridge over a larger stream. Watch for a massive, columnar black oak (more than 3.5 feet in diameter) left of the rather level trail. Its bottom section bears what appears to be a lightning-strike scar. To the right near the property line, barbed wire, now rusty and deeply imbedded in tree trunks, once confined livestock. Below the trees, a shrub called leatherwood, 2 to 5 feet high with incredibly rubbery limbs (its bark was once used by American Indians for bowstrings), is common.

Turn left and immediately reach a Y intersection. Go right to follow Caves Trail and begin a very gradual climb among numerous gray birches and hop hornbeams, 3 to 8 inches in diameter. One of the first indications of marble bedrock pokes up on the left in the form of a layered boulder capped with mosses and evergreen wood fern. Turn left, around the rock. When you reach the height of land, follow the contour over now rolling topography where a steep drop-off looms to the left. In winter, homes along Oblong Road are visible from this high point as you begin your descent. The tracks of gray squirrels leading from trees to excavated food caches—probably acorns—are obvious then.

In January, in addition to strings of deer tracks, a row of paired fisher tracks crossed the path. The Berkshire population of fishers—large, dark weasels—certainly seems to be on the upswing. A livestock barn is visible on the right on private property as the trail bears left and passes among tight-skinned black birches. Traffic noise from Oblong Road is evident as you reach an intersection; bear left to continue on Caves Trail.

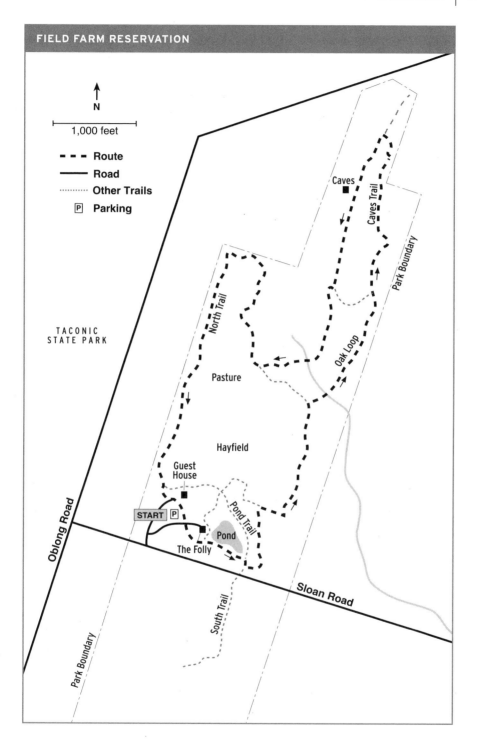

FIELD FARM RESERVATION

N

1,000 feet

- - - Route
——— Road
·········· Other Trails
P Parking

TACONIC
STATE PARK

Caves

Caves Trail

Park Boundary

North Trail

Oak Loop

Pasture

Hayfield

Guest
House

Oblong Road

START  P

Pond Trail

Pond

The Folly

South Trail

Sloan Road

Park Boundary

A tiny brook flows through a deciduous woodland of birch, beech, ash, and oak on its way to join the Green River.

The woods are dominated by big-tooth aspen (named for its leaves), and before long you'll reach a flowing brook on the right that mysteriously disappears beneath the marble bedrock that the trail crosses. Belowground—out of sight—the flow, aided by acid precipitation, dissolves the marble, carving out "caves" within the rock. To your left rises the rocky spine that you recently walked over. Several examples of these so-called caves appear as you continue south.

The tilted marble outcrops contain excellent den sites for porcupines, a favorite menu item of fishers. I was able to follow one porky's trail from its den through the snow to a stand of young beech trees. Here the rodent had climbed high to gnaw the nutritious bark off trunks and limbs. After leaving the caves area, the trail bears left and arrives at a junction with Oak Loop. Turn right and pass an up-tilted outcrop on the left. Wild strawberry plants, moss, and saxifrage adorn the rock. The path undulates easily over flat terrain and approaches an attractive brook babbling through woodland of black and gray birches, beech, ash, and oak. Watch for a patch of primitive horsetails looking like jointed green soda straws after you cross the wooden bridge. And note the witch hazel shrubs just before the wire-fence gap. A screech-owl nest box is affixed to a trunk on the right.

Beware of the stout thorns of multiflora rose thickets that fringe the pasture. Both it and prickly Japanese barberry shrubs are sure signs of soil disturbance. A few eastern junipers (a.k.a. red cedar) are also former pasture indicators. Stay right and follow the blazes. This area may be damp, as water flows off the slightly higher pasture ahead during wet seasons. When you reach the T intersection, turn right on North Trail and right again at the sign for it. The grassy path leads among more apple trees and multiflora rose.

Reenter the forest, pass through another fence gap, and bear left where large ash trees display their characteristic crosshatched bark. After bearing right, you'll start a gradual climb and switchback up an easy slope. On the right stand a few healthy American beeches, their smooth gray trunks unblemished by the fungus. On the left, another very large oak—this one a red—rises as two trunks in a victory sign forked low to the ground. Gigantic sugar maples with wire imbedded in them stand on the right. One very large hickory has barbed wire protruding from a depth of 9 inches.

When you reach the pasture corner, continue straight. Panoramic views of the Greylock Range and the Hopper (Trip 10) become ever more splendid as you walk on. You'll probably want to linger here. A lone nest box placed for the declining American kestrel stands like a sentinel out in the field. The Guest House bed-and-breakfast is visible ahead. Continue straight, through the sculpture garden, and across the gravel drive back to the parking area on your right.

## MORE INFORMATION

Open year-round, daily, sunrise to sunset. Free admission, but a $2 donation suggested for nonmembers over age 12. A chemical toilet is situated opposite the map kiosk. Dogs must be leashed at all times. Mountain biking is not permitted. The Guest House at Field Farm offers year-round bed-and-breakfast accommodation. Guided tours of the Folly are conducted on Saturdays, noon to 4 P.M., Memorial Day until early October; tour fees are $5 adult, $3 child. The Trustees of Reservations, Field Farm, Sloan Road, Williamstown, MA 01267; West Region office 413-298-3239; westregion@ttor.org; http://www. thetrustees.org.

## TRIP 13
## NOTCHVIEW RESERVATION

$ 🚶 🐕 ⛷ 🗺

**Location:** Windsor
**Rating:** Moderate–Difficult
**Distance:** 5.5 miles
**Elevation Gain:** 520 feet
**Estimated Time:** 3.0–4.0 hours
**Map:** USGS Cheshire, USGS Pittsfield East; trail map available online

**Twenty-seven miles of trails traverse 3,108 acres of high-elevation woodlands, dense evergreen stands, hilltop fields, and clear, swift-flowing streams. But Notchview is best known as a cross-country ski mecca.**

### DIRECTIONS

From the intersection of Routes 9 and 8 in Dalton, follow Route 8 for 6.2 miles to Route 8A on the left. Continue another 1.1 miles (for a total of 7.3 miles) to a paved roadway on the left at a modest sign for Notchview Reservation. Turn left and drive 0.1 mile to the large head-in parking area on the left.

### TRAIL DESCRIPTION

Begin by registering (a must in winter) at the Arthur D. Budd Visitor Center, where restrooms and excellent trail maps are available. Cross-country skiers will welcome the visitor center's warming and waxing facilities. An impressive kiosk with a display map and a weather station stands just beyond the building. After dropping your fee in the money pipe to the left of the kiosk, begin by turning right onto the mowed Circuit Trail and stride or snowshoe through a grassy field frequented by breeding eastern bluebirds and tree swallows (in the nest boxes) as well as bobolinks May through July. Venerable apple trees provide perches for the colorful birds and bountiful fruit for many species of wildlife.

Near the staff residence on the right, the wide grassy trail bears left past two old garages, but continue straight on a less defined path—Orchard Trail (no sign here). Soon a series of old concrete steps leads up into a now dense spruce stand. A row of honey locusts, their leathery brown seedpods littering the ground, bound the orchard. Walk or ski among apple trees straight ahead toward a woodland edge of young ash trees, yellow birches, and gray birches.

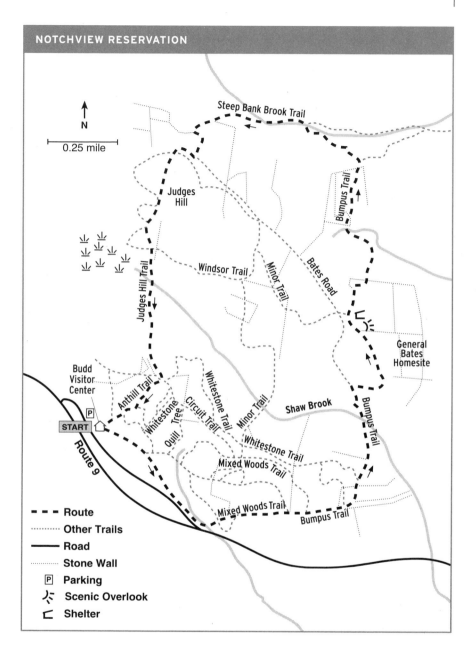

## NOTCHVIEW RESERVATION

N
0.25 mile

Steep Bank Brook Trail

Judges
Hill

Bumpus Trail

Judges Hill Trail

Windsor Trail

Minor Trail

Bates Road

General
Bates
Homesite

Budd
Visitor
Center

P

START

Anthill Trail

Whitestone
Circuit Trail

Whitestone Trail

Quill Tree

Minor Trail

Shaw Brook

Whitestone Trail

Bumpus Trail

Mixed Woods Trail

Mixed Woods Trail

Bumpus Trail

Route 9

- - - Route
.......... Other Trails
——— Road
.......... Stone Wall
P   Parking
人  Scenic Overlook
匸  Shelter

Traverse damp ground through reed canary grass. In autumn, American larch or tamarack takes on a golden hue before dropping its needles, making it the area's only native deciduous conifer. Bear right along the forest edge toward a monumental stone wall that uses small amounts of mortar. The builders incorporated some truly gargantuan boulders into its construction! Upon

**A fieldstone chimney and foundation are all that remains of the General Alfred Elliott Bates estate.**

reaching blacktopped Old Route 9, turn left, following it gradually down a few hundred yards past towering Norway spruces to its terminus at the current Route 9. Turn left and follow a graveled roadway under more spruces and over a brook with a culvert. The water plays over rocks to create a soothing music. Ash, big-tooth aspen, black cherry, and young, flat-needled balsam firs line the roadway along with stone walls.

Continue past Mixed Woods Trail under a canopy of sugar maple, white pine, ash, and prickly-needled spruce. You'll reach two round, stone gate pillars of the former Bumpus estate. Puff 'N Trail leads up to the left. Instead, pass through the portal to a Y split. The red-blazed Orchard Trail turns left up toward sloping Sawmill Field, but bear right on the wide wood road bordered by a stone wall among ash, yellow and white birches, American beech, cherry, aspen, and young spruce. The faint yellow blazes are difficult to discern, but the wide, often wet path is easy to follow. During particularly wet conditions, you may wish to traverse the field edge rather than the road.

Remnants of electric fence, now engulfed by tree trunks, delineate a former pasture. Be alert for a ruffed grouse (a.k.a. partridge) that may explode in a blur of wings. At the far end of Sawmill Field stands Trela Shelter. Turn right onto signed Bumpus Trail—actually a gravel road here. The trail was named for Judge Cephas Bumpus. It bears left along a bordering stone wall composed of quartzite and gneiss rocks and crosses a drainage. A massive white ash grips the brook bank on the right, and sugar maples crowd the roadway. Beeches and maples populate the hillside after the Mixed Wood Trail, while evergreens thrive in the moister soil right of the level roadway. Several smooth-skinned beeches display vertical black scars left by bear claws. Black bears are very fond of the triangular beechnuts and will climb high to feast on them.

Stone walls indicate a former field corner on the left just before an intersection with the Whitestone Trail. This part of the reservation retains an atmosphere of its former estate identity—first that of Louise Bumpus and later that of Lt. Col. Budd's Notch View Farm. Continue straight and pass two stone foundations (the Bumpus place) situated on the right and then through a break in a stone wall into a predominantly beech wood. At the intersection of Bumpus and Whitestone trails, take a right to remain on Bumpus and follow the slope contour on a somewhat rough treadway. Native red spruces intermix with maturing hardwoods—including yellow birch. Straight-boled red spruces tower over their numerous offspring. Wind throws (i.e., trees uprooted by wind) litter the forest floor; a mossy coat cushions some fallen spruces. What a wild contrast this primeval forest presents to the leafy estate lanes you recently passed over!

As you make your way gradually downhill, a flaky-barked black cherry more than 2 feet in diameter and bearing a yellow blaze stands trailside, but the abundance of spruce saplings imparts a fairyland ambience. Bear left to the sound of flowing water and arrive at Shaw Brook. Ice clings to fallen branches, creating a multitude of fantastic shapes during frosty seasons. Cross the clear-flowing stream on a wide plank bridge, and ascend the slope via switchbacks past ancient, gnarly sugar maples. Soon you'll reach the graveled Shaw Road. Enter the woodland opposite, and go right to continue on Bumpus Trail, an old wood road (muddy in spots) under a canopy of maples and ashes—some with imbedded bits of rusty barbed wire.

Bear left and enter the southern end of Bates Field along a sugarbush of venerable sugar maples. To the east lie distant, verdant ridges. Follow the wide mowed path along the field edge through goldenrod, milkweed, and invasive buckthorn shrubs. A standing fieldstone chimney and stone foundation up on the right remain from the General Alfred Elliott Bates estate. Bates was paymaster general of the U.S. Army in the first decade of the twentieth century. Beyond it are redbrick remains of a former pump house and wooden shed. Persistent woody, brown-beaded stalks of last season's sensitive fern flag the path's many moist spots as you continue the gentle climb. Turn right at the intersection toward the red-roofed Thomas Carl Pierce Shelter, from which a splendid view of the Westfield River notch beckons to the northeast—the best vista along the route. The white dome of a radar facility rests like a gigantic egg on the distant ridgeline.

Return to the main trail, continue straight, and bear right at an intersection with Minor Trail, walking a short distance farther to Whitman Trail on the left. Scattered gneiss boulders—much too large for use in wall building—attest to the passage of glacial ice eons ago. Follow Bumpus Trail straight along field border, rather than entering mixed woodland where car-sized glacial boulders reside. Note the tree with a white blaze nearly identical to the rectangular blaze of the Appalachian Trail. Bear right, walk gently downslope, and pass through a gap in the stone wall on the now single-track Bumpus Trail. As you descend beneath young beech, cherry, ash, sugar maple, and spruce trees, the sound of flowing water soon becomes audible. Listen for the flutelike refrain of hermit thrushes in early summer.

Patches of shining club moss contrast with the brown, lifeless forest floor in late autumn, as do the angular chunks of milky quartz partially clothed in moss. Beneath the now larger trees stand green-barked striped maple and some hobblebushes. Here the paint blazes are quite fresh and easy to follow. Soon you'll cross the gurgling 3- to 4-foot-wide brook on stones. At a corner of the stone wall, bear left to follow along the fence for 30 feet, then turn right to pass through it. Stone walls are numerous—you'll pass through or over a number of these reminders of early-nineteenth-century agriculture. A harsh climate and rocky soils essentially ended those erstwhile efforts by 1900.

Bumpus Trail finally bears left for good and follows the hill's contour. This slope has a few trees of admirable size, perhaps because it is rich moist woodland and logging on the steep incline would have been too costly. An unnamed brook tumbles along loudly below to the right. After a sharp right turn, descend steeply toward the stream and find yourself in the deep shade of eastern hemlocks, big yellow birches, and hobblebush. This descent is not recommended during icy conditions!

The Steep Bank Brook and Bumpus trails intersect at the clear, fast-flowing waterway. Turn left and cross a feeder stream on rocks—watch your step. Proceed along the opposite bank within this picturesque little ravine. In the next 0.6 mile or so, you'll weave up and down and back and forth across the stream, which affords ample intimate and photogenic views. This section is truly a delight to the senses. Upstream watch for a magnificent old white ash, fully 3 feet in diameter, with cross-hatched bark, on the right. The tough, relatively lightweight wood is perfectly suited for ax handles and baseball bats, but this giant seems too grand for such prosaic uses. The massive trunk contains hollows that in daytime may well house a denning furbearer.

At the confluence of two streams, cross the brook again and follow along its left branch. After another crossing, watch for an impressive yellow birch on the right that shades a sandy pool. This species requires cool, moist sites. A bit farther, a truck-sized gneiss boulder looks uncannily like the domed shell of a giant turtle. The mossy covering only adds to the deception. Head uphill, following white blazes in the company of stone walls, and arrive at the gravel Bates Road. Turn right and amble along for 300 feet to Judges Hill Trail on the left.

Climb steadily through mixed woods of red maple, beech, ash, yellow birch, cherry, and red spruce on a footpath marked by yellow blazes. The glossy deep green leaves of ground-hugging goldthread remain green all year. Level out on the summit of Judges Hill (elevation 2,297 feet) at the ruins of a building—a fieldstone chimney and foundation—to the left. According to local historian Bernard Drew (who grew up at Notchview), the promontory is named for Judge James Madison Barker, the founder of a sporting and social club called the Windsor Club. Club members—Judge Bumpus and General Bates among them—cooked luncheons here. An ingenious table made from a large stone slab resting on smaller stones sits in front of the fireplace. When the building was constructed, there was an unobstructed view from here; now it is totally wooded.

Begin a gradual descent; bear left at the fork (the white-blazed Judges Loop Trail goes right). Your yellow-blazed Bumpus Trail zigs and zags, then crosses Judges Loop Trail again. The wide path finds level ground amid beeches and maples. After a couple of bog bridges and an intersection with Windsor Trail, the wide pathway becomes Judges Hill Trail and undulates to Shaw Road. After negotiating a small stream, you may detect the spicy aroma of balsam; the shady forest has the wild feel of northern New England. This wood road can be very wet at times, and wooden culverts guide water under the steadily but gently climbing path.

Upon reaching Shaw Road, cross and continue on the level Judges Hill Trail in the deep shade of red spruces. A wayside exhibit on land stewardship greets you at a trail intersection, but continue straight for 200 feet to Anthill Trail. Turn right and tread a path cushioned by needles and mosses. Goldthread, named for its orange roots, is notably abundant on the shady woodland floor. The lack of sunlight and the acid soil limit what can survive beneath the evergreens. Whitewash at the base of one tree alerted me to what might have served an owl as a roost. Notice too the superabsorbent sphagnum moss—a sure indicator of saturated soil.

At a small white cement-block building outfitted with antennas, bear right and continue gently downhill to a junction where you should bear right again.

At the next junction—with Circuit Trail—turn left toward the visitor center; be sure to sign out.

## MORE INFORMATION

Trails open year-round, sunrise to sunset. The fee for nonmember adults is $2; children 12 and under are free. During ski season, the fees are $10 for adults and $3 for children 6–12; children under 12 are free. Dogs must be leashed at all times. Skiing with dogs is allowed only south of Route 9. Seasonal hunting is permitted north of Bates Road and south of Route 9. The Trustees of Reservations, Notchview, Route 9, Windsor, MA 01270; 413-684-0148; notchview@ttor.org; http://www.notchview.org.

## TRIP 14
## ASHUWILLTICOOK RAIL TRAIL–
## CHESHIRE TO ADAMS

**Location:** Cheshire
**Rating:** Easy–Moderate
**Distance:** Up to 9.6 miles
**Elevation Gain:** 35 feet
**Estimated Time:** 4.5 hours
**Maps:** USGS Cheshire

**This out-and-back section combines lakeside views, Hoosic River wetlands, and a dramatic hike into an enjoyable outing. It can easily be shortened to suit your tastes.**

## DIRECTIONS

From the south: From the Allendale Shopping Center in Pittsfield, drive north on Route 8 for 5.1 miles through Lanesborough and into Cheshire; look for Farnam's Road on the left. Follow Farnam's Road across the rail trail for 0.1 mile to the paved parking on the right.

From the north: From the intersection of Route 8 and Maple Street at the statue of President McKinley in the center of Adams, take Route 8 south for 7.2 miles to Farnam's Road on the right and drive 0.1 mile to paved parking on the right.

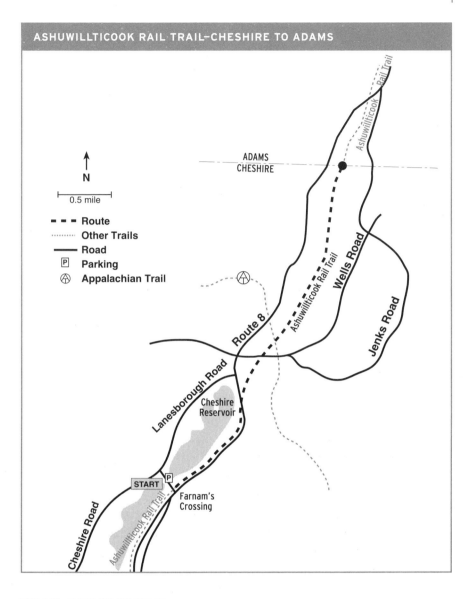

ASHUWILLTICOOK RAIL TRAIL–CHESHIRE TO ADAMS

## TRAIL DESCRIPTION

From the parking area (Farnam's Crossing), follow the sidewalk back along the left side of the roadway past the comfort station and picnic tables to a green iron gate; turn left. A kiosk is located on the left; trail maps may be available there. Miles are stenciled in white paint on the asphalt, while kilometers are noted on wooden posts. Much of the rail trail, like the original rail line, follows arrow-straight, level stretches, which makes a fast pace possible, if you wish.

When you stop, be sure not to block the path. There is a gravel-and-grass shoulder that you can step onto when examining fauna or flora. Basic rail-trail etiquette mandates that users stay to the right. Cyclists approaching from behind will ring a bell to alert you to their presence or call out that they are passing on the left; rollerbladers will also call out when passing. Because courtesy is the rule, there is surprisingly little conflict between user groups on the Ashuwillticook! And virtually no litter.

From the beginning, you'll be treated to postcard scenes of the most northerly of three basins that make up Cheshire Reservoir (also known as Hoosac Lake) and the verdant hills that form a terrific backdrop. The reservoir is the source of the northward flowing Hoosic River, a tributary of the famous Hudson. As you've probably noticed, the lake is popular with anglers. To the right of the level, asphalted path are quiet cattail-lined pools where painted turtles bask on logs. What appears to be a green slime coating on the surface in summer is actually a combination of two of the world's tiniest flowering plants: duckweed and the almost microscopic watermeal.

An array of shrubs—some native, some exotic—borders the right side. Among the exotics are Morrow's honeysuckle, its branches heavy with translucent red berries by midsummer, and autumn olive, which has silvery leaves. In contrast, staghorn sumac, dogwood, buttonbush, speckled alder, horsetails, and wild grape are natives. Among the native trees are willow, eastern cottonwood, quaking aspen, white ash, and maple. Colorful dragonflies dart about or hover in space, always keen for an insect meal or just patrolling their stretch of pond or lakeshore. Watch for the elegant black-and-white-winged widow skimmer, the orangey-brown Halloween pennant perched atop a weed stalk, the slaty skimmer, and the common green darner.

You'll reach a paved road at the 4-mile mark and pass through double gates (be alert for traffic). The tall white steeple of the First Baptist Church in Cheshire rises beyond the lake. At about the 11-kilometer post, you'll be treated to your first glimpse of Mount Greylock and the Veterans War Memorial Tower on its summit. Recycled-plastic benches are situated at strategic intervals along the route, providing creature comfort. From the benches you can scan the lake for ducks and geese or perhaps a flying great blue or green heron.

Soon you'll come upon a pair of wayside exhibits relating the history of this publicly owned 500-acre lake created in 1866 to provide reliable waterpower to mills downstream. Water from a red maple swamp on the right drains under the trail into the lake. A concrete post with a large white W near its rounded top stands like a forgotten sentinel on the right—a railroad whistle post. It prompted engineers to blow the locomotive's whistle as they approached a highway grade crossing. You'll see other such posts along the route, each one a quarter mile from a crossing. The original Pittsfield and North Adams Railroad line, constructed in 1845, was moved to higher ground before the lake was filled.

At the 12-kilometer marker you can gaze back to where you parked your vehicle. A tad farther is a 5-mile stencil on the asphalt (from the Berkshire Mall). A vegetated slough is bordered by a dense growth of speckled alder shrubs, and even a few highbush blueberry plants. You'll reach a small concrete spillway adjacent to Route 8—the south branch flows unimpeded from here until just before the Adams town line. Pass by the now familiar twin metal gates. A traffic signal makes crossing the busy highway less hazardous, but use caution. Next, cross the Hoosic, peering down into its clear flow over a gravel bottom—fine habitat for coldwater fish species. Unfortunately, Japanese knotweed, a leafy invasive exotic, crowds the bank.

You'll arrive at a narrow road crossing with the usual vehicle-excluding gates, followed by a nice view of Cheshire quartzite outcrops along the Appalachian Trail known as the Cobbles, almost 900 feet above the river. Pass homes and an old depot building, retrofitted as an auto repair shop. An official paved rail-trail parking area is located here at Church Street, which you cross. A monument to a serviceman killed in action in Afghanistan stands on the left. Soon you'll reach the 6-mile stencil and the 14-kilometer marker. From here, you'll be intimate with the river for the better part of the next 1.5 miles. The ample heart-shaped leaves of basswood trees shade the riverbanks, while massive willows thrive in saturated soil. In summer watch along the stream for a spectacular damselfly with an electric-blue abdomen and jet-black wings—the ebony jewelwing.

The floodplain of the Hoosic is rich in shrub swamps and marshlands that are home to myriad creatures. Listen for the gulps of green frogs, and the *fee-bee-o*, the last note dropping, of the little alder flycatcher singing from the swamp. You may note a pattern here. Marshes lined with cattails constitute the narrower portion of the floodplain west of the trail, while shrub-filled swamps occupy the wider portion of the floodplain east of the old railroad bed. Cross over the outlet from the marsh. A wire "cage" has been installed to keep beavers from plugging the pipe that permits a constant water level. You'll see more of these as you continue north. A red maple swamp and an extensive shrub swamp known locally as the Jungle stretch for some distance eastward and northward near the 15-kilometer marker.

**Great blue herons nest in rookeries on the Berkshire plateau but hunt for fish and frogs in valley wetlands.**

Mount Amos, part of the state's Stafford Hill Wildlife Management Area, lies close by to the east. At some point, a row of trees on the right was toppled like matchsticks by westerly winds, their naked root-balls oddly lined up. A sign that beavers are integral members, and major shapers, of this large wetland system appears in the small beaver dam on the right not far from the 7-mile stencil. A wayside exhibit flanked by benches asks the question "What is a wetland?" and then catalogs wetlands' numerous virtues. Perhaps the brightest red in nature belongs to the lovely lobelia called, appropriately enough, cardinal flower. A few spikes fluoresce here in late July along the Hoosic. Keep your eye on them as ruby-throated hummingbirds pay regular visits to sip sweet nectar.

Enter a shady and cooler forest environment of maples and oaks near the 17-kilometer post and 8-mile mark. An old redbrick building on the left is labeled Adams Pumping Station, although you are still in Cheshire. The right shoulder bristles with the green soda-straw stems of horsetails. Their hollow stems contain significant silica, which explains their other name—scouring rush. You'll reach another pair of green metal gates at a bridge over the Hoosic River. Bassett Brook, which originates on the east face of Saddle Ball Mountain, adds its flow here. Cross the small roadway and pass through a gleaming schist bedrock cut blasted to accommodate the rail bed.

A steady roar alerts you to an approaching spillway, where the river abruptly creates rapids and riffles downstream, totally changing the stream's character. This area is known locally as Cheshire Harbor, not for any nautical reason, but because local Quaker families harbored escaped slaves in their homes as part of the Underground Railroad. Stroll a bit farther to a bench and wayside exhibits about the trout—native and introduced—that inhabit the river. This is the hike's endpoint. The Adams line is literally a stone's throw farther north. You might want to take a breather here before retracing your steps all 4.8 miles back to Farnam's Crossing.

## MORE INFORMATION
Open dawn to dusk, year-round. Access is free of charge. Dogs must be leashed and under control; owners must clean up after their pets. Motorized vehicles (except electric-powered vehicles used by people with disabilities), horses, alcoholic beverages, fires, hunting, trapping, feeding of wildlife, and removal of park resources are prohibited. Accessible restrooms are available at the Farnam's Crossing (Cheshire) parking area. Massachusetts Department of Conservation and Recreation (DCR), Regional Headquarters, P.O. Box 1433, 740 South Street, Pittsfield, MA 01202; 413-442-8928; http://www.mass.gov/dcr. DCR's Universal Access Program, 413-545-5353.

## TRIP 15
## DUNBAR BROOK

**Location:** Florida, Monroe
**Rating:** Difficult
**Distance:** 6.25 miles
**Elevation Gain:** 1,010 feet
**Estimated Time:** 4.0 hours
**Maps:** USGS Rowe; trail map available online at the Monroe State Forest website

**Old-growth trees, massive boulders, and a roaring flow make the Dunbar Brook Trail a path of superlatives in the northeastern corner of the Berkshires.**

## DIRECTIONS

From the intersection of Routes 2 and 8 in North Adams, follow Route 2 east past the Hairpin Turn, Western Summit, and Whitcomb Summit to Whitcomb Hill Road on the left at 7.5 miles. Follow Whitcomb Hill Road (staying right at the intersection with Monroe Road) for 2.5 miles to the junction with River Road. Turn left and drive on River Road across the railroad tracks (active rail line—exercise caution when crossing) at the Hoosac Tunnel and continue another 4 miles to a gravel parking area (day use only) on the left across from the Dunbar Brook Picnic Area.

## TRAIL DESCRIPTION

From the parking area, where a stylized map and recreation area rules are posted, follow the rough track (left if you parked head-in) up the inclined power-line corridor for about 150 feet to a footpath on the right, where you enter a dark hemlock wood. Blue blazes mark the trail. Do not follow the wooden staircase fitted with railings, which goes down to the small concrete dam that spans the brook.

Amble along the hill's contour beneath shade-casting hemlocks along a rocky slope. Dunbar Brook, an evocative tributary of the nearby Deerfield River, flows below. The brook, like the forest, has a wild, untamed look. Yellow birches rise from the gneiss boulders they firmly grasp. As you descend toward the untamed flow, you'll be struck by the sheer size of some of the boulders in the streambed. But the sound of water cascading over rocks is what first captures your attention.

An outcrop bordering on your left drips moisture from its mossy coat. More boulders—some the size of trucks—protrude from the slope; others, rounded by flowing water, litter the stream. Yellow birches soon become more numerous, and one large tree leans over the trail. Along the path, foamflowers send up frothy white heads of modest flowers in late spring. The foamflower's leaves resemble those of geranium. The shrub with white blossoms earlier in spring and paired heart-shaped leaves is hobblebush. Climb higher above the brook and enter a mixed forest. A very tall and straight white ash stands sentinel-like on the right. Big-tooth aspen, red maple, and beech join the deciduous mix as you approach Dunbar Brook more closely. Early yellow violet, red trillium, baneberry, jack-in-the-pulpit, starflower, and wild ginger are among the woodland wildflowers you may spot.

When you reach an intersection, put aside the temptation to bear right and cross the stream on a wooden span; instead, turn left to ascend the steep slope (you'll be crossing the bridge to close the loop later). Blue blazes lead in both

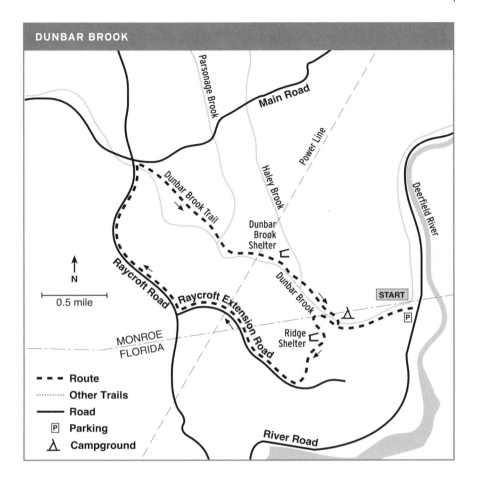

**DUNBAR BROOK**

Parsonage Brook

Main Road

Power Line

Dunbar Brook Trail

Haley Brook

Deerfield River

Dunbar Brook Shelter

N

0.5 mile

Raycroft Road

Raycroft Extension Road

Dunbar Brook

START

P

MONROE
FLORIDA

Ridge Shelter

- - - Route
......... Other Trails
——— Road
P  Parking
⛺ Campground

River Road

directions. The path undulates; then switchbacks take you up the steep incline. You'll experience nearly two-thirds of the hike's total elevation gain here. Dotting the slope are some impressive trees—sugar maples, yellow birches, and especially an ash—that escaped the ax thanks to the slope's acute angle

You'll see Ridge Shelter on the right; bear left just before it. A privy is located 100 yards farther along this old wood road on the right. Blazes are a bit spotty here, but the path is reasonably easy to locate on this level stretch. A pond on the left, transitioning to a bog, has virtually filled in with fallen leaves and branches. Arrive at gravel Raycroft Extension Road (a snowmobile corridor) and turn right. Although a road, it is more of a wide path through pleasant deciduous woodland that now includes oaks. Since you're far from the roaring waters of Dunbar Brook, the voices of neotropical songsters such as the scarlet tanager, the American redstart, the ovenbird, the red-eyed vireo, and the rose-breasted grosbeak are audible in late spring and early summer.

White birch—one of the most attractive of our northern trees—is plentiful along the roadway, and red spruce becomes common at this elevation. If you reach the intersection with a wood road bearing left down to Smith Hollow Shelter in late spring and early summer, listen carefully for the ascending flutelike song of Swainson's thrush, a species found only at high elevation in Massachusetts. Continue on Raycroft Extension Road through mixed woods dotted with big gneiss boulders, and then traverse a power-line right of way, where in late May the fragrant pink blossoms of mountain azalea dazzle the nose as well as the eye. Back in the forest, plantations of Norway spruce and red pine were established in the 1930s. Note the 6-inch-long cones of this exotic spruce littering the ground. Where sunlight penetrates along the road, Canada mayflower and clintonia bloom in spring.

Arrive at the gravel Raycroft Road and turn right onto this route—more traveled by motor vehicles, including all-terrain vehicles (ATVs), which are not permitted in the state forest. Nonetheless, potentially heavy ATV traffic on summer weekends is a good reason to plan your hike for a weekday. Sugar maples and light green hay-scented ferns line the road, while gneiss boulders protrude from the forest floor. Patches of cobblestones from early paving remain here and there, and then the road becomes rougher. Large, platy-barked yellow birches bear little resemblance to youthful, brassy skinned individuals. Two brooks flow through culverts under the roadway. Cabin-sized boulders—one characteristically serving as an anchor for a yellow birch—are eye popping. Continue the descent and bear right. On the left a blue-blazed path leads up to the wooded summit of Spruce Mountain.

As you continue downward on Raycroft Road, the sound of flowing water becomes apparent. More monumental boulders appear—one with a sheer face toward the road. You'll reach a flat pullout area on the right adjacent to Dunbar Brook. The roadway soon crosses it on a new wooden bridge. Dunbar Brook trailhead is to the right immediately after you cross, and may be obscured by a lumber debris pile. Enter the mixed forest of hemlock, beech, and yellow birch. The roaring, cascading stream gushes through tight squeezes between and over rocks, creating an evocative scene. But be careful if you move closer for a better view, as the rocks are slippery and the current unforgiving! Note how eons of flow have abraded and sculpted the bedrock. Between here and where you parked, the brook drops some 700 vertical feet.

The path is a bit difficult to follow initially, but that improves. It's difficult to miss the stone ruins of a millrace on the left where diverted water once turned a millwheel. Look for a blue blaze that leads across a feeder stream's rocky tumble where American yew bushes (a favorite of deer) thrive. The

**Dunbar Brook pours over gneiss boulders polished to a fine patina by the abrasive actions of the swift current.**

yew's needles resemble those of hemlock but are longer and a lighter shade of green. Climb up under a canopy of large hemlocks and northern hardwoods away from Dunbar Brook on a needle-cushioned treadway. Bear right when you reach a wider wood road that traverses mature woodland dotted with more boulders. One on the right is the size of a small house! There is little undergrowth except where big trees have fallen to admit light. Look for the clover-like leaves of wood sorrel. In June, its five-petaled, pink-veined blossoms resemble those of spring beauty.

Now temporarily out of sight of the brook, the path follows the grade downward, sometimes with moderate steepness. Spruce Mountain is visible through a screen of trees to your right. Watch for the large pink slippers of the moccasin flower during early June in the acidic soil. Red spruce is regenerating very well here, as evidenced by the abundant seedlings and small trees. No doubt the most imposing boulder along the route—verdant with moss and capped by polypody ferns—lies where the trail turns sharply right and skirts its overarching face. Other boulders are a veritable nursery for hemlocks and spruces. Tiny orange-throated Blackburnian warblers sing their lisping refrains from high in the evergreens during the breeding season.

As you continue a steady and sometimes rather steep descent, the sound of rushing water becomes evident again. Level out above the brook and bear left to parallel it. Seepage from the steep slope on your left may make for soggy footing. The rocky streambed, the cascades, and the crystalline pools are very photogenic. Walk over level ground where red-backed salamanders hide under logs by day and search for tiny morsels by night, while poisonous red efts wander blissfully in broad daylight. Cross a feeder stream on rocks rather by a decrepit log bridge. The trail widens under a leafy canopy. A boulder with a thick milky quartz intrusion on the right just before the power-line cut may catch your eye.

Raspberry, meadowsweet, interrupted fern, birch, and red maple fill the linear light gap. Back in mixed woodland, you'll be awed by two massive white pines—one twin-trunked—on the right. Tiny prince's pine, a club moss, and lots of ground-hugging partridgeberry, with coral red berries, form a miniature woodland beneath. On the downslope side the old roadway was built up to create a fine path. Soon Haley Brook joins in from the left. A mammoth split white ash towers on the left. Indian cucumber-root (which has an edible tuber), false Solomon's seal, and red trillium do well in the rich soil as you reach Dunbar Brook Shelter. Turn left and walk about 60 feet to cross a short wooden bridge over Haley Brook. Native stone abutments indicate that a bridge of higher capacity once spanned the stream. Beyond, where the path splits, be sure to stay right, close to Dunbar Brook, rather than heading uphill.

Another pair of massive, straight-boled, 100-plus-foot white pines tower above you here. Monroe State Forest is known for its old-growth pines. Soon bear right to cross Dunbar Brook on a long log bridge outfitted with AstroTurf to improve traction. Turn left and rejoin the trail that you trod earlier, back to the parking area.

## MORE INFORMATION

Open sunrise to sunset, daily, year-round. Free access. Chemical toilets available at Dunbar Brook Picnic Area across River Road. Carry in, carry out all trash. Snowmobiling is allowed when conditions permit. All-terrain vehicles and alcoholic beverages are not permitted. Monroe State Forest, Tilda Hill Road, Monroe, MA 01350; 413-339-5504 (Mohawk State Forest); http://www.mass.gov/dcr/parks/western/mnro.htm. Trailhead parking area and restroom facilities at Dunbar Brook Picnic Area owned and managed by USGen New England, Inc., P.O. Box 9, Monroe Bridge, MA 01350; 413-424-7229.

## TRIP 16
## WINDSOR JAMBS TRAIL

**Location:** Windsor
**Rating:** Easy–Moderate
**Distance:** 2.1 miles
**Elevation Gain:** 140 feet
**Estimated Time:** 2.0 hours
**Maps:** USGS Ashfield, USGS Cheshire; trail map available online at the Windsor State Forest website

**On this trip you will pass through a fairyland forest where thrushes make music fit for Pan and hike along a narrow gorge that roars with the power of fiercely flowing water.**

## DIRECTIONS

From the intersection of Routes 8 and 9 in Dalton, take Route 9 east for 11.3 miles to West Cummington. Turn left onto West Main Street; use caution, as the turn is at the bottom of a steep hill. Drive for just over 0.1 mile and turn left onto River Road, which you follow for 3.0 miles to the day-use area entrance on the left. Cross a small bridge over the Westfield River and park in the spacious paved lot.

## TRAIL DESCRIPTION

After paying the $5 parking fee at the small office, where drinking water is also available, stroll across the bridge that spans the Westfield River and cross the paved River Road. Turn right to wend your way through the campground under planted Norway pines toward the toilet facilities located at the far end. A water spigot is located there also. The trail commences just ahead under eastern hemlocks and is indicated with a blue triangular plastic blaze. The interlacing hemlock canopy lets little light reach the ground in this forest, so few plants are able to make a go of it in the shaded acidic soil. Two exceptions are mosses and touch-me-not (a.k.a. jewelweed), which forms thick stands in moist depressions. When its seedpods are ripe, they explode with the slightest touch, flinging seeds many feet.

Shade-tolerant Norway spruces do form little nurseries below their parent trees. Perhaps they are the result of a squirrel's forgotten food cache. Turn left

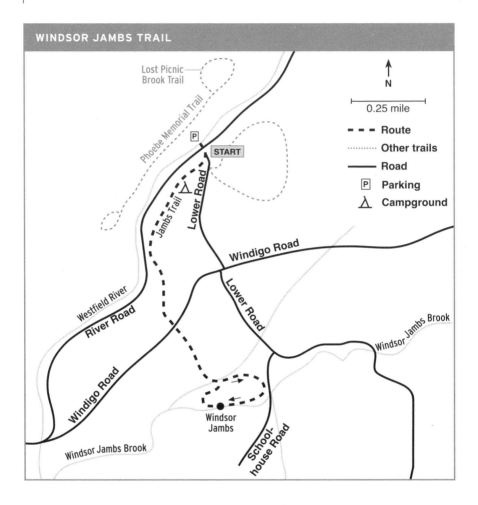

**WINDSOR JAMBS TRAIL**

Lost Picnic Brook Trail
Phoebe Memorial Trail
Jambs Trail
Lower Road
START
P
N
0.25 mile
Route
Other trails
Road
P Parking
Campground
Windigo Road
Westfield River
River Road
Lower Road
Windigo Road
Windsor Jambs Brook
Windsor Jambs
Windsor Jambs Brook
Schoolhouse Road

and cross the first of several spring-fed swales on split logs. A few flowers do dwell in the shade, including pink lady's slipper and Indian cucumber-root. Red-backed salamanders emerge at night to search for tiny prey, but they while away the daylight hours sequestered under moist logs. A thick layer of dead needles puts a spring in your step as you stride past clintonia flowers that bloom yellow in May and produce ceramic-blue berries in July. Hence this plant's other name—blue-bead lily. The forest soon changes to a mixture of sugar maple, red maple, and yellow birch. You'll pass stands of New York fern, which tapers at the bottom as well as the top, and spinulose wood fern. Wood sorrel forms clover-like patches, but the pretty midsummer flowers don't resemble clover at all. By the way, in summer, insect repellent is almost a must in the shady dampness.

Wind-thrown hemlocks have obscured the crossing for another swale, but with a little judicious stepping and following the blue blazes, you'll soon gain the other side. As you glance around, note the hummocky surface— what botanists call classic pit-and-mound topography, referring to a landscape characteristic of wet hemlock stands. When a tree falls, its root-ball decays to form a mound adjacent to the pit where the roots used to be. In such natural communities, the Swainson's thrush plays its panpipes in an upward spiraling refrain, adding a touch of magic to this forest. This bird winters from southern Mexico to Argentina and is quite an uncommon nester in the state. I was thrilled to hear two on a mid-July visit. In fact, the evergreens harbor a number of uncommon Northern Forest birds, including the tiny golden-crowned kinglet.

A diminutive forest of waist-high spruces and balsam firs stands enchantingly on the left, while quartzite boulders are scattered about. Stride up under Norway spruces—their 5- or 6-inch-long cones litter the ground. When you reach stonework, turn left and pass through an emerald carpet of mosses and Canada mayflower. A harsh chattering or barking may alert you to the presence of an impish red squirrel, unhappy with your intrusion. Another clue to the rodent's presence are cone middens—3-foot-high mounds of discarded spruce-cone scales within which the creatures construct burrows. Middens are visible at the base of trees on the left.

Timber-thinning operations are under way to permit more light and moisture to reach the forest floor. A newly thinned spruce stand is not particularly attractive, however. You'll reach the gravel Windigo Road and cross it, bearing left to where a sign helps relocate the path. Soon you'll enter another thinned plantation. The number of tree rings exposed by the saw places the date of their planting to about the time the Civilian Conservation Corps was active in the area. Lower Road is visible to the left. Soon you'll enter a natural woodland of white pine and sugar maples and pass through a damp area on a bog bridge.

Beyond the swale, soft haircap moss literally carpets the forest floor under the spruces. Seedling white pines have taken root in this carpet, as have lowbush blueberries, to create a storybook forest. Just before you bear left, a pile of quartzite stones shows that this land was once cleared. This is the red squirrel's stronghold, as evidenced by numerous monumental middens up to 12 feet in diameter. The mammals emerge from burrow entrances in the piles and race up into the protective tree branches, where they scold unwelcome visitors. Walk gently downhill over the cushioned path to the sound of flowing water. A

**Windsor Jambs Brook careens through a narrow passage to create cascades and falls that delight the eyes and ears.**

previously thinned area is filled with ferns and mosses. Bear right to descend fairly steeply along the slope to Windsor Jambs Brook in a hemlock ravine.

Cross the stream on rocks and use bog bridges to negotiate a seep luxuriant with wood sorrel. A sign on a tree points uphill in the direction of the Upper Jambs. Continue uphill moderately, bearing left under a mixed evergreen-deciduous canopy, and then more steeply to reach the Upper Jambs paved parking area on the left. Ahead runs a green cyclone fence along the length of the gorge. It is not particularly aesthetically pleasing, but it affords visitors a real measure of security. Begin your encounter with Windsor Jambs on the left at the upper end of the fence, and walk to the right along the edge of the defile. A sign at the top informs visitors that the upper Westfield, along with its tributaries, has been designated a Wild and Scenic River by the federal government.

You will want to dawdle here to appreciate the best views of the falls and cascades. The rock walls are flaky metamorphic phyllite, turned on end to create vertical faces that cleave off as a result of the freeze-and-thaw cycle.

And through this stone chute, the brook charges and careens with abandon, especially after snowmelt. When you reach a dead-ending outcrop, backtrack around and above it to continue your stroll along the fence. Thankfully, the fence is low enough that an adult can gaze (and photograph) over it. You'll arrive at a fabulous view of the major falls, rollicking and cascading into a tannin-stained pool. Sapling mountain maples have sprouted in the gorge between stone slabs. One rectangular chunk is some 9 by 20 feet.

You may not have noticed, but the spruces over your head are now native red spruces. The cones of this species are only 1.5 inches long. Hemlock and spruce are perpetuating themselves very well here. Descend easily to the terminus of the fence and level off for a closer look at the stream. Look to your right for a view upstream into the gorge. The major source for the impressive flow is Windsor Pond, only 1 mile east.

To continue on the trail, bear right under yellow birches and sugar maples (blue blaze on tree) and cross a tributary stream on stones. Stroll in company with a smaller brook and through a shallow ravine, passing through a fern glade. The route soon turns right to cross the brook on stones, but the crossing is obscured by fallen timber. Continue through the damp ground and rejoin the trail that you entered on to close the Upper Jambs Loop. Turn left to retrace your steps to the campground, the parking area, and your vehicle.

## MORE INFORMATION

Open sunrise to sunset, daily, year-round. A fee of $5 per vehicle is charged May through Labor Day for the day-use area. Free for ParksPass holders; vehicles with handicapped, POW, disabled veteran plates/placard; and seniors 62 and above with Massachusetts Senior Pass. Pets must be on a 10-foot-maximum leash, and attended at all times; must have proof of current rabies vaccination. Swimming is permitted at the day-use area only. Motorized off-road vehicles, alcoholic beverages, and swimming or climbing at Windsor Jambs are prohibited. Windsor State Forest, River Road, Windsor, c/o 555 East Street, Williamsburg, MA 01906; 413-684-0948 (413-268-7098 off-season); http://www.mass.gov/dcr/parks/western/wnds.htm.

## MORE THAN JUST NUTS

During my day job at the Massachusetts Audubon Society, I regularly field questions regarding what mammals visitors are likely to observe during their hikes. My pat answer is that few mammals are out and about during the midday hours; chipmunks and squirrels are all that anyone should probably expect to see. Except for European tourists, who seem to especially adore our chipmunks, that response comes as a bit of a letdown. At the same time, people aren't all that keen to come face-to-face with a black bear. The truth is that squirrels—most of which are decidedly diurnal—are fascinating critters.

Six members of the squirrel family are native to the Berkshires. Probably the most familiar is the eastern gray squirrel, a ubiquitous and often un-invited guest at backyard birdfeeders. Eastern chipmunks are likewise well-known to almost everyone. Red squirrels are common, but they are more likely to inhabit mixed evergreen-deciduous woods than suburban yards; we might think of them as country cousins to the bigger grays. The two nocturnal members of the group are mysterious, seldom-seen gliders—the southern and northern flying squirrels. And then there is a most un-squirrel-like relation. Also known as groundhog or even whistle pig, the woodchuck is actually a marmot, a rotund, burrowing member of the squirrel family. You're most likely to find woodchucks nibbling clover in a hayfield and then beating a hasty retreat into the safety of an adjacent woodlot.

Most squirrels are skillful aerialists. The impish, chatty red squirrel is an especially adept climber. The chunkier gray squirrel also spends much of its time aloft. Chipmunks have mastered life on the ground as well as in trees. Almost all squirrels (except the hibernating woodchuck) store food for leaner times. The image of a gray squirrel retrieving stored acorns, or red squirrels nibbling on a spruce cone as if it were an ear of corn, are familiar. But the carnivorous habits of squirrels are little known. It may shock some people to learn that squirrels—red squirrels especially—are among the primary robbers of birds' nests, consuming both eggs and young. It seems squirrels have a real taste for meat. I once watched spellbound as a chipmunk ate a mouse it was clutching in its forepaws. So, far from being boring, squirrels are well worth keeping an eye on!

## TRIP 17
## SPRUCE HILL

**Location:** Florida, North Adams
**Rating:** Moderate
**Distance:** 2.6 miles
**Elevation Gain:** 670 feet
**Estimated Time:** 1.5–2.0 hours
**Maps:** USGS North Adams; trail map available online at the Savoy
Mountain State Forest website

**This trip takes you to a rocky perch offering magnificent vistas of
Mount Greylock and the Taconics, perhaps the finest views after a
short hike in the entire region.**

### DIRECTIONS

From the intersection of Routes 8 and 2 in downtown North Adams, follow
Route 2 (the Mohawk Trail) east for 5.7 miles (via the Hairpin Turn). Turn
right onto Central Shaft Road just before the Florida town line. Stay to the
right at each of the next two forks and drive an additional mile (passing the
Savoy Mountain State Park headquarters on the right) to a wide gravel pull-off
area on the right with space for some ten vehicles.

### TRAIL DESCRIPTION

Initially walk down the rutted Old Florida Road, but turn right onto Busby
Trail after just 100 feet. Busby Trail is also a dirt road that suffers from off-road
vehicle traffic in spite of the prohibition. The level blue-blazed path is bordered and shaded by sugar maples, white and gray birches, striped maple, and
hobblebush shrubs. Before long, you'll find yourself in a power-line easement
filled with raspberry canes, gray birches, and sapling red maples. Chestnut-
sided warblers whistle their *pleased, pleased, pleased to meetcha* standard and
nest in shrubs here May through July.

Back in the forest, the blue-blazed trail detours left for a short distance,
paralleling the rutted and often wet road for a couple of hundred yards. Continue through a northern hardwood forest of birch, beech, maple, and hemlock. Patches of the Massachusetts state flower, trailing arbutus, grace both
sides at one point, their pale pink flowers emerging for a short time in early

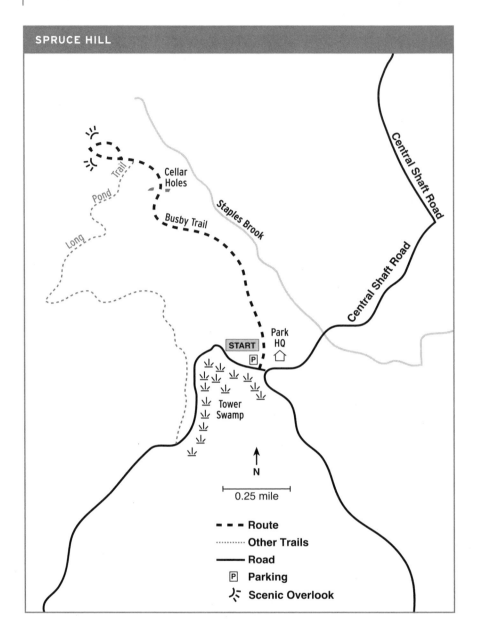

**SPRUCE HILL**

Cellar Holes

Trail

Pond

Long

Busby Trail

Staples Brook

Central Shaft Road

Central Shaft Road

START

Park HQ

P

Tower Swamp

N

0.25 mile

- - - **Route**
............ **Other Trails**
——— **Road**
P **Parking**
⚐ **Scenic Overlook**

May. More common, however, are the little paired leaves of partridgeberry and the heart-shaped leaves and spike of tiny white blossoms of Canada mayflower. Soon the roadway rises a bit and becomes drier and more pleasant.

Traverse another power-line cut filled with arrowwood (note the straight branches), bilberry, raspberry, and birch. A schist boulder in the road sparkles due to its mica content. The cut—devoid of trees—reveals the lay of the land as it dips and then rises to a ridgeline on the right. Ignore the narrow roadway that joins Busby Trail from the right a bit farther along, and begin a gradual ascent. So far, you've had to expend little effort. During the 1930s the legendary Civilian Conservation Corps planted groves of Norway spruces here and at many other locations. These trees are now maturing and provide habitat for birds and mammals that prefer conifer stands—such as fiery orange, black, and white Blackburnian warblers and impish red squirrels, which feast on birds' eggs as well as spruce seeds and fungi. There are virtually no spruces on Spruce Hill itself, and virtually all those that you encounter along the trail have been planted.

Listen for the sound of flowing water to your right and soon gaze upon a small brook. The stone remnants of former bridge abutments are visible along the far bank, as is a stone wall. You'll find white ash trees here, identifiable by their cross-hatched bark; they do well in moister ground. In fact, other than the spruce plantations, deciduous trees predominate. Bear right and cross a narrow drainage—wet in spring. The clean white trunks of paper birch are most attractive. Flowing water has eroded a gully and toppled a tree on the right, exposing rock and forming a modest falls during wet seasons.

Tread up and over flat schist bedrock; the remains of an unmortared wall stand on your left. The old road becomes rockier before you arrive at a jumble of rectangular cut blocks of schist on the left that indicate a former foundation. A few feet farther and on the opposite side gapes a well-preserved cellar hole. A yellow birch threatens to cleave apart stones of the right wall. It's interesting to contemplate what farm life would have been like here some 200 years ago.

Busby Trail now turns sharply left—where the shiny, pointed leaves of trout lily carpet the ground profusely—and begins to climb. The treadway becomes briefly sandy under a canopy of black cherry, ash, birch, and beech, and here is where you'll finally have to exert yourself. The sand too sparkles with flecks of the mineral mica. Soon you'll cross a stone wall built of good-sized schist blocks—moving them into place would have been no easy chore. A luxuriant growth of skunk currant about 18 inches high fills the sunny forest floor where you turn left. Shining club moss forms a patch of green "bottle brushes" on the right.

The path winds through attractive woodland. Listen for the lisping *beer, beer, bee* songs of tiny black-throated blue warblers in late spring and early summer as you approach ledge outcrops. They nest low among the wiry branches of hobblebush, which in spring are lovely with bunches of white

**This farmstead cellar hole along the Busby Trail creates an opportunity for reflection on farm life here two centuries ago.**

flowers resembling doilies. At the first trail split, follow the blue blazes straight ahead; at the second, turn right. Rock tripe—a type of lichen that morphs to green after becoming wet—looks like peeling brown paint on the rocks when dry.

You'll reach a steep but well-built stone staircase that leads up over the ledge. A bouquet of exquisite painted trillium—three petals, three leaves—clamors for attention partway up in May. Bear left and continue a more moderate climb under stunted beech trees into a wonderful spring wildflower garden. Clintonia (blue-bead lily), bunchberry (a tiny, ground-hugging dogwood), wild oats, and lowbush blueberry have turned this into a fairyland forest. The paired heart-shaped leaves and flat white flower clusters of hobblebush are abundant. The tiny fertile flowers produce red berries, and in fall the leaves turn lovely shades of maroon.

After a few short switchbacks, and one last ascent over a ledge outcrop, emerge into the open. Follow the blue blazes over bedrock and through a hobblebush thicket to the left, for the best views from exposed, slanted schist bedrock at an elevation of 2,566 feet. What a fantastic vista from this perch

## MASTERS OF WINGED MIGRATION

Well into the twentieth century, hawks in parts of this country were indis-criminately shot as vermin. A young man who began his career in Massa-chusetts, Maurice Broun, started to change all that in 1934 at a newly estab-lished sanctuary in eastern Pennsylvania called Hawk Mountain. Broun was the first warden there, having previously served two years as the inaugural warden of the Pleasant Valley Bird and Wildflower Sanctuary in Lenox from 1929 to 1931. After a stint on Cape Cod, Broun spent the rest of his long and notable career on the Kittatinny Ridge, where he and his wife, Irma, confronted the shooters and spent countless hours educating all who would listen about the virtues of raptors.

It's difficult now to imagine a time when such slaughter was condoned. Today people compete to count the hawks that soar past them on ridge tops rather than blowing them out of the sky. Almost every state has one or more established hawk watches where official counters track the seasonal movements of thousands of raptors. In this way, the relative abundance of each species can be gauged. It's serious science, but it's also a lot of fun. For some, it becomes an addiction.

In addition to Pennsylvania's Hawk Mountain, another storied East Coast site is Cape May, at the extreme southern tip of New Jersey. From late Au-gust to early December, earnest, eagle-eyed counters scan the skies, record-ing every individual of every species they see. When the watch is conducted over a period of many years, definite trends and patterns emerge. The pre-cipitous drop in American kestrels and the notable increase in Cooper's hawks first showed up through the counts.

Although Berkshire County is not along a major flyway, an observer at one of several Berkshire locations in mid-September to early October, and under favorable weather conditions—the recent passage of a cold front—may spot dozens or even hundreds of migrant raptors daily. Berry Hill in the Pittsfield State Forest (Trip 19) is one of those locations. Pittsfield's Edna Dunbar counted raptors from her lawn chair there for years. And Spruce Hill is another. This lofty perch is the perfect place to observe and tally raptors as they glide down the valley along the Hoosac Range. Once you've tuned into the autumn raptor spectacle, you'll be gazing skyward often to marvel at the masters of winged migration.

on the Hoosac Range! The Greylock Range is sprawled out to the west, with Ragged Mountain lying at its feet, and the Taconics stand beyond Greylock. North Adams lies in the Hoosac Valley to your right, with Pine Cobble poking up beyond. To the left is the town of Adams. At your feet, lowbush blueberry plants crowd the perimeter and show creamy bell-shaped blossoms in spring, and a few wind-trimmed mountain ashes hold forth to the right.

You'll want to linger here and soak in all the stunning scenery. If you are fortunate enough to have planned your hike for mid-September to early November, be on the lookout for migrant hawks passing by from right to left. You are most likely to observe broad-winged hawks (sometimes in "kettles" of dozens of birds in September), sharp-shinned and Cooper's hawks, black turkey vultures, and ospreys. The fall foliage spectacle in October is also reason enough to visit then. When ready to return, retrace your steps 1.3 miles back to where you left your vehicle.

## MORE INFORMATION

Open 8 A.M. to dusk, year-round. Busby Trail access is free. Pets must be on a 10-foot-maximum leash and attended at all times. Must have proof of current rabies vaccination. Motorized off-road vehicles and alcoholic beverages are prohibited. Savoy Mountain State Forest, 260 Central Shaft Road, Florida, MA 01247; 413-663-8469; http://www.mass.gov/dcr/parks/western/svym.htm.

## TRIP 18
## EUGENE D. MORAN WILDLIFE MANAGEMENT AREA

**Location:** Windsor
**Rating:** Easy
**Distance:** 3.8 miles
**Elevation Gain:** 115 feet
**Estimated Time:** 2.0–2.5 hours
**Map:** USGS Cheshire; map available online

**Area birders know Moran, a high and wild place, as perhaps the most reliable spot to find winter visitors such as the northern shrike and the rough-legged hawk.**

## DIRECTIONS

From the intersection of Routes 9 and 8 in Dalton, take Route 9 east for 6.2 miles to the intersection with Route 8A in Windsor. Turn left onto Route 8A and drive 0.9 mile north to the large paved parking area on the left.

## TRAIL DESCRIPTION

From the voluminous parking area, walk south and around a greenish-yellow metal gate, turning right and down a gravel road through mowed fields. About 100 feet to the left stands a gray granite monument erected in 1977, honoring sportsman Eugene D. Moran, for whom the property is named. From here you gaze down on an extensive wet meadow with mixed woodland beyond.

Return to the roadway and continue down it past shrubby willows (many sporting pinecone willow galls, induced by tiny flies, at their branch tips), dogwoods, alders, and planted crab apple trees that offer up red fruits to pine grosbeaks in winter. You'll soon reach the impounded Windsor Brook—note the remains of an old beaver dam to your left. Cross the bridge and climb the opposite slope to a large meadow where tall grasses and goldenrods wave in the breezes. In winter, scan the treetops for a northern shrike—a gray, black, and white robin-sized songbird with a hooked beak and carnivorous diet.

About 150 feet to the left, overgrown concrete foundations of farm buildings stand as mute testimony to this land's former use. It's obvious that at least one held livestock. But continue on the main track on either side of a rocky hedgerow of shrubs and small trees. The fields in summer bloom pink with meadowsweet. Cranberry viburnum's clusters of translucent red berries catch the eye in winter.

Soon the old roadway enters a fairly dense stand of red spruce and balsam fir. The firs have flat needles and are especially aromatic. The spruces stand in orderly rows, having been planted as Christmas trees during the 1960s. The conifer trunks are straight and crowded, creating a shaded boreal atmosphere. Light gaps are filled with fast-growing sapling spruces and firs. You're walking on level ground here. Some gray birches, aspen, maple, and elm appear. The birches and aspens are pioneers that rush in to fill sunny open spaces. During periods of wet weather, including snowfall, this path is often wet and muddy in spots.

The old cart way narrows a bit and heads up gradually between more fields—a 1-acre field on the right and a larger one on the opposite side—where apple trees border the path. The abundant fruits provide white-tailed deer, bear, and many other animals a tasty repast. In winter, look for tracks in the

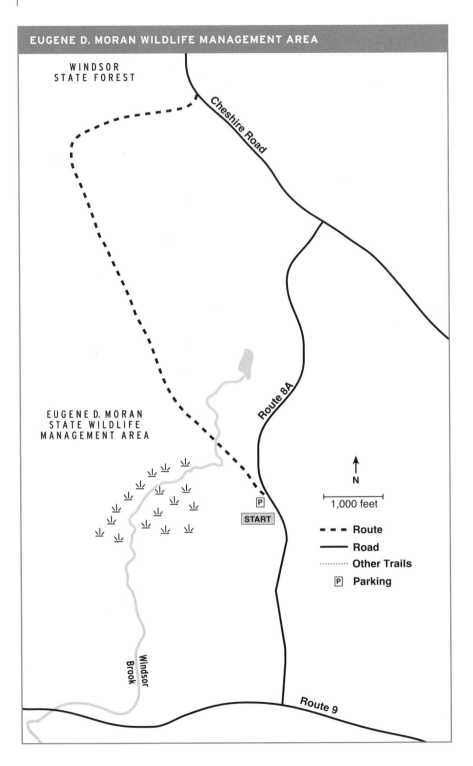

EUGENE D. MORAN WILDLIFE MANAGEMENT AREA

WINDSOR
STATE FOREST

Cheshire Road

EUGENE D. MORAN
STATE WILDLIFE
MANAGEMENT AREA

Route 8A

P

START

N

1,000 feet

Windsor
Brook

Route 9

- - - Route
—— Road
·········· Other Trails
P  Parking

**A granite monument to Eugene D. Moran overlooks a wet meadow that teems with life in spring and summer.**

snow-covered ground around the trees. Perched red-tailed hawks sometimes scan the fields for a furry meal.

Continue past the fields and a fallen stone wall on the left. Now sugar maples and black cherries border your route. Both produce valuable wildlife food, collectively known as mast. Faint blue blazes and ax cuts delineate the Windsor State Forest boundary. Step over fallen logs and enter the mixed woodland of evergreens (spruce and fir) and deciduous trees (cherry, maple, yellow birch, and American beech)—fine habitat for ruffed grouse. Stone walls on both sides provide another glimpse into the area's agricultural history. For a short span the path narrows through goldenrods, while the short, beady stems of sensitive fern delineate perennial wet spots.

In winter, watch for signs in the snow of deer mice. Their paired tracks are several inches apart with an obvious tail drag mark between. The footpath, now cut into the bank, curves right. A small logged area has regenerated to cherry, ash, maple, and balsam fir. The formidable root-ball of a big fallen red spruce on the right looks out at the path. Make your way along a raised cart path through a shrub swamp. Former logging roads veer off the main route, but stay straight.

A tunneling masked shrew left small holes, the diameter of a pencil, poked in the snow with tiny tracks leading away. These tiny insectivorous mammals have incredible metabolic rates and spend their brief lives in a virtually constant search for food. The much larger tracks of big-footed snowshoe hares should also be relatively easy to find on snow-covered ground. These "varying hares" attain a nearly perfect camouflage in winter—white coats.

Soon you'll reach paved Cheshire Road. A timber harvest was conducted here on the state forest under official auspices in 2007. To return, retrace your steps, but consider a slight diversion to the left along the perimeter of the large meadow that begins at the end of the rocky hedgerow. A wide mowed path along the edge will give you a slight change of scene. In winter watch the skies for big, hovering rough-legged hawks—visitors from the far north.

## MORE INFORMATION

Free admission. Open dawn to dusk. Open to hunting in season. The hunting season for ring-necked pheasant, stocked here, is generally mid-October through November. MassWildlife Western District Office, 400 Hubbard Avenue, Pittsfield, MA 01201; 413-447-9789; http://www.state.ma.us/dfwele/dfw. Windsor State Forest, Massachusetts Department of Conservation and Recreation, Western Regional Office, 740 South Street, Pittsfield, MA 01201; 413-442-8928; http://www.mass.gov/dcr/parks/windsor.

# 2

# CENTRAL BERKSHIRES

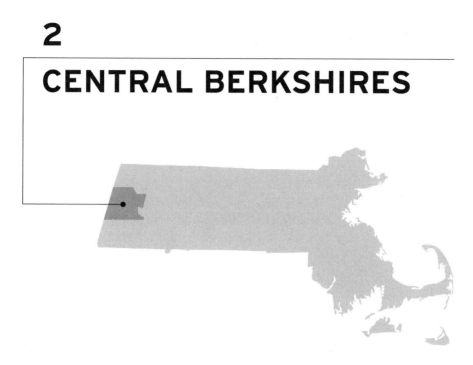

**THE CENTRAL BERKSHIRES HOLD THE COUNTY'S** most populous city, but also the commonwealth's most expansive state forest. The Taconic Range continues along the border with New York on the west, while to the east, the high, undulating, and sparsely settled Berkshire plateau stretches for mile after forested mile. Between them, the Housatonic River carves a wide valley through relatively soft marble bedrock.

Sixteen of the hikes in this guide are to be found in this section. The high points are not as lofty for the most part as those in the northern or southern Berkshires, but there are fine vistas to be enjoyed nonetheless. A number of hiking destinations in this section are far from run of the mill; these include the historic destinations of Shaker Mountain (Trip 20) and Keystone Arch Bridges Trail (Trip 34). A significant number have moving or still water as a major focal point; these include the accessible Ashuwillticook Rail Trail—Lanesborough to Cheshire (Trip 21), spectacular Schermerhorn Gorge Trail (Trip 29), the accidental Washington Mountain Meadow Trail (Trip 31), the little-known gem of Basin Pond (Trip 32), and tranquil and scenic Upper Goose Pond (Trip 33). Summit vistas are available too; among the hikes with a long view are Pittsfield State Forest (Trip 19) and Pleasant Valley Wildlife Sanctuary—Lenox Mountain (Trip 26).

## TRIP 19
## PITTSFIELD STATE FOREST

$  🐕  〽️

**Location:** Pittsfield, Lanesborough, Hancock
**Rating:** Moderate–Difficult
**Distance:** 5.0 miles
**Elevation Gain:** 1,000 feet
**Estimated Time:** 4.0–4.5 hours
**Maps:** USGS Pittsfield West and Stephentown, NY; trail map available online

**This trip is a trifecta of water attractions—lovely cascades and two of the state's highest natural water bodies: scenic Berry Pond and Tilden Swamp, a former bog turned beaver pond.**

### DIRECTIONS

From Route 7 at Park Square in the center of Pittsfield, turn west onto West Street and travel 0.5 mile to a T intersection; turn left to continue on West Street. Drive for an additional 2.2 miles to Churchill Street on the right. Follow Churchill Street for 1.7 miles to Cascade Street on the left. (Note: Cascade Street actually intersects Churchill Street twice; stay on Churchill until the second intersection with Cascade.) Drive on Cascade Street 0.7 mile and then bear right to reach the Pittsfield State Forest contact station (trail maps available here). Continue another 0.7 mile to the Lulu Brook Day Use Area and a spacious gravel parking area on the left. The trailhead is located across paved Berry Pond Circuit Road at an iron gate.

### TRAIL DESCRIPTION

Walk to the far (north) end of the parking lot and cross the paved Berry Pond Circuit Road diagonally to a brown iron forest gate adjacent to where Lulu Brook flows under the road. A sign marks the start of Lulu Brook Trail. Note that this trail apparently ends after approximately 1 mile, although Pittsfield State Forest maps show it continuing unbroken to its junction with Honwee Loop Trail about 0.25 mile farther. You can, however, follow the flow closely for as long as possible and then walk 25 feet to the right, meet and continue on the Honwee Loop Trail, a rough and rocky former roadway.

Another option is to begin your hike on Honwee Loop Trail. That trailhead is also situated across from the parking area, but about 75 feet before Lulu

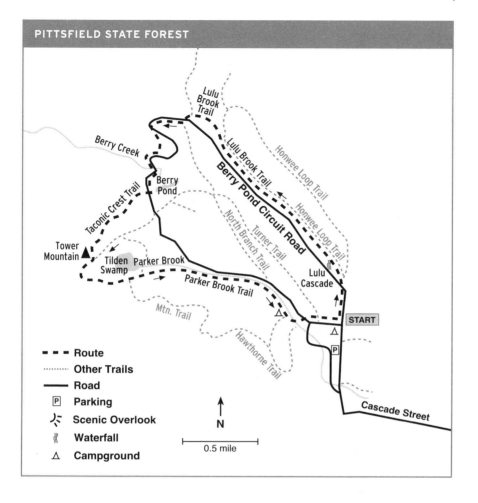

PITTSFIELD STATE FOREST

Lulu Brook Trail

Berry Creek

Lulu Brook Trail

Honwee Loop Trail

Berry Pond Circuit Road

Honwee Loop Trail

Taconic Crest Trail

Berry Pond

North Branch Trail

Turner Trail

Tower Mountain

Tilden Parker Brook
Swamp

Parker Brook Trail

Lulu Cascade

Mtn. Trail

Hawthorne Trail

START

P

Cascade Street

- - -   **Route**
..........   **Other Trails**
———   **Road**
P   **Parking**
人   **Scenic Overlook**
《   **Waterfall**
△   **Campground**

N

0.5 mile

Brook Trail. This wide, easy-to-follow path is frankly not as interesting as the Lulu Brook Trail, since from it the stream and its cascades are seldom visible. If you don't mind treading a sometimes narrow, more precipitous, and occasionally damp trail, you will be amply rewarded by an intimacy with the brook not possible from the upper path. The two paths closely parallel each other, so getting lost is unlikely. This hike follows Lulu Brook Trail (not recommended in icy conditions).

After walking for only a couple of minutes, you'll arrive at Lulu Cascade. The path briefly ascends a moderate slope and levels out on a schist ledge above the brook. This is not a large waterfall, but it's enchanting nonetheless, as the brook plunges into a crystal-clear pool surrounded by mossy boulders. But watch your footing. Over the course of the next mile or so, you'll be treated to additional, smaller cascades. A big egg-shaped milky quartz boulder, resistant to erosion and flecked with moss, may catch your eye a bit farther on. Occasional blue plastic triangles mark the trail. You'll walk upstream on an undulating trail through a ravine cut by the stream, under a canopy of hardwoods—oak, ash, maple, birch, and beech, joined by hemlock. Striped maple and hobblebush fill out the understory. Tall meadow rue—spindly stalks with thumbnail-sized leaves topped by starry white flowers—enlivens the banks in summer.

The path alternately climbs along the leafy slope and dips to brook level. Watch for ground-hugging trailing arbutus (the Massachusetts state flower) and partridgeberry along the upper level. At one point along the stream, there juts a tilted schist ledge from which flat slabs have cleaved. On humid summer days, fog may hang above the cold flow. The abundant moisture makes this a verdant place. When the trail suddenly ends at a left-leaning birch sporting a faded blue blaze, turn right and reach Honwee Trail in 25 feet. Follow this rough roadway on a steeper grade for another 0.25 mile and level out at an intersection marked by a few large white pines. The gravel road on the right leads to Honwee Mountain. Stay straight on what is now Lulu Brook Trail.

From here the old road morphs into a wide woodland path through patches of ferns under hardwoods and pines. You'll see a few yellow blazes too. An easy descent leads to a junction with an eroded all-terrain vehicle (ATV) trail. Turn left and cross the brook on a wooden bridge. Bear left to reach the paved Berry Pond Circuit Road. Turn right and walk up along the roadway on a grade that requires more effort as you continue. Mountain azalea bushes bloom pink in late May in a glade of hay-scented fern. The azaleas put on quite a show that includes a delicious aroma! The road curves left. Soon you'll arrive at the Taconic Crest Trail on the right, but continue on the road for another 150 feet to a second blaze (also marked with a white square in a blue diamond) on the right and a sign for Azalea Fields.

Turn right onto the grassy path as it follows the field edge, where raspberry canes proliferate in the sunshine. Enter the young woodland with Canada mayflower and ferns, and shortly you'll arrive at a level clearing—the summit of Berry Hill—and a T intersection. Shad trees, red maple, mountain ash, and shrubs—arrowwood, bilberry, meadowsweet, and lowbush blueberry, in addition to azaleas—thrive atop the bedrock. Turn right and walk gently down through a tunnel of vegetation to a gravel pullout area off the paved circuit road; this pullout offers wonderful glimpses west into New York State. Listen too for the evocative guttural croaks of common ravens cavorting on the air currents.

After taking in the views, walk downhill along the grassy shoulder of the paved road to the state's highest natural water body, Berry Pond, at 2,150 feet.

Showy white blossoms of fragrant waterlilies dot the surface. Close to shore, look in summer for pumpkinseed sunfish fanning their tails to create circular depressions in which the female deposits her eggs for the male to guard. On a late-June visit, we witnessed several pairs courting within the dozen nests visible in a small area. Continue along the shoreline and follow the gravel roadway straight where the paved road bears right. The gravel leads past campsites to the circuit road again, which you cross.

The Taconic Crest Trail continues on the far side up into beech, maple, and oak woodland. As you level out among the hardwoods, notice that many red oaks have twin trunks—the probable result of stump sprouting following logging decades ago. Semi-open gaps are now filled with yellow-green hay-scented fern and raspberries. Delicate maidenhair fern may attract your attention just before some eye-catching milky quartz ledge outcrops softened by emerald green mosses. The panpipe-like voice of the hermit thrush often reinforces the quiet under this leafy canopy. The canopy, however, is lower at this elevation.

You'll reach a level shrubby clearing on the summit of Tower Mountain (2,193 feet). Some distant views to the west are possible, but regenerating woody vegetation has nearly obscured this vista. Abundant lowbush blueberry patches start producing ripe fruit by the end of June—a tasty consolation. No doubt black bears visit here as well. The Taconic Crest Trail turns right, but instead, turn left on a narrow path that leads down through shrubby growth of wild raisin and raspberry. Back in the forest the path wends through attractive fern growth from which young trees—especially red maple—rise up.

You'll arrive at a rutted gravel ATV road under a mix of hardwoods and white pines. Turn right and bear gently left to reach an easy-to-overlook blue-blazed woodland path on the left that leads toward Tilden Swamp. Follow it through a young deciduous forest with a fairly dense understory. A few pole-sized American chestnuts have managed to reach 4 or 5 inches in diameter. These root sprouts are a sad reminder of a species that once dominated the forest community prior to the onset of the chestnut blight in the 1920s. Pass a side trail that joins on the right and continue downslope. The water's surface is visible through the trees—mostly oaks.

At the junction with Parker Brook Trail on the right, continue a few more feet to Tilden Swamp. Since the mid-1990s, beaver activity has turned the former swamp (or more accurately bog) into a pond. Here at the pond's southeastern end, you can inspect the tall, arched dam constructed by the world's second-largest rodent, and North America's largest. Pitcher plant, round-leaved sundew, leatherleaf, and other bog plants once grew profusely in the

**Scenic Berry Pond, located 2,150 feet above sea level, is the state's highest natural body of water.**

acidic conditions. Since the flooding, however, only a few bog remnants survive along the largely inundated shoreline. Yellow bullhead lilies protrude now from the water in summer, while dragonflies and damselflies zip about this peaceful spot. Pickerel frogs prowl the shoreline, and bullfrogs bellow from deeper water. But beaver ponds are part of a natural cycle, and one day a bog may return to Tilden Swamp.

Parker Brook is the outflow from the pond. Retrace your steps to the trail of the same name and turn left to follow it. After just a few steps the unmarked Pine Mountain Trail descends on the left to a new wooden footbridge across Parker Brook, but continue straight to follow the brook downstream under a lush canopy of beech, maple, birch, and oak. The narrow water-cut gorge is quite deep, and the pliable branches of hobblebush are bountiful on its steep side slopes. Miniature woodland protrudes from the leaf litter in one area on the right in the form of nonflowering shining club moss—all in all, a botanical delight. Colorful wood warblers are a joy to the eye as they search for leaf-munching caterpillars in the foliage. One of these birds to be found here is the lovely Canada warbler, which sports a necklace of black feathers on its citron-yellow breast.

Hemlocks increase in number before you reach an intersection with a trail on the right. Turn right, down the wider, more traveled path, which may have been a road at one time, and soon you'll come to a junction with an old roadway that runs up to Hawthorne Trail. Stay straight, passing clumps of partridgeberry whose red fruits are eaten by grouse, and head to a four-way intersection. Turn left to cross Parker Brook on a wooden span. Before doing so, check out the schist outcrops on the right along the stream under an umbrella of hemlocks.

Beyond the brook the path meets another trail on the left under oaks, and then another on the right. Bear right, walk by more chestnut sprouts and past campsites to the one-way, paved circuit road, where rows of Depression-era Norway spruces stand. Bear right, walk 50 feet, and turn left onto a wide gravel road heading modestly uphill. You'll amble by a number of side paths, including Turner Trail on the left. Mature oak trees tower on the right. After you pass a metal forest gate, you'll reach the paved road; turn left, following it straight back to the Lulu Brook Day Use Area and your vehicle on the left.

## MORE INFORMATION

Open sunrise to 8 P.M., daily, year-round. A $5 day-use fee per vehicle is charged early May to mid-October. Parking is free for ParksPass holders, vehicles with handicapped, POW, disabled veteran plates/placards, and for seniors 62 and above with the Massachusetts Senior Pass. Picnicking is permitted at the Lulu Brook Day Use Area, where there is also a restroom building. Alcoholic beverages are prohibited on all state lands. Pittsfield State Forest, 1041 Cascade Street, Pittsfield, MA 01201; 413-442-8992; http://www.mass.gov/dcr/parks/western/pitt.htm.

## A BEAR IN THE WOODS

Few creatures engender more trepidation than black bears. I'll readily admit to an elevated pulse every time I see one of these magnificent mammals. You're more likely to come upon one while motoring toward the trailhead, but trail encounters do occur. For me, they are always memorable, an elevated pulse and increased perspiration notwithstanding.

Black bears are formidable beings and, indeed, larger than life. An adult male generally weighs in at about 350 pounds, but record-sized individuals have tipped the scales at 600 or more. Although they may be brown or blond, I've never seen any shade other than black in these parts. The considerably larger grizzly bear does not dwell in our woodlands.

Healthy black bears are very rarely aggressive. They generally detect our scent, or hear us coming, and beat a hasty retreat. If you do meet one, remain calm and back off, allowing the bear to save face and retreat. You can thrill to the encounter once the animal has departed! A mother bear with cubs or yearlings merits special concern, but not panic. Giving the animals a wide berth is the best action.

Some bears, unfortunately, have learned to associate humans with food, and this is potentially dangerous—usually for the bear. Bears that are coaxed near human habitation by garbage, birdseed, or even deliberate handouts are far more apt to be struck by automobiles, shot, or otherwise treated badly. And a diet of human food is certainly not a recipe for good health for a bear. Sadly, as more and more of us choose to live in proximity with bears, the odds of conflicts increase.

Black bears are now quite common. While only 100 or so roamed area woodlands in 1978, now, just three decades later, that number is around 3,000. Several factors seem to be at work. The fact that our woodlands have come of age is probably foremost. A breeding nucleus was always present in northern New England, and as that population increased, competition forced animals south.

If you spend much time on the trail, you will find bear "sign"—a polite word for fecal matter. An ample pile of large-diameter, dark, blunt-ended droppings is almost certainly of bear origin, especially if major constituents are seeds and berry pits. Coming upon bear sign is a tangible reminder that we share this land with some rather amazing creatures—what conservationists like to refer to as "charismatic megafauna."

## TRIP 20
## SHAKER MOUNTAIN

**Location:** Hancock
**Rating:** Moderate
**Distance:** 6.5 miles
**Elevation Gain:** 790 feet
**Estimated Time:** 3.0–4.0 hours
**Maps:** USGS Pittsfield West

**This hike leads from the beautifully maintained Hancock Shaker Village to ruins and religious sites atop the neighboring hills in what is now the Pittsfield State Forest.**

## DIRECTIONS

Traveling north on Route 7, before reaching Park Square in the center of Pittsfield, turn left onto Route 20 (a.k.a. West Housatonic Street) and follow it west for 6.0 miles to the entrance for Hancock Shaker Village on the left. (Note: Route 20 passes through the village, so you'll see the main buildings before you reach the entrance sign; do not try to enter at the east end of the village, which is an employee entrance.) Park in the paved lot and walk eastward to the visitor center to register.

## TRAIL DESCRIPTION

When you register at the lovely modern visitor center (restrooms available), you will be asked to give your name and contact information, and to check in upon your return. Passes for hiking are given free of charge. Consider leaving a donation to support the good work being done by this nonprofit. Pick up the Boy Scout Trail interpretive material, which gives a great deal of information about this Shaker community. You may want to tour the village's many historic buildings now or upon your return, but be sure to leave sufficient time to complete your hike. You might also want to consider making the hike on a weekday to avoid all-terrain vehicles (ATVs). Note that the Pittsfield State Forest is open to hunting in season.

After registering, walk through the visitor center and out toward the famous stone round barn. Turn left just before the barn and exit through a gap in the fence. Caution: Here you have to cross Route 20; use the painted crosswalk. On the other side, walk down a gravel farm road to the first interpretive sign

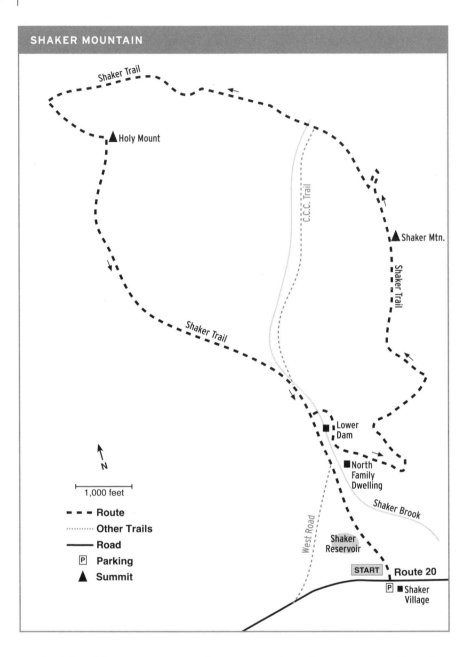

## SHAKER MOUNTAIN

Shaker Trail

Holy Mount

C.C.C. Trail

Shaker Mtn.

Shaker Trail

Shaker Trail

Lower
Dam

North
Family
Dwelling

Shaker Brook

West Road

Shaker
Reservoir

START    Route 20

P    Shaker
Village

N

1,000 feet

- - - Route
............ Other Trails
——— Road
P    Parking
▲    Summit

on the left of the Boy Scout Trail, constructed in the 1960s. Note the white circle within a green triangle that blazes the Scout Trail.

At the split, bear right and soon you'll arrive at the Shaker Reservoir (concealed by the earthen berm to your left), which was constructed in 1790. Continue through the rectangular field of grasses and goldenrod to reach West

**Hancock Shaker Village's iconic Round Stone Barn is the centerpiece of the Shakers' City of Peace, the hike's starting point.**

Road. Bear right and follow the gravel road under a canopy of oak, maple, hickory, black cherry, and black birch along pleasantly gurgling Shaker Brook. A low stone wall, the first of many, accompanies you on the left. In fall, Christmas fern and spinulose wood fern add splashes of deep green to the leaf-covered forest floor. You'll reach an interpretive marker indicating the footings of a bridge that once led over the brook to the North Family Dwelling, a shaker communal dwelling that housed 20 to 40 or more people.

A bit farther up the roadway you arrive at the Lower Dam, which supplied waterpower to the village. A slope rises up to the left, and yellow birch makes an appearance as the road begins a gradual ascent. Soon you'll come to a wooden footbridge across Shaker Brook; use it to get to the eastern side. *Note: Be sure to follow the trail in this counterclockwise direction rather than continuing straight, as the trail is unblazed in that direction!* You'll now have to bear right and walk a short distance downstream to the North Family Dwelling site; past occupation is made evident by the extensive carpet of shiny green periwinkle (*Vinca*) leaves carpeting this large site. Just past this site, you'll find the trail to Mount Sinai (Shaker Mountain) on the left.

Follow the contours and switchback to ascend the fairly steep slope. You'll encounter white pines, some quite large, and then shady woods of hemlock mixed with oak. In late spring look for the yellowish pinecone-like form of squawroot—a parasite on oak roots. At a branch in the cart road, turn left. Soon you'll arrive at a four-way intersection with a rather steep road and a utility line that leads up to an airplane beacon near the summit. Cross this rocky roadway and bear left; soon you'll arrive back at a second, higher intersection with the same road. Cross it again and continue gradually up on the blazed Scout Trail toward the Hancock Shaker community's religious site atop Shaker Mountain, marked by an interpretive sign. In spring and fall special religious services were held here. This brushy area has four sections of white picket fence demarcating the four corners of the site. American chestnut sprouts are numerous within. A bit farther I found chestnut husks in the trail—a rare sight these days!

Continue uphill, passing through an attractive growth of young white pine and hemlock. The predominant trees, though, are oak, with black cherry, American beech, and white birch. You'll reach a major intersection of forest roads showing heavy ATV use. Turn left and then immediately right (not straight ahead) to continue on the Scout Trail toward the Shakers' Holy Mount. Continuing straight leads down the ravine between the two promontories—the most direct route back to the village. Smooth gray schist bedrock protrudes from the treadway as you make your way across the head of the valley. Screened views down the valley and distant hills beyond are possible after leaf fall. Stately oaks now rise where the long stone wall on your right once bordered open pastures.

You'll reach an intermittent stream and cross it on stones; a stand of attractive young hemlocks rises to your right. Hardwoods—white ash, sugar maple, and black cherry—thrive on the slope. After frost has killed other ferns, a luxuriant growth of spinulose wood fern has the forest floor to itself. ATV activity can turn this path into a flowing brook during wet seasons as you head uphill.

At the intersection, turn left. Many of the rocks in this different stone wall contain milky white quartz, visible through the mossy covering. Beech trees become more common now, and below them thrives a Lilliputian forest of club mosses. These attractive nonflowering plants reproduce by spores as well as by runners. On the left, beyond the rock wall, hay-scented fern grows profusely. After you start climbing again, you'll soon pass through a stone-wall gap (wide enough to permit a team of oxen to pass) and enter a flat area of low-stature red maple, oak, cherry, and beech. This is the Lebanon, N.Y., Shaker community's Holy Mount. Extensive stone walls demarcate an enclosure of several acres. Follow the wall to a short path on the left that leads to a "perfect stone wall," the best example of the stone wall builder's craft on this hike. Once, both these summits were denuded of timber and long views were possible. It is said that the Shakers from the two communities would call to each other across the valley between the two religious sites, 1 mile apart.

Return to the main trail and turn left. The path, which leads downhill, is needle-cushioned beneath a stand of young, somewhat gnarled white pines. Raspberry brambles also indicate a former clearing. You'll encounter more stone walls and wide gaps, which allowed carts to pass, as you descend moderately to the Sacred Gap, a natural amphitheater where the brethren gathered for prayer and reflection. A small rock dam impounded water from a spring. Turn left and follow the woodland path up through hardwood forest and then down, arriving at a Civilian Conservation Corps (CCC) fire road (open to motorized vehicles) that parallels bubbling Shaker Brook. Turn left and follow the CCC road for a short distance to a split. The roadway rejoins a bit farther and then bears left. A big black oak bears the long scar of a possible lightning strike on the right. A little farther, at the base of a white ash on the left, sharp-lobed hepatica offers delicate purplish blossoms in early spring.

At the intersection, turn left on the Shaker Trail and proceed uphill. Be mindful of loose rocks underfoot. Continuing straight on the road leads to a brook crossing. A stone wall borders the path on the right, and wintergreen leaves enliven the verge. The route leads up fairly steeply for a bit, then heads downward to a major intersection. Shaker Brook is just beyond. Turn right and follow West Road downstream to the site of the High Dam, where dry masonry walls are visible on the opposite bank. The water that once flowed out from here powered an overshot wheel built in 1810 and destroyed by flooding in 1976. A little more walking brings you back to the footbridge over Shaker Brook to close the loop. From there, retrace your steps down West Road back to the village.

## MORE INFORMATION

Hours are 10 A.M. to 4 P.M. daily. Motorized vehicles, firearms, hunting, and fishing are not permitted. Restrooms and a café are located on the village grounds. Hancock Shaker Village, 34 Lebanon Mountain Road, Hancock, MA 01237; P.O. Box 927, Pittsfield, MA 01201; 413-443-0188; http://www.hancockshakervillage.org. Pittsfield State Forest, 1041 Cascade Street, Pittsfield, MA 01201; 413-442-8992; http://www.mass.gov/dcr/parks/western/pitt.htm.

## TRIP 21
## ASHUWILLTICOOK RAIL TRAIL–
## LANESBOROUGH TO CHESHIRE

**Location:** Lanesborough, Cheshire
**Rating:** Easy–Moderate
**Distance:** 7.4 miles
**Elevation Gain:** 20 feet
**Estimated Time:** 3.5 hours
**Maps:** USGS Cheshire

**The Ashuwillticook Rail Trail's southernmost section is studded with biologically rich wetlands that host a panoply of birds and dragonflies. The hike ends at the picture-perfect Cheshire Reservoir.**

## DIRECTIONS

From the south: From the Allendale Shopping Center in Pittsfield, drive north on Route 8 for 2.5 miles to Berkshire Mall Road on the left. A large paved parking lot straddles the road. The trailhead is located to the right.

From the north: From the intersection of Route 8 and Maple Street at the statue of President William McKinley in the center of Adams, take Route 8 south for 10.9 miles to Berkshire Mall Road on the right. A large paved parking lot straddles the road. The trailhead is located to the right.

## TRAIL DESCRIPTION

This portion of the rail trail is extremely popular, and the parking lot is often filled with vehicles by late morning. To have the best chance of spotting wildlife, you should arrive early in the morning. As is true in most populated areas these days, visitors should lock their cars and avoid leaving behind any valuables. Start by heading north, in the direction of a brick restroom building. Just beyond it on the left stands a kiosk where trail maps may be available. A donation pipe is situated near it. (For basic rail-trail etiquette, see Trip 14.)

You'll pass through a gap in a green metal gate and immediately peer into a wooded swamp with skeletal white pines and ribbon-leaved cattails on the left—just the sort of habitat favored by many aquatic and semi-aquatic creatures. Although modest, these are the headwaters of the Hoosic River, a northward-flowing tributary of New York's mighty Hudson. Binoculars are recommended for this hike, as the many open wetlands invite wildlife and

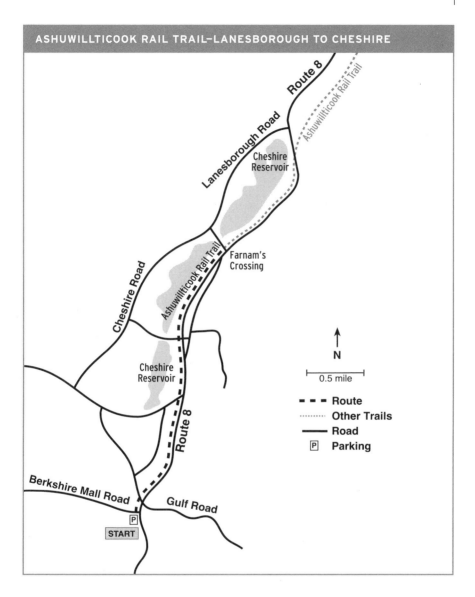

ASHUWILLTICOOK RAIL TRAIL–LANESBOROUGH TO CHESHIRE

thus wildlife viewing. During the warm months you're apt to observe familiar mallards, elegant wood ducks, handsome if overpopulating Canada geese, and perhaps a stately great blue heron. On a late July visit I counted 25 different species before walking the first half-mile. Smaller birds to spot include feisty eastern kingbirds, skulking gray catbirds, olive-drab warbling vireos, male red-winged blackbirds flashing red epaulets, and crested cedar waxwings. Look for painted turtles sunbathing on logs and various species of camouflaged frogs, including bellowing bullfrogs and banjo-plucking green frogs.

There is also smaller game to be sought. Butterflies are numerous in summer, sipping nectar through soda-straw tongues from blooming plants along the edges. Harder to miss are the darting darners and skimmers—the dragonflies. Some to watch for are common whitetail, ebony jewelwing, and widow skimmer. And don't worry: they are harmless. Extensive patches of bullhead lily pads blanket sections of the marsh. Their egg-yolk-yellow flowers never seem to fully open, while their stalks are rooted in the muddy bottom 3 or 4 feet down.

Soon you'll stride beneath an overpass that funnels motor vehicles to the north end of the Berkshire Mall and enter a shaded section of trail bounded by oaks, maples, black birches, ashes, and white pines. Shrub swamps and marshy sloughs continue on both sides of the asphalt. Trees felled by North America's largest rodent (and the world's second largest), the beaver, are in evidence in the red maple swamp. Red maples are among the most tolerant of trees. They thrive in poor, dry soils as well as in saturated ones, in bottomlands as well as on mountaintops. Along the right edge of this wooded wetland is a small assembly of the delicate and lovely maidenhair fern. Along a lengthy straightaway, a marshy pond on the left known as Berkshire Pond is filled shore to shore in late summer with both of our native lilies, the aforementioned bullhead species and the exquisite white fragrant lily. Recycled-plastic picnic tables and benches overlook the lily pond.

As you move out of sight of the water, attention shifts to nonflowering plants, including lush fern growth—sensitive and interrupted species—and the otherworldly green stalks of horsetails. Both these plant groups have existed virtually unchanged on earth for hundreds of millions of years. As you pass a few homes, be alert to a patch of poison ivy on the right before the next road crossing at Old State Road, where you'll walk around green metal gates. Quite handily, trail distances in miles are stenciled on the pavement, while signposts indicate kilometers covered. Perhaps the last remaining artifacts of the rail line besides the railroad bed itself are cement whistle posts. A large white W adorns the top of each post. They were an enigma to me until a kindly gentleman enlightened me. The posts told the engineer when to let go with his locomotive's whistle. And they're situated a quarter mile on either side of a road crossing.

You will reach another whistle post and the Cheshire town boundary marker on your right. At this point it's very obvious that you're walking along a former railroad track bed, as it drops off steeply to either side. Pass under utility lines supported by very tall, paired wooden poles that cut a swath over the hills to either side. The next road crossing, right after a miniature duck pond with domestic fowl and complete with paired gates, is the intriguingly

**Female mallards nest in marshlands and forage for plant and animal foods in shallow water.**

named Nobody's Road. The origin of the name is anybody's guess. There is a nice panorama of North Mountain to the east beyond Route 8. After the 8-kilometer marker and a copse of large water-loving willows, you'll cross the modest, clear-flowing Gore Brook. Its flow nourishes an alder and red maple swamp. Savage Hill, at 1,924 feet above sea level, represents the height of land to the west.

The view becomes expansive moments later as you gain the southern end of the middle lake basin. While cattails and lilies provide habitat and food for aquatic mammals and birds, to the north the surface is more open. Two series of benches and picnic tables face the lake at this especially scenic location. Check out the little pool on the right, where bluegills are often visible. The rusty corrugated-metal hulk of the former Farnam's Quarry stands forlornly at the far end of this basin of Cheshire Reservoir. Marble was once quarried and processed into lime there. Camp Mohawk's beach lies on the opposite shore. Reenter the refreshing woodland shade.

Near the lakeshore a clump of young quaking (or trembling) aspens, the favorite food of beavers, may all be sprouts from the same rootstock—a clone if you will, something aspens are apt to do. Their heart-shaped leaves are attached to twigs by means of long, laterally flattened stems, which causes them to flex and rustle or tremble with the wind. Maple, ash, and oak are more

## BEJEWELED MARVELS

There are living relics from the ancient past all around us. Consider the dragonfly, a creature little changed from the Carboniferous era 300 million years ago. One difference between today's modest-sized insects and the denizens of steamy, tree-fern-filled forests of eons past is that the latter were gigantic, with wingspans reaching 2 feet.

Today's damselflies and dragonflies, while only a fraction the size of their ancient relatives, are identical in many ways. They are among the most colorful, active, and fascinating insects to grace the planet's surface. World-wide, two groups are taxonomically lumped in the order Odonata (from the Greek for "tooth," referring to their jaws). They number some 6,500—more species than all the earth's mammals. All are voracious insect hunters, both as aquatic larvae crawling over pond bottoms and as adults performing aerial maneuvers that are nothing short of stupefying.

Odonates ("odes" for short) sport four wings that operate independently, allowing a degree of maneuverability unknown among other aerialists. They can fly forward, backward, up, or down; change course instantly; and do loop-the-loops. Then too, their eyesight is nothing short of phenomenal. The huge, nearly wrap-around compound eyes that comprise a large proportion of their heads impart a nearly 360-degree field of view. Other flying insects stand little chance of evading this predator.

Approximately 110 species in two major groups are known to live in Berkshire County. Damselflies, which are both male and female, are generally slow fliers that fold their wings together over their long thin abdomens at rest. Dragonflies in contrast are generally larger, more robust, stronger fliers that at rest extend their wings straight out. An eye-catching trait common to both groups is their stunning coloration. Every shade imaginable can be found, from brown and green to red and orange, yellow, blue, and even purple. These flashy and often intricate color patterns help the sexes recognize each other. In the majority of species, male and female can be readily identified by body coloration and wing pattern.

Most active during warm, sunny weather from May to October, odonates are usually fairly easy to find patrolling pond and stream borders and hawking insects over fields. There are now a number of excellent identification books available to help you get started. After birds grow quiet during the heat of summer, try turning your attention to these bejeweled marvels.

dominant here, and some of the oaks are quite large. After another whistle post, giant cottonwoods dominate the scene. These fast-growing relatives of aspen produce truckloads of minute seeds, each attached to a mass of cottony fluff that enables them to fly on the air currents. Wind carries them far from the parent trees. In summer cottonwood seeds pile up in windrows.

You'll arrive at Farnam's Road between the familiar green metal gates. A restroom building is located to your left, along the shore of the reservoir's upper basin. There are more benches and picnic tables here, so this is a nice spot for a relaxing break before you retrace your steps 3.7 miles to the parking area at Berkshire Mall Road.

## MORE INFORMATION

Open dawn to dusk, year-round. Access is free of charge. Dogs must be leashed and under control; owners must clean up after their pets. Motorized vehicles (except electric-powered vehicles used by people with disabilities), horses, alcoholic beverages, fires, hunting, trapping, feeding of wildlife, and removal of park resources are prohibited. Accessible restrooms are available at the Berkshire Mall Road parking area in Lanesborough and at Farnam's Crossing, the turnaround point in Cheshire. Massachusetts Department of Conservation and Recreation (DCR), Regional Headquarters, P.O. Box 1433, 740 South Street, Pittsfield, MA 01202; 413-442-8928; http://www.mass.gov/dcr. DCR's Universal Access Program 413-545-5353.

## TRIP 22
## CANOE MEADOWS WILDLIFE SANCTUARY

**Location:** Pittsfield
**Rating:** Easy
**Distance:** 2.0 miles
**Elevation Gain:** 20 feet
**Estimated Time:** 1.5 hours
**Maps:** USGS Pittsfield East; trail map available online

**Shouldering the Housatonic River, this sanctuary offers the wildlife watcher a rich biological diversity only 1 mile from the heart of the county's major population center.**

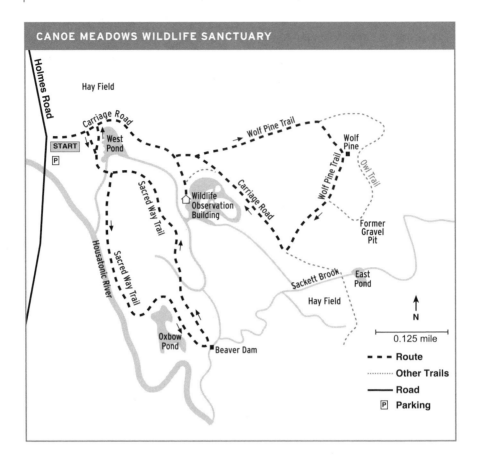

CANOE MEADOWS WILDLIFE SANCTUARY

Holmes Road

Hay Field

Carriage Road

START

West Pond

P

Wolf Pine Trail

Wolf Pine

Owl Trail

Wolf Pine Trail

Sacred Way Trail

Carriage Road

Wildlife Observation Building

Former Gravel Pit

Housatonic River

Sacred Way Trail

Sackett Brook

East Pond

Hay Field

N

Oxbow Pond

Beaver Dam

0.125 mile

- - - Route

··········· Other Trails

——— Road

P Parking

## DIRECTIONS

From the center of Pittsfield at Park Square, follow East Street east for 0.5 mile to its intersection with Elm Street. Turn right onto Elm and follow it for 0.75 mile to Holmes Road on the right. Follow Holmes Road 1 mile (crossing Williams Street), and turn left into the sanctuary entrance.

## TRAIL DESCRIPTION

Do not leave valuables in your vehicle, and be sure to lock it. An orientation panel, with a colorful trail map, stands just beyond the split-rail fence. To the left is an admission box where nonmembers are asked to place a nominal fee.

Proceed down the gravel carriage road (this was once a private estate) bounded on the left by a hayfield with residences just beyond. A brass plaque affixed to a boulder on the right commemorates the sanctuary's donation to Mass Audubon by Cooley Graves Crane in 1975. Soon you'll turn right onto Sacred Way Trail. The trail and the sanctuary hark back to a time when the native Mahicans summered here, setting up hunting and fishing camps in the area. The sanctuary's name is thought to be derived from the fact that American Indians were known to leave their birch bark canoes in the meadows along the Housatonic.

Walk through a gently sloping meadow reverting to shrubs. Annual mowing prevents a wholesale woody takeover. Nest boxes to your right house tree swallows (iridescent blue-green above and snowy white below) and house wrens in late spring and early summer. West Pond (dredged by steam shovel in the 1930s) often hosts mallards, black ducks, belted kingfishers, and herons in all but the winter months. The wooded hills beyond are part of the October Mountain State Forest.

Adjacent to a row of planted red pines on the right, a posted notice informs visitors about the presence of polychlorinated biphenyls (PCBs) in the property's floodplain soils. PCBs are suspected carcinogens that were manufactured by General Electric (GE) from the early twentieth century to about 1972 for use in electrical transformers. The oily fluid found its way into the Housatonic River, where the polymers cling to the sediment. During spring and fall flood events, the pollutants are deposited in floodplain areas adjacent to the river. A portion of Sacred Way Trail passes through the floodplain. The U.S. Environmental Protection Agency (EPA) has concluded that recreational use of the trails, such as walking, does not pose a hazard to humans. Visitors are urged not to handle, ingest, or inhale soil. A consent decree signed in 2000 by GE and the EPA mandated cleanup of the first 2 river miles below the GE plant. This cleanup, which has included dredging, had as of 2008 advanced downstream to within 1 mile of Canoe Meadows.

Bear left to a concrete bridge that provides a nice vantage point from which to scan the pond (the trail is wheelchair accessible to at least this point). Painted turtles often crowd logs in the water, soaking up the sun's rays. In July the invasive, exotic purple loosestrife chokes the pond's outlet stream. This lovely but deleterious invader all but crowds out native aquatic vegetation. After crossing, bear right to follow Sacred Way Trail through shoulder-high reed canary grass, goldenrods, and pink-blooming joe-pye weed. Islands of willows serve as song posts and nesting sites for aptly named willow flycatchers in late spring and early summer; listen for their sneezy *fitz-bew* calls. The path closely follows the outlet stream, where gray catbirds skulk in the dogwood shrubs May through September. Canoe Meadows is regarded as one of the county's most productive birding spots, even in winter.

Soon the path climbs out of the floodplain, passing the short Cutover Trail on the left. Blue blazes mark the outbound route, while yellow ones indicate

**A pair of iridescent blue-green and white tree swallows examine a potential nest site at Canoe Meadows.**

the return. Continue straight and parallel the Housatonic for a stretch. The field on your left, thick with pink-flowering meadowsweet in summer, is being invaded by light-loving old-field white pines. The river is shaded by silver maples and basswood, while oaks and black cherries thrive in the sandy "upland." The trail bears left and arrives at an oxbow pond once part of the main channel. Be alert for the presence of muskrats and cavity-nesting wood ducks here. Follow the path above the pond amid a lovely stand of white birches. Soon you'll bear left and reach Sackett Brook, the property's southern boundary. It is dammed by beavers upstream of its confluence with the Housatonic.

Turn left and head north. Young gray birches grow thickly in the sandy, sterile soil. Goldfinches, and in some years redpolls, feast on the female catkins, littering the snow with chaff. When the other end of Cutover Trail comes into view, bear right and traverse a boardwalk that snakes among arrowwood and willow shrubs. Male redwing blackbirds sing their reedy songs and show off their scarlet epaulets in spring. Raccoons, coyotes, and foxes sometimes leave their calling cards on the decking. Before long, you are back at West Pond (this section is often soggy and sometimes impasssable) and the concrete bridge.

Recross the bridge and follow right along the pond margin instead of heading back to the parking area. Turn right at Carriage Road and walk beneath planted red pines. Poison ivy grows profusely on the right just before you enter the woodland. Turn right at a signpost for the Wildlife Observation Building. This observation blind is situated at the end of a short boardwalk on a peninsula that overlooks a shrub swamp. You may be fortunate enough to spot a river otter from within it. Kingfishers and ducks are more likely, however. Return to Carriage Road and turn right to continue.

At the Wolf Pine Trail intersection, turn left. You'll soon be walking on a raised old roadway in the dense shade of hemlocks where tiny winter wrens sing their exuberant songs from mossy logs and spot-breasted wood thrushes offer up their flutelike refrains during the breeding season. This waterlogged woodland is markedly different from the sunny Sacred Way Trail. At the intersection with Owl Trail, bear right and continue on Wolf Pine, soon reaching the trail's iconic namesake on the left. A short spur leads to the base of this spreading giant. With myriad trunks reaching out and up, it's obvious this "wolf tree" reached maturity in what was then an open and sunny field. It has a certain Hansel-and-Gretel feel about it.

After Wolf Pine, the trail continues under a dense canopy of pine and hemlock, where owls sometimes roost during the day and noisy crows harass them, to reach Carriage Road. A hayfield across the road, like others on the sanctuary, is cut seasonally by a neighboring farmer to keep open. Turn right and walk through a grove of stately "cathedral" hemlocks. Brown creepers hitch up their rough trunks year-round in search of hidden insects, while tiny golden-crowned kinglets flutter amid the boughs plucking bugs and spiders from the dark green foliage. Emerge from the deep shade where shrub swamps border both sides on the roadway. The observation blind is visible across the pond to your left. A bit farther, opposite the Wolf Pine trailhead, butterflies are plentiful in the small field in late spring and summer.

Past the path to the blind, you'll be following Carriage Road back the way you came, around West Pond and back to your vehicle.

## MORE INFORMATION

Open year-round, except Mondays, 7 A.M. to dusk. Note that a cable prevents entry at other times. Pets, hunting, fishing, trapping, and collecting are prohibited. Nonmember admission fees are $3 adults, $2 for children (3–12) and senior citizens. Pittsfield residents are free. Guided bird walks are presented Friday mornings spring and fall (fee for nonmembers). Berkshire Wildlife Sanctuaries, 472 West Mountain Road, Lenox, MA 01240; 413-637-0320; berkshires@massaudubon.org; http://www.massaudubon.org.

## TRIP 23
## WARNER HILL

**Location:** Dalton, Hinsdale
**Rating:** Moderate
**Distance:** 6.3 miles
**Elevation Gain:** 430 feet
**Estimated Time:** 3.5 hours
**Maps:** USGS Pittsfield East

**This is an enjoyable hike on the Appalachian Trail through northern hardwoods interspersed with evergreens. Warner Hill's partially cleared summit yields a pleasing view of Mount Greylock.**

### DIRECTIONS

From the intersection of Elm and East streets in Pittsfield, follow East Street east for 3.0 miles to Division Road at the Dalton town line. East Street becomes South Street in Dalton. Drive north on South Street for 0.85 mile to Grange Hall Road on the right. Follow Grange Hall Road for 1.25 miles and park on the wide gravel shoulder on the left.

### TRAIL DESCRIPTION

Cross to the south side of the road (be alert for traffic speeding downhill around the curve) and ascend the rather steep slope on the white-blazed Appalachian Trail (AT) under a deciduous canopy of white ash, red maple, black cherry, and American beech. Note the interesting gneiss rock outcrop studded with quartz crystals. As you level out, gray birches indicate that this was once an open field, since birch seeds require bright sunlight to germinate. Prince's pine and cedar club moss—ancient nonflowering plants—add a fairyland quality to the forest floor. On the right stands a fine yellow birch, one of the classic northern hardwood forest indicators.

You will come upon the remains of a fireplace chimney built of native stone and mortar left of the path, just before descending into a gully. A few planted Norway spruces confirm former human occupation. After a modest climb up the far side, reach a blue-blazed trail on the left that leads to Kay Wood Shelter, where a pit toilet and picnic table are located. A locked metal case near the structure is designed to keep hikers' food safe from black bears. The shelter's picturesque setting on a moss-and-lichen-covered gneiss outcrop makes the

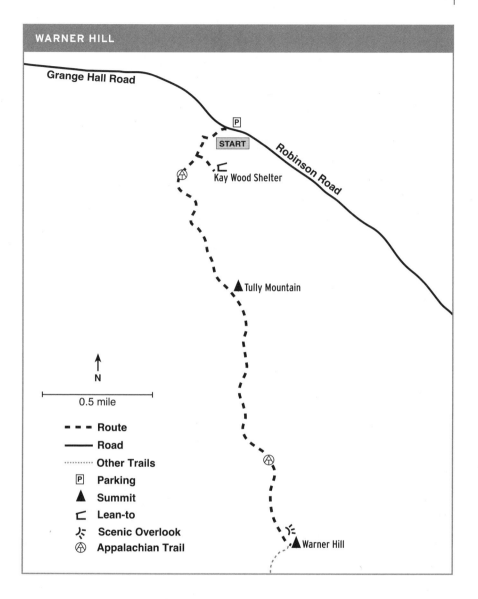

**WARNER HILL**

Grange Hall Road

P

START

Robinson Road

Kay Wood Shelter

Tully Mountain

N

0.5 mile

- - - Route
— Road
········· Other Trails
P Parking
▲ Summit
⊏ Lean-to
⅄ Scenic Overlook
Ⓐ Appalachian Trail

Warner Hill

0.3-mile round trip well worthwhile. The shelter is named for Dalton resident Kay Wood, who hiked the entire AT at age 71.

Return to the main trail, turn left, and climb along the slope. Screened views of the Taconic Range's rounded summits to the west are possible after leaf fall. Unfortunately, at that time of year, the sounds of Pittsfield are audible as well. Note the wind-thrown black cherry whose root-ball holds stones in a tenacious grasp. Soon you'll negotiate small boulder fields, their stones cleverly utilized in construction of the treadway. This hilltop is grassy. Actually, it's

**Kay Wood Shelter, named for a local woman who hiked the entire Appalachian Trail at age 71, was constructed in 1987.**

thickly vegetated with sedges—which are similar to grasses but have triangular rather than round stems.

Soon you'll emerge into a power-line gash filled with blackberry brambles and meadowsweet shrubs whose elevation of 1,981 feet makes a nice view of Lenox Mountain possible. The path beyond the right of way is straddled by emerald clumps of club mosses and a profuse growth of spinulose wood fern, both of which remain green year-round. Walk over a gently undulating trail and through a shallow bowl. A dark green hemlock grove to your left contrasts with the comparatively light green shades of maples, cherries, and beeches. Past a tiny drainage rill you'll come across the aptly named staghorn club moss and a luxuriant growth of shining club moss. Club mosses, when brushed against in late autumn, emit a smoky cloud of microscopic spores. The highly flammable spores once provided the flash for early flash photography.

Watch your footing as you traverse a small damp area on a couple of plank bridge sections, since some boards may be loose. Modest gray, sinewy ironwood trees share the damp earth with yellow birch. An amazingly well-camouflaged ruffed grouse suddenly burst forth from its hiding place as we passed on one visit, catching us by surprise, as they always do. Now begin a gradual climb to the level, wooded summit of Tully Mountain at an elevation of 2,085 feet. No distant views here. Twin venerable, flaky-barked yellow birches stand trailside on the left. Although these two are no longer yellow, young trees with thin, peeling, brassy bark are especially attractive. As you stride over an exposed chunk of gneiss bedrock, note the 6-inch-thick milky quartz intrusion that filled a fracture when buried deep underground hundreds of millions of years ago.

Along this high-elevation stretch are pockets of boreal evergreens—especially red spruce. In a damp swale, goldthread and wintergreen bloom in spring and summer, respectively. Both display white blossoms. Those of goldthread are star shaped, while tiny bells adorn wintergreen. Follow along ledge outcrop, the slope dropping off to the left, and descend into a hobblebush stand. Its big heart-shaped leaves are among the first to reveal their multiple hues in autumn. Conifers become more common now, interspersed with hardwoods. Cross two small streams separated by about 50 feet as the trail continues to undulate easily, and then pass through a bowl hemmed in by dramatic gneiss ledges—a sort of miniature canyon where prickly porcupines must certainly den among the boulders. Climb out at the far end, bearing left around a low outcrop, and pass an old wood road after you level off.

There are more screened views to the right of forested ridges after leaf fall. Black birches are suddenly common as you descend into a col then amble up and cross a wood road. Bear right rather than following the road up, and descend gently to where a ledge juts up at an awkward angle. Wild strawberries, whose small fruits are relished by many creatures, have gained a foothold in pockets of soil atop the rock. Soon you'll pass through a number of fallen stone walls and enter a scruffy, unkempt woodland of gnarly old apple trees and viburnum shrubs. Cross an unmarked path and begin a gradual climb amid more apple trees and 6-inch-diameter shad blow (a.k.a. juneberry).

A luxuriant growth of hay-scented fern fills the open sunny slope just below the summit of Warner Hill. The light green fronds of summer wither to an auburn hue after frost ends their growing season. The trunks of red maples and other trees in the clearing show black charring—perhaps from a campfire that got out of control. A white sign on a tree tells you that you've finally reached your objective, while a rock cairn marks the 2,050-foot summit of Warner Hill (the AT turns right at this point and descends another mile to Blotz Road). Sprouting gray birch and highbush blueberry spring from pockets of soil amid the rust-stained summit rocks, but this modest growth still permits a fine view north 16 miles to the Greylock Range. The rotating white blades of the wind turbine at the Jiminy Peak ski resort in Hancock are visible to the northwest. When ready, retrace your steps northward to your vehicle along Grange Hall Road.

## TRAIL TRIBULATIONS

The Appalachian National Scenic Trail, or simply AT for short, is one of the more extensive footpaths in North America. The first of several such continental trails, it was the brainchild of Massachusetts native Benton MacKaye. Although MacKaye conceived the idea in 1921, his dream was not fully realized until 1937. Stretching for 2,175 miles from Springer Mountain in northern Georgia to the craggy summit of 5,267-foot-high Katahdin in Maine's Baxter State Park, the AT is walked by hundreds of thousands of hikers yearly. But only a few hundred hardy souls, known as thru-hikers, complete the roughly 5-month journey each year. Many more set out in the attempt. And numerous others complete state segments or spend a month or more on the trail annually until they have traversed its entire length.

A significant number of the hikes described in this guidebook follow portions of this fabled footpath. Its 6-inch-high, 2-inch-wide white blazes are iconic. The trail invariably passes over some of the most scenic ridgelines in the Berkshires, from the Vermont border to the Connecticut line—a distance of roughly 90 miles. Interestingly, today's AT is more rural than the original, as many segments have been relocated farther from roads and onto acquired conservation land. Changes and improvements continue.

Along the AT's 2,000-plus-mile route, a string of rough shelters provides respite for long-distance hikers. In summer you're likely to encounter at least a few of these hardy souls on their way north. Many adopt an emblematic moniker or trail name that you'll find at the bottom of journal entries at AT trail registers. The majority set out from Georgia in March, before winter has fully retreated. Their goal is to reach Katahdin in September before winter reasserts itself. Therefore, most pass through the Berkshires in June, some pausing in the relative luxury of Bascom Lodge (closed at press time, but Massachusetts Department of Conservation was working to find an organization to rehabilitate and reopen it) atop Massachusetts's tallest peak, where hot showers and warm meals are a welcome change from their daily routines. If you can get a thru-hiker to stop long enough to chat, you'll almost certainly enjoy the experience.

Although under the jurisdiction of the National Park Service, which designated the footpath as a National Scenic Trail in 1968, in Massachusetts a cadre of dedicated volunteers of the Appalachian Mountain Club's Berkshire Chapter maintains the AT for all of us. They deserve our gratitude.

## MORE INFORMATION

Motorized vehicles, horses, and hunting are not permitted along the AT. Camping is permitted in designated areas only. The AT in Massachusetts is maintained by volunteers of the Berkshire Chapter of the Appalachian Mountain Club's Appalachian Trail Management Committee; Rich Wagner, Regional Trail Coordinator, P.O. Box 2281, Pittsfield, MA 01202; 413-528-8003; http://www.amcberkshire.org/at; at@berkshire.org; 413-528-6333.

## TRIP 24
## DOROTHY FRANCES RICE
## SANCTUARY FOR WILDLIFE

**Location:** Peru
**Rating:** Easy–Moderate
**Distance:** 3.8 miles
**Elevation Gain:** 570 feet
**Estimated Time:** 2.0 hours
**Maps:** USGS Pittsfield East

**Red spruce, balsam fir, and northern hardwoods clothe this home to moose and beaver. Although inhabited and altered by humans for centuries, this land has a wild feel.**

## DIRECTIONS

From the junction of Routes 8 and 143 in Hinsdale, drive east on Route 143 for 4.3 miles (past Ashmere Lake) into Peru, to the intersection with South Road. Take a right onto South Road and follow it for 0.9 mile to the parking area and entrance on the left.

## TRAIL DESCRIPTION

Park outside and clear of the locked gate. Walk eastward down level, grassy Rice Road flanked by large white ash trees and sugar maples. Soon you'll reach a short mowed path on the left that leads to a beaver dam and a picturesque pond created by the masterful rodents. Be alert for beavers as well as abundant bird life in the surrounding vegetation. Continue east on the road lined with red spruce, red maple, black cherry, and striped maple. Luxuriant fern growth crowds the borders. Continue straight at a second mown path on the left, but

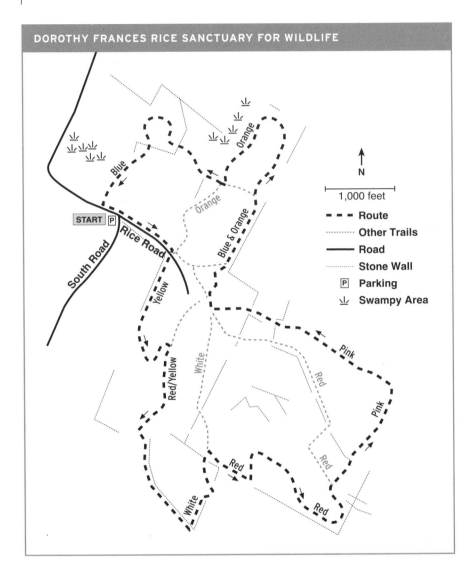

**DOROTHY FRANCES RICE SANCTUARY FOR WILDLIFE**

only for about 30 feet—the Yellow Trail enters the forest through a gap in the stone wall on your right. This intersection is easy to miss!

Some trees, such as the red maple at this location, are identified with descriptive tags. Follow the single track, blazed with yellow paint, through woodland that now includes fragrant young balsam firs. With orange roots and glossy dark green leaves, goldthread lines the path. Cross an intermittent brook bed on a boardwalk (watch for loose boards) and amble up a low slope thick with New York ferns; their fronds taper at both ends. In autumn, the red maple canopy is ablaze with color. Although somewhat overgrown late in the season with goldenrod, ferns, and raspberry canes, the path is reasonably easy to follow.

The Yellow Trail bears left, ascends gradually, and follows along the opposite side of the shrubby clearing. A thick growth of young red spruce imparts a North Woods feel. Gray birch, cherry, and red maple have colonized the clearing, providing browse for white-tailed deer (listen for their snorts) and moose. I didn't encounter a moose on my October outing, but one of the big animal's cloven hooves had left an impressive 6-inch-long track in the mud of a sedge-filled area.

Arrive at the Red Trail and turn right (posted with red and yellow arrows), and very shortly you'll come to the intersection with the White Trail at a grassy woods road. Turn right and follow the red-and-white blazes gradually downhill between stone walls. Light green hay-scented fern carpets the ground. At another posted intersection turn right on the White Trail, and soon you'll enter shaded coniferous forest. Some hemlocks here are sizable. Their needles are short and flat, rather than sharp-tipped like those of red spruce. A flowing brook gurgles through this attractive mixed woodland, which includes the northern hardwood yellow birch. Twin leaved, red-fruited partridgeberry and tiny prince's pine add beauty. Soon you'll cross a stream where rockwork hints at former human engineering. Follow along the slope's flank. The melancholy cries of a red-shouldered hawk caught my ear as the bird soared above the maturing American beech, yellow birch, and white ash woodland.

The trail follows the sanctuary's boundaries closely here and throughout the hike. Numerous stone walls add additional demarcation. As the trail levels out, red oak and lowbush blueberry indicate drier, more acidic soils. An intriguing assemblage of northern species (yellow birch and red spruce) and a southern one (red oak) commingle here. Walk through a small selectively cut area. At a white ash with three trunks, pass through a gap in the stone wall and soon you'll arrive at an old logging road at the intersection with the Red Trail. Turn right. Note the many beeches with black, disfigured bark—the work of a fungus that enters through holes made by minute sap-sucking insects. Soon a slope guides you down to a damp spot populated by tall cinnamon ferns. A young stand of red maple characterizes this stand.

At the intersection with the Pink Trail, turn right, pass through a rectangular logged clearing, and reenter the forest of red maple, red spruce, beech, and yellow birch. Then climb more steeply to a vista point complete with a log bench. A lovely view of distant ridges to the southwest makes this the perfect place for lunch or a snack. When ready to resume your hike, continue walking along the slope and descend fairly steeply. Mica crystals in the gneiss (pronounced

**A beaver pond and bordering vegetated wetlands at the start of the hike provide fine habitat for myriad creatures.**

"nice") rocks sparkle. Reenter the dark woodland and pass through three more stone-wall gaps and over a brook bed to reach a wide mowed path that leads to a clearing in the center of the property. A large painted trail map, a picnic table, and an apple orchard are located adjacent to the Rice cabin (not the original). Oran and Mary Rice established this sanctuary in the late 1920s in their daughter's memory. In 1974 the New England Forestry Foundation was entrusted with it. You can pick up a trail map at the map board.

At this point you may wish to make a short side trip on the pink/white-blazed Pond Trail for another chance at observing beavers. Freshly cut stumps attest to their presence. Lush woodland bordering the ponds—along with the alder, birch, winterberry, maleberry, and arrowwood shrubs fringing them—makes for particularly productive birding. In the water, red-spotted newts (poisonous to fish) use their vertically flattened tails to propel themselves in search of insect prey.

To continue the hike, approach the cabin and bear right. Multiple trails intersect near the shed. Follow the Blue Trail (blazed blue/orange/yellow at this point) straight ahead. Reenter the mixed woods and reach the intersection with the Yellow Trail. Continue on the blue/orange-blazed trail, bearing right. Note the large red spruces, one of which has fallen across a stone wall, exposing its shallow root-ball. At the Y intersection, follow the Orange Trail to the right. Young balsam firs—5 to 8 feet high—crowd each other on the forest floor. The classic Christmas-tree form (and heavenly fragrance) of this lovely conifer can be found only in the highest elevations of Berkshire County. In contrast, the balsam fir is a major component of Canada's vast boreal forest. And as in the North, the four-veined leaves of little bunchberry plants thrive in the shade of the conifers. White, four-petaled blossoms that become pink as they age make this, the tiniest dogwood, stand out in spring.

Follow the treadway through mixed woodland. Eastern hemlocks sport shorter needles than balsam fir. A wet depression is carpeted with sphagnum moss that can hold 50 times its weight in water. Traverse a seepage area on a boardwalk that leads into woodland equally composed of hardwoods—maple and birches—and evergreens. Left of the intersection with the Blue Trail stands an impressive yellow birch with a 2-foot-diameter trunk. Turn right and follow the now blue/orange-blazed path. An even older yellow birch with peeling bark on the right has produced seeds relished by finches for many decades. Soon you'll reach another junction at the edge of a sapling-filled clearing. Stay straight on the Blue Trail, as the Orange Trail turns left.

After the clearing, reenter the woodland of beech, black cherry (flaky black bark), and red maple. A bit farther on, red spruce and balsam fir make a handsome evergreen pair again. Chatty red squirrels noisily voice their annoyance when humans intrude on their domain. Nutritious conifer seeds make up an important part of their diet. Note the red maple snag riddled with big, deep pileated woodpecker excavations. Our largest woodpecker seeks prey in such carpenter-ant-infested trees. At this point, where blazes are uncharacteristically few, bear right on the more obvious path. Soon blue blazes commence once again. Heart-shaped leaves of hobblebush transform from green to maroon, yellow, and orange in autumn. Next season's twin leaf buds are already formed and obvious, projecting above the branches.

On the right is a rock-lined structure—a cistern perhaps—where the roots of a gray birch anchored it to the rocks years ago. Shortly you'll reach South Road; turn left and walk to your vehicle some 125 feet away.

## MORE INFORMATION

The sanctuary is open daily for hiking and cross-country skiing year-round, dawn to dusk. Access is free. Hunting, fishing, camping, trapping, fires, and motorized vehicles are prohibited. New England Forestry Foundation, P.O. Box 1346, Littleton, MA 01460; 978-952-6856; info@newenglandforestry.org; http://www.newenglandforestry.org.

## STICKY-FINGERED AMPHIBIANS

You are bound to hear two distinct tiny voices as you hike through Berkshire woodlands and past the county's wetlands. Unlike the proverbial well-behaved child, the little creatures to whom these voices belong are more often heard than seen, but some people mistake their calls for those of birds. One might believe that tree frogs as a group should rightfully be confined to rain-drenched tropical jungles, but two species call our area home.

The most familiar is less than 1 inch long when fully grown, but the male of the species possesses a high-pitched voice that, in chorus with its brethren, can blow your socks off. I'm referring of course to the spring peeper. The high-register peeper chorus produces the defining sound of our early spring wetlands—a sleigh-bell symphony of sorts. These tiny frogs, equipped with toe-tip discs that permit them to climb up onto vegetation, gather in courtship assemblies where males call out for all they're worth in efforts to attract a mate. Night after night, even when temperatures hover around 40 degrees, the tiny beings belt out their love notes.

Peepers call again in late summer and early fall—singly this time, and sounding less like a pure whistle. To the uninitiated, their calls, especially then, may be mistaken for those of birds. Tracking the notes to their source, however, is nigh impossible because just as you seem to be closing in, he ceases and desists. At that time of year it may be easier to find one low to the ground in a damp meadow. But only careless movement on its part will draw your attention to its tiny tan-colored form emblazoned on the back with a fairly prominent X.

Our other local tree frog is a bit larger and even more of a camouflage artist. Few people ever see gray tree frogs because their coloration and pattern so closely matches lichen-covered tree trunks as to be uncanny. As a general rule, to find small creatures in nature, employ a child in the search. Unlike spring peepers, gray tree frogs don't whistle; they purr. Hence, they are often mistaken for raccoons or even red-bellied woodpeckers, other Berkshire denizens that produce uncannily similar vocalizations in our woodlands. Gray tree frogs breed later in the year than spring peepers, and they seemingly call from taller vegetation. So be alert for the calls of these climbing amphibians in our midst.

## TRIP 25
## PLEASANT VALLEY WILDLIFE
## SANCTUARY–BEAVER PONDS LOOP

**Location:** Lenox
**Rating:** Easy
**Distance:** 1.5 miles
**Elevation Gain:** 115 feet
**Estimated Time:** 1.0 hour
**Maps:** USGS Pittsfield West; trail map available at office, online

**An active and easily observed beaver colony is a highlight of this
loop route through a scenic valley on the east flank of Lenox
Mountain.**

## DIRECTIONS
From the south: From Exit 2 (Lee) off the Mass Pike (I-90), turn right after
the tollbooths and drive north on Route 20 (which just after Cranwell Resort
becomes Route 7/20) for 6.6 miles to West Dugway Road on the left. Follow
West Dugway Road (which becomes West Mountain Road) 1.6 miles to the
sanctuary's gravel parking area.

From the north: From the center of Pittsfield at Park Square, take Route
7/20 south for 4.9 miles to West Dugway Road on the right, then follow the
directions above.

## TRAIL DESCRIPTION
All visitors are asked to register at the farmhouse (built c. 1790) that serves as
the sanctuary office. Registration cards and visitor guides are available inside
as well as outside after hours. Check the board for recent wildlife sightings,
and examine the nearby orientation panel, which includes a large artist's rendi-
tion of the trail system.

Turn right onto the wide graveled drive and walk northward toward a
bright red barn on the left where attached public restroom facilities and potable water are available year-round. The wheelchair-accessible All Persons'
Trail begins here and ends at nearby Pike's Pond. Continue straight, however,
on Bluebird Trail past the education center (home of the sanctuary's summer
day camp). In the brushy field opposite, tree swallows and sometimes eastern

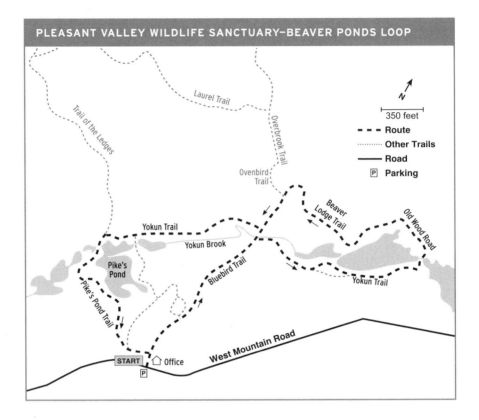

PLEASANT VALLEY WILDLIFE SANCTUARY–BEAVER PONDS LOOP

bluebirds nest. In July, the sweet-smelling pink flower heads of common milk-weed lure myriad butterflies, including various hairstreaks and skippers, and of course monarchs. The looming Lenox Mountain ridge beckons.

Walk straight ahead past a formidable eastern cottonwood at the intersection of Alexander Trail and through another field prickly with raspberry canes before entering a stand of tall white pines bordered by a remnant stone wall. Ahead is Yokun Brook, a tributary of the Housatonic River and the sanctuary's only perennial stream. Rather than crossing the brook, turn right onto Yokun Trail. Both the trail and the brook take their name from a notable Mahican leader of the early eighteenth century. The path winds through low-lying woodland of white ash, black cherry, and birch. Opposite the far end of the short Alexander Trail, turn left onto a loop spur that leads to the first of a series of beaver ponds that descend in staircase fashion along about 1 mile of Yokun Brook. Signs of the big rodent's handiwork are evident, including a sizable cherry tree felled years ago. In 1932, beavers were reintroduced at this location after an absence of almost 150 years. A well-vegetated beaver dam is close at hand near the bench. Continue on the short loop to the main trail and turn left. You'll soon pass hollows on the right where gravel was once mined. To your left is a larger beaver-engineered pond, and near its far end is a conical mass of sticks and mud—a beaver lodge.

Each lodge is home to one family. These vegetarians do not hibernate through the depths of winter, but rather retrieve twigs that they have stock-piled in the pond mud near the lodge. Twigs (especially the nutritious bark) serve as their sole food until more succulent vegetation becomes available during spring green-up. If you are here in early morning or at dusk, you may observe a curious beaver cruising about with only its head and a bit of its back visible above the surface.

When you reach Old Wood Road turn left and linger on a long wooden bridge that traverses a small pond between two beaver dams. The upstream dam to your left is 3 to 4 feet high, while the smaller one on the right is con-siderably lower. Glance down and you'll surely see beaver scat—oval pellets of compressed sawdust. At the far right end of the bridge, the closed blue-purple blossoms of bottle gentians bloom in early fall.

Beyond the bridge grow a few mountain laurel shrubs and some impressive white pines. The shrub layer contains an abundance of spiny Japanese barberry shrubs—an invasive exotic. Some have been uprooted, but many persist. At the four-way intersection, turn left onto Beaver Lodge Trail. In the vicinity of the boardwalk, be alert in summer for the takeoff of an American woodcock—a chunky "shorebird" sporting a nearly 3-inch-long, crochet-hook-like bill with a flexible tip used to adroitly pull earthworms from the moist soil.

Winterberry bushes have established themselves in a beaver-dug channel on the left beyond the winding boardwalk. The coral-red berries add a wel-come splash of color to the late-fall scene. During warm seasons, a multitude of ferns (mostly New York fern) carpet the sunny openings and white birch trunks reflect the sun's rays. A visitor once photographed a moose calf seques-tered in this shrub wetland! Soon you'll pass the first beaver pond you reached, but from the opposite side. Here the path curves right onto a low mound above another small pond where the trail's namesake beaver lodge sits hidden by woody vegetation until after leaf fall. A bench near a couple of mighty white pines some 150 years old or more serves as a nice spot for a snack.

Continue on Beaver Lodge Trail around the swamp and into a stand of pines and hemlocks where golden-crowned kinglets reside during the cold months. At the shaded junction with Bluebird Trail, turn left and cross another boardwalk. Here at the base of Lenox Mountain, turn left to cross a short span over an intermittent brook where one late autumn I surprised a bathing adult goshawk. Truth be told, I was at least as surprised as the raptor! Ahead towers

**Beavers can weigh up to 70 pounds and live in family groups headed by the adult female.**

a stand of cathedral pines, their straight and lofty trunks soaring 100 feet above the needle-cushioned forest floor. Their girth suggests considerable age. You'll discern a definite hushed atmosphere in their shade. Back at gushing Yokun Brook, turn right onto the southern section of Yokun Trail and amble up under a pine canopy to a point above the brook where the soothing sound of flowing water is omnipresent. Carpenter ants once inhabited a long-dead pine, deeply riddled with pileated woodpecker excavations. It was recently felled.

The trail continues through mixed woodland that now includes red oak and yellow birch. I once caught a glimpse of a mink as the slender weasel bounded upstream where the path reaches brook side. The vernal green of pleated false hellebore leaves pushing up through the brook's moist floodplain soil is a very welcome sight in April after a long, snowy winter. You'll emerge into the sunlight at another beaver pond. Two young fawns—camouflaged by their dappled coats—once drew considerable attention from school groups as they lay quietly on the small island where their mother had left them while she foraged.

At the intersection turn left onto Pike's Pond Trail. Green frogs bask on the muddy bank and emit squeals as you approach, while in the woods, eastern chipmunks utter a fluty whistle and scamper for their burrows when danger threatens. They harvest the abundant acorns, beechnuts, and beaked hazelnuts for winter dining belowground. The path is bordered in places by mountain azalea shrubs that waft intoxicating perfume from their tubular pink flowers in late May. After the path crosses a protruding schist outcrop, it bears left to a picturesque bridge. Trailing arbutus, the Massachusetts state flower, blooms here in early May. Its sandpapery leaves and delicate pink blossoms hug the ground in sunny openings.

About a month after the azaleas put on a feast for the senses, mountain laurel shrubs come into their own. Although not fragrant, their clusters of nickel-sized white-and-pink blossoms are a sight to see. Beyond the bridge on the left, beavers have felled a red oak—hardly a preferred food—but without doubt a testament to their prowess as loggers! The trail bears left to continue around the pond—best viewed as the path climbs a few feet to higher ground at two substantial sugar maples. Note the active beaver lodge (adorned with fresh mud and cut vegetation in fall) on the island. Saw-billed hooded mergansers nest in big wooden boxes fastened to trees for use by cavity-nesting mergansers and wood ducks.

Move away from the pond and walk beneath a stand of planted Depression-era red pines where red squirrels chatter. The path curves left into a small shrub wetland traversed by a boardwalk bordered by alder, larch, and luxuriant ferns. Interrupted ferns stand shoulder high on drier ground, while lacy royal ferns and lush cinnamon ferns (with cinnamon-hued fertile fronds) crowd the decking. At its far end, turn right to walk a few feet back to the parking area.

## MORE INFORMATION

Trails open year-round, dawn to dusk. Open seven days per week from July to Columbus Day; closed Mondays the rest of the year, except open on all Monday holidays. The office is open on the same days as the grounds, 10 A.M. to 4 P.M. Nonmember fees: $4 for adults, $3 for children (3–12) and senior citizens. Mass Audubon members and Lenox residents free. Pets, vehicles (including bicycles), horses, hunting, trapping, fishing, and collecting are not permitted. Berkshire Wildlife Sanctuaries, 472 West Mountain Road, Lenox, MA 01240; 413-637-0320; Berkshires@massaudubon.org; http://www.massaudubon.org.

## BRINGING BACK THE BEAVER

You won't find the beaver on a short list of most-beloved animals. In fact for many, the mere mention of the rodent's name engenders disdain. But why? The answer may be, at least in part, that beavers are sometimes in direct competition with us for waterfront property. These vegetarian creatures are adept at constructing engineering marvels that in their way rival our own, and their persistence and ingenuity are legendary.

From the time of European settlement, beavers were killed for their splendid pelts. Long, glossy guard hairs protrude above a dense, luxuriant underfur that insulates the animal against damp and cold–just the right attire for a creature that doesn't hibernate and that spends a good portion of its waking hours submerged in cold water. Beavers constituted the bread and butter of the fur trade that provided impetus for the exploration of much of North America. By the late eighteenth century though, beavers had been eliminated from Massachusetts.

In the late 1920s and early 1930s, after the beaver had been absent almost 150 years, there were some people who sought to repatriate the former native and thereby recalibrate the balance of nature. Thus, in 1932, Pleasant Valley Bird and Wildflower Sanctuary warden S. Morris Pell acquired–after considerable effort–one adult female and two adult males from the Blue Mountain Lake region of New York. Pell and his helpers constructed a sturdy fenced enclosure around 1.5 acres of willows and alders bordering Yokun Brook. The beaver trio was introduced to their new quarters at 5 P.M. on October 8; by dawn the next morning they had constructed their first dam and pond.

Beavers build ponds to safeguard themselves from land-bound predators. Although certainly not defenseless on terra firma, in its watery realm the pudgy beaver transforms into a study in grace. An enlarged liver enables it to remain submerged for up to 15 minutes. And just like humans, they use the water's buoyancy to float cargo, be it building material for dams and their homes, called lodges, or food in the form of leafy twigs.

Beaver wetlands have many virtues. They absorb storm runoff like the proverbial sponge and release it slowly, minimizing flooding. Wetlands serve as nature's purification plant for runoff entering groundwater aquifers. And beaver wetlands provide homes for a litany of other creatures, from mosquito-eating dragonflies to fish and wood ducks. If frogs and newts could vote, beavers would win the popularity contest hands down.

## TRIP 26
## PLEASANT VALLEY WILDLIFE SANCTUARY–
## LENOX MOUNTAIN LOOP

**Location:** Lenox
**Rating:** Difficult
**Distance:** 3.0 miles
**Elevation Gain:** 825 feet
**Estimated Time:** 2.0 hours
**Maps:** USGS Pittsfield West; trail map available online

**On this trip you'll ascend Lenox Mountain's east-facing slope over bony ledges to its summit and then descend over gurgling brooks and along tranquil hemlock ravines.**

## DIRECTIONS
From the south: From Exit 2 (Lee) off the Mass Pike (I-90), turn right after the tollbooths and drive north on Route 20 (which just after Cranwell Resort becomes Route 7/20) for 6.6 miles to West Dugway Road on the left. Follow West Dugway Road (which becomes West Mountain Road) 1.6 miles to the sanctuary's gravel parking area.

From the north: From the center of Pittsfield at Park Square, take Route 7/20 south for 4.9 miles to West Dugway Road on the right, then follow the directions above.

## TRAIL DESCRIPTION
After checking in at the office (trail map available here), cross the gravel drive and begin at the south end of Pike's Pond Trail, immediately opposite the office. Sanctuary trails are blazed blue outbound and yellow returning. Bear right and turn left immediately to traverse a boardwalk through a boggy area of ferns and alders where the liver-colored spathes of skunk cabbage push up through the cold earth as early as February and the shiny yellow petals of marsh marigolds fairly glow in May. After skirting a planted red pine stand, the path descends very gradually toward its namesake, Pike's Pond, constructed in 1932 to increase the sanctuary's habitat diversity. Named in memory of William Pike, whose family funded construction, it is an excellent vantage point from which to observe beavers, especially at dusk. Note the active lodge on the island.

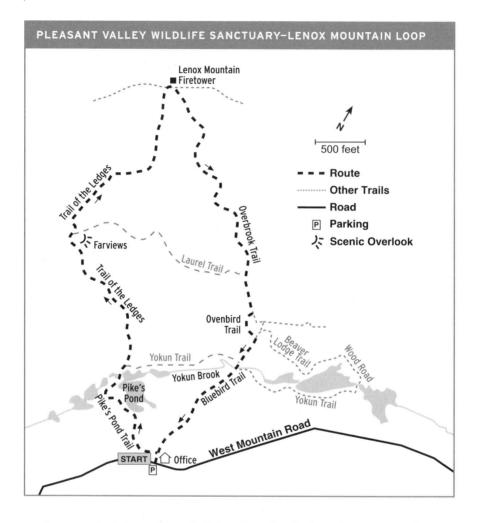

**PLEASANT VALLEY WILDLIFE SANCTUARY–LENOX MOUNTAIN LOOP**

Lenox Mountain
■ Firetower

N

500 feet

– – – Route
············· Other Trails
——— Road
P Parking
Scenic Overlook

Trail of the Ledges

Farviews

Overbrook Trail

Laurel Trail

Trail of the Ledges

Ovenbird
Trail

Beaver
Lodge Trail

Wood Road

Yokun Trail

Yokun Brook

Pike's
Pond

Bluebird Trail

Yokun Trail

Pike's Pond Trail

START ▮ ⌂ Office    West Mountain Road
P

Soon on the left you'll reach Yokun Brook, which at this point is a beaded necklace of small beaver ponds. Emergent bur reed with spiky inflorescences populates the shallows. A bridge leads across one pond to the foot of Lenox Mountain. After treading over a tilted outcrop of schist, turn left onto the Trail of the Ledges, the start of your ascent. Remnant stone walls attest to sheep grazing here as recently as 100 years ago. Shortly you'll arrive at the Waycross Trail intersection. But continue straight up—between here and a vista point called Farviews, at 1,850 feet elevation, you'll ascend 500 vertical feet in less than one-third of a mile. During wet seasons, water trickles over mossy ledge outcrops on the left. Beyond the Ravine Trail junction on the right, some slopes approach 45 degrees. As some over-rock scrambling is required, hikers are advised not to descend on this section.

**Snowshoers consult a trail map to estimate their location along Overbrook Trail on the way to the Lenox Mountain summit.**

A transitional forest of oak, white pine, birch, beech, and maple clothes the lower slopes of the ridge. Crow-sized pileated woodpeckers seek out mature trees infested with carpenter ants, while yellow-bellied sapsuckers (the only local woodpecker that regularly migrates long distances) dine on the sweet sap of birches and maples and the insects attracted to the flow. In contrast, a loud, bubbling song matching the exuberance of the brooks after snowmelt, issues from the mousy winter wren. Mountain laurel increases as one gains elevation, and laurel and eastern hemlock predominate at Farviews. From here you can gaze down to the sanctuary buildings in the valley and eastward all the way to October Mountain State Forest.

Although you are only about halfway to the top, you've achieved 60 percent of the total rise. The remaining section to the summit is not as steep; the narrow trail leads to several more pleasing vista points with views to the east and north. As you continue up the slope, notice that the stature of the timber decreases as you go. Shallow soils and a harsher climate stunt the trees' growth. As a rule of thumb, temperatures decrease 1 degree for every 400 feet one ascends. Finally, you'll emerge into a small "grassy bald" where the now derelict state fire tower looms 70 feet up from the summit bedrock. Ironically, it was the victim of a lightning-induced fire in March 1998.

The red maples aren't very tall, but they're high enough to block any easterly view. The best view from the 2,126-foot summit is westward: Almost directly below is Richmond Pond. Beyond that, the Taconic Range runs the length of the New York–Massachusetts border. The Taconics are among the continent's oldest mountain ranges, having been thrust up more than 400 million years ago when what is now Africa rammed into what is now North America. Geologically speaking, Lenox Mountain is considered an outlier of the Taconics. On a clear day the Catskills, 40 miles to the southwest, will appear as a distant bluish ridge. Walk a few feet down the westward flank and gaze to your right (north) for a glimpse of Mount Greylock (elevation 3,491 feet; see Trips 4, 8, 9, and 10).

When ready to descend, walk toward the back (east side) of the fire tower and enter the forest—the start of Overbrook Trail. After a few feet, you should see a white sign on a tree indicating that this is the return path to Pleasant Valley Sanctuary. Amble through a peaceful mixed woodland and listen in summer for the ethereal song of the 7.5-inch-long hermit thrush, a leading contender for best avian singer. The initial grades are moderate with some steeper slopes to come, but none approaching the house-roof-like angles of the ascent. You'll cross a shallow intermittent brook five times en route to the Great Hemlock Trail intersection. Just above the first crossing is a picturesque 12-foot-high cascade.

After heavy winter snowfalls, hemlocks are weighed down by the accumulation of snow on their needle-dense boughs, producing a fairyland effect. A winter ascent on snowshoes via this trail can be very enjoyable. Among the few birdsongs you may hear then are the sibilant, three-note calls of tiny golden-crowned kinglets. Hemlocks crowd the ravines, but deciduous species like red oak, big-tooth aspen, American beech (most show signs of a fungal disease that disfigures its normally smooth gray bark), and black and yellow birches also are numerous. Striped maple and hobblebush grow in their shade. Just above Great Hemlock Trail you'll be walking along the rim of a hemlock ravine where some of the conifers are tall and massive. The feel is a bit primeval here. The inner bark of hemlock was once used to tan leather, but these trees escaped harvest due to their location. It is hard to imagine now that most of the mountain was once denuded. Timber was cut to produce charcoal, lumber, and firewood as well as to clear land for pasture. Indeed, merino sheep once grazed this hillside!

You'll reach a four-way intersection with Laurel Trail on the right and Great Hemlock Trail on the left. Continue straight ahead on Overbrook down along a cascading brook among stately hemlocks. The trail bears left and widens into a former wood road. Turn right briefly onto Ovenbird Trail. In late spring and summer, the loud *teacher-teacher-teacher* refrain of the ovenbird is ubiquitous. This species builds a roofed nest with a side entrance like an old-fashioned oven. The path descends steeply for a short spell to an intermittent brook at the base of the mountain at Bluebird Trail. Cross the brook on a short bridge and head toward an imposing grove of white pines. Some are 3.5 feet in diameter and tower nearly 100 feet tall.

Soon you'll arrive at Yokun Brook, the property's only year-round stream. Two-lined and dusky salamanders call it home, as do brook trout. A pair of Louisiana waterthrushes is among the first warblers to return from the tropics in late April, constructing their nest along its banks. The birds bob their hindquarters incessantly as they walk along. Continue over the brook and under more pines to a sloping field. Ahead on the left, clumps of common milkweed attract myriad butterflies in summer. A rotund eastern cottonwood seems to stand guard at the intersection with Alexander Trail. From here it is about 200 yards along the field edge back to the office, passing the education center building on the left and the sanctuary barn on the right en route. Restrooms (potable water available) are attached to the near end of the barn.

## MORE INFORMATION

Trails open year-round, dawn to dusk. Open seven days per week from July to Columbus Day; closed Mondays the rest of the year, except open on all Monday holidays. Office is open same days as grounds, 10 A.M. to 4 P.M. Nonmember fees: $4 for adults, $3 for children (3–12) and senior citizens. Mass Audubon members, Lenox residents free. Pets, vehicles (including bicycles), horses, hunting, trapping, fishing, and collecting are not permitted. Berkshire Wildlife Sanctuaries, 472 West Mountain Road, Lenox, MA 01240; 413-637-0320; Berkshires@massaudubon.org; http://www.massaudubon.org.

## TRIP 27
## JOHN DRUMMOND KENNEDY PARK

**Location:** Lenox
**Rating:** Moderate
**Distance:** 4.8 miles
**Elevation Gain:** 355 feet
**Estimated Time:** 2.5–3.0 hours
**Maps:** USGS Pittsfield West, USGS Stockbridge; trail map available online

**This is a fine family hiking trip to points of historic interest, including the site of the famed Aspinwall Hotel, a marble balanced rock, and terrific long views.**

### DIRECTIONS
From the south: From Exit 2 (Lee) off the Mass Pike (I-90), turn right after the tollbooths and drive north on Route 20 (which just after Cranwell Resort becomes Route 7/20) for 6.6 miles to West Dugway Road on the left (note sign for Pleasant Valley Wildlife Sanctuary). Drive down West Dugway Road for just over 0.1 mile to the park's gravel parking area on the left, with space for approximately twelve vehicles.

From the north: From Pittsfield's Park Square, drive south on Routes 7/20 for 4.9 miles to West Dugway Road on the right. Follow West Dugway Road for just over 0.1 mile to the park's gravel parking area on the left.

### TRAIL DESCRIPTION
Examine the kiosk, which contains a brief history of the property and use regulations. Although almost all trail intersections are signed and posted with maps, the intricacy of the trail system requires attentiveness. Turn right and follow a sandy path into a forest of maple, ash, oak, birch, and cherry. Pass a side trail on the left and walk up a slight grade on Cold Spring Trail to the trail's namesake, a stone-lined, octagonal reservoir that captures and holds spring water that once supplied the luxurious Aspinwall Hotel. You can investigate a short dead-end path to the spring's source on the right, where a dense growth of hardy kiwi festoons the grotto of marble boulders, reminiscent of Mayan ruins lost to the jungle!

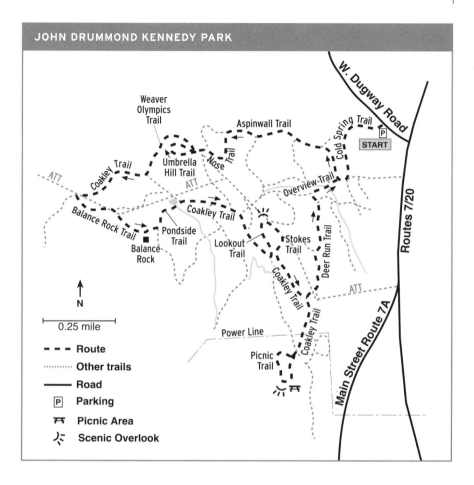

JOHN DRUMMOND KENNEDY PARK

Weaver Olympics Trail

Aspinwall Trail

W. Dugway Road

Cold Spring Trail

P

START

Coakley Trail

ATT

Umbrella Hill Trail

Nose Trail

ATT

Overview Trail

Routes 7/20

Balance Rock Trail

Coakley Trail

Pondside Trail

Balance Rock

Lookout Trail

Stokes Trail

Deer Run Trail

ATT

N

Coakley Trail

0.25 mile

Coakley Trail

Power Line

Picnic Trail

Main Street Route 7A

- - - Route

·········· Other trails

——— Road

P Parking

Picnic Area

Scenic Overlook

Back at the main trail, turn right and follow the old roadway, bearing right past kiwi-infested light gaps. In late summer, ripe black cherries litter the path. You'll reach the wide Woolsey Trail at a four-way intersection with a map kiosk and bench. Edward J. Woolsey bought the nucleus of what would become Kennedy Park beginning in 1853 with a dozen land acquisitions totaling 500 acres. For years, townspeople referred to it as the Woolsey Woods. Turn right, walk a few feet, and almost immediately turn right on Aspinwall Trail, named for the former 400-room hotel that was built in 1902 and succumbed to fire in 1931. Note the spreading gray birch with six trunks (two already dead) that pioneered this site.

The old road becomes rougher as it bears left and continues up a gentle grade. Ignore the side paths. The still numerous gray birches are being outcompeted by more shade-tolerant hardwoods. A tall plant with lacy, fernlike leaves common throughout these rich woods is sweet cicely. Its roots exude a licorice-like aroma. Rock outcrops appear in the gully on the left, and a big sugar maple stands opposite at the fringe of a dark hillside grove of hemlocks and yellow birch. An easy climb soon steepens markedly, passing Hemlock Trail on the left. Continue to a T intersection with Nose Trail, but stay left on Aspinwall Trail. Beyond, boulders and gneiss ledges up to 15 feet high and showing squiggly white quartz bands are capped by the 7-inch fronds of common polypody fern. Lowbush blueberry plants are scattered about this now drier forest floor.

You'll arrive at a five-way intersection. Continuing straight takes you, via a short loop, to the forested top of Umbrella Hill, the park's high point at 1,634 feet. After returning to the main trail, turn left and then left again onto wide, level Weaver Olympics Trail. This trail is named for Lenox nordic skier and Olympian Patrick Weaver, who competed in 1998 at the Winter Olympics in Nagano, Japan, and at the 2002 Winter Games in Salt Lake City. A plaque in his honor is affixed to a boulder. In late summer white wood asters form a decorative fringe along these paths. Pass under a young canopy of red maple and black birch, past decaying stumps of former logging, and ignoring side trails, reach an intersection. Bear right and in 75 feet join the Main, or T. F. Coakley, Trail. Thomas Francis Coakley was a renowned local horseman who developed most of the current trails and maintained them until his death in 1952.

Turn right and soon you'll gaze upon a spreading "wolf" pine on the right that grew up in what was once an open field. Another tree worthy of attention is a massive, deeply furrowed oak on the left. Below, tall meadow rue blooms frothy white in summer, while thin-leaved sunflower exhibits its cheerful yellow petals in late season. At the Y intersection with Balance Rock Trail, turn left and head up a wide, rough road past rock outcrops, ignoring a descending side trail on the right. Maple-leaved viburnum and sapling sugar maples pose an identification challenge; distinguish the toothier leaves of the viburnum. A screened glimpse of Parson's Marsh is possible right, just before you traverse an AT&T transcontinental telephone cable right of way. A thick patch of horse balm produces pointed airy stalks of pale yellow blossoms that appear vaguely orchid-like in late summer, though the plant is a mint.

At the next trail split, either choice brings you to Stonehenge Trail, on the left, which leads to a mound topped by 12 concrete pilings, each 4.5 feet high, and a presumably older set of lower, cement-and-stone footings. These may have supported a tank that once fed water, by gravity, to the hotel. After exploring the site, return to Balance Rock Trail; walk straight, past Kirchner Trail on the left, and bear right on the old roadway through oak woodland

**Spring-fed Cold Spring reservoir once supplied water to the famed Aspinwall Hotel, which burned to the ground in 1931.**

with a "grassy" groundcover of sedges. Note that the downslope margin of the roadway was fortified with stones. At the Y, a short side path leads right, to Balance Rock. A grayish potato-shaped boulder rests atop a sculpted base of the same composition, creating an attractive natural sculpture. The marble is weathering rapidly to produce granular sand. Retrace your steps to the main trail and a big white oak on the left at the intersection. Continue moderately downhill on Balance Rock Trail, choosing either fork where it splits to soon arrive at Pondside Trail.

Turn left or stay straight depending on which fork you took onto Pondside Trail, passing through remnants of a fallen stone wall, and walk under beech, maple, and ash trees to reach a small murky pond on the left where tadpoles metamorphose into wood frogs. Turn right, back on T. F. Coakley Trail, and watch for a small patch of wild ginger. Ginger's heart-shaped leaves obscure the ground-level maroon blossoms pollinated by beetles attracted to the fetid odor. You'll reach Under Mountain Trail on the right, but continue straight on Coakley Trail past the unsigned Aspinwall Trail on the left near an exposed bedrock ledge. Soon you'll arrive at a major Y intersection with two benches and a posted map. A sign attached to a trunk on the left reads Woolsey. Continue straight on Coakley Trail—in the direction of Church on the Hill (at least for now).

Bypass Cutoff Trail by walking straight on the old roadway that contours the hillside where false Solomon's seal thrives. Turn left onto Lookout Trail, a gravelly old road studded with bedrock outcrops as it morphs into a twin track through dry oak woodland. Your destination is a wooden gazebo built in 1992 at a nice all-season vista point for Mount Greylock, and other promontories not visible until after leaf fall. The various summits and cardinal points are noted within the structure. This is a fine place for a snack. Upon leaving the gazebo, turn left along the AT&T right of way. Ignore the subsequent left junction with Lookout Trail, descending easily instead to Stokes Trail. Follow Stokes Trail right through attractive mixed woods, and soon you'll find yourself back on Coakley Trail. Bear left and remain on the wide roadway. After leveling off, pass the Upper Deer Run Trail junction, a fine spot for woodland wildflowers.

Pass through an overhead power-line cut flanked by pleasing views of farms and forested ridges. At the major four-way intersection, bear right onto hard-surfaced Main or Coakley Trail. Bear right again after about 50 feet onto a woodland path—Picnic Trail, passing various cement structures, stone ruins, cellar holes, and foundations of Aspinwall Hotel outbuildings. Follow the path up a steep hemlock-shaded hillside with a precipitous drop on the right. The flat grassy hotel lawn, now a picnic area, offers gorgeous and expansive southerly views that include Monument Mountain (Trip 36) at the left end and Mount Everett (Trip 44) farther south to the right. The hotel's hanging gardens once graced the slope below a metal cyclone fence, now draped with Virginia creeper vines.

Turn left and walk about 70 feet under white pines to a grassy rectangle where the posh hotel, built in 1902, and which hosted the rich and famous of the early twentieth century, once stood. Cross the lawn and turn left onto an asphalted hotel access road. Saunter down to the major intersection, bear left to the Y, and take the right fork, retracing your steps to the power-line cut where sunflowers attract pollinating insects in late summer. At the Upper Deer Run Trail turn right. Bishop's weed (a.k.a. goutweed), an invasive exotic, forms a trailside monoculture. After the AT&T cable right of way, reach an intersection with Deer Run Trail. Turn left. A stone wall runs along the rather inclined slope to your right. Pass the Weaver Trail on the left. The stone wall continues on the right as various metal objects and other refuse from the hotel operations become visible. I noted an oyster shell among the detritus.

The trail becomes briefly steeper and narrows between mossy outcrops. Ignore a side trail and reach a T intersection with spacious Woolsey Trail. Turn right, cross drainage, and descend easily past Wilderness and Aspinwall trails,

## ALIEN INVADERS

They're green, they came from far, far away, and they are threatening to take over. Aliens from Mars? No, invasive exotic plants! Ask land managers today what their biggest concern is regarding species diversity, and it's a good bet they'll answer, "Invasive species." Continent-wide, invasive exotics are second only to habitat loss on the list of threats to biological diversity.

Well-known invaders include purple loosestrife, Eurasian water milfoil, the exotic form of common reed, Japanese barberry, oriental bittersweet, and garlic mustard. A rogue's gallery, to be sure. What makes a perfectly respectable plant (or animal for that matter) from one part of the globe such a menace in another? In their homelands each species faces a long-evolving system of checks and balances to rampant growth. However, when translocated from their native haunts to foreign soil (either by accident or intentionally), the plants may have little or no insect or mammal herbivores, no fungi, and no diseases to keep them in check. Therefore, the possibility exists that a new arrival, sans controls, will outcompete the natives already there.

In Kennedy Park, the adjacent Pleasant Valley Wildlife Sanctuary, and a few other locations, a newly recognized threat has the potential to do serious damage to our forests. That threat is hardy kiwi (*Actenidia arguta*). If you've never heard of it, you're not alone. So recent is this realization that it has yet to be added to the official state registry of invasive exotic plants as of the printing of this book.

Hardy kiwi hails from Southeast Asia, a region from which a number of other very troublesome plants, including oriental bittersweet, arrived. Both species have found our soils and climate to be very welcoming since they mimic those of their homelands. Like bittersweet, hardy kiwi is a climbing vine, but one that is even more aggressive, and that says a lot! Kiwi spreads mostly by runners, but it also produces tasty, grape-sized, green seed-filled fruits that are distributed by birds and mammals looking for a treat. Although it doesn't constrict the trunks of trees the way bittersweet does, it grows so prolifically as to completely engulf woody natives and rob them of sunlight. Kiwi-filled light gaps are a frightening vision of complete alien dominance. Natives have little chance against kiwi. Although restricted in its range currently, it is poised to become a major threat to deciduous forests in the Berkshires, so be on the lookout!

both on the left. Back at the four-way intersection with map kiosk, turn left on Cold Spring Trail to return to your vehicle.

## MORE INFORMATION

Open sunrise to sunset, daily, year-round. Dogs, horses, mountain bikes, and skiing all allowed. Dogs must be under owner's control at all times. Motorized vehicles, alcohol, fires, tree cutting without permission, hunting, and trapping are not permitted. John Drummond Kennedy Park Restoration Committee, Town of Lenox, Lenox Town Hall, 6 Walker Street, Lenox, MA 01240; 413-637-5500; http://townoflenox.com/Public_Documents/LenoxMA_Parkland/kennedy.

## TRIP 28
## BURBANK TRAIL

**Location:** Richmond, Lenox
**Rating:** Moderate
**Distance:** 3.2 miles
**Elevation Gain:** 540 feet
**Estimated Time:** 1.5–2.0 hours
**Maps:** USGS Pittsfield West; trail map available online at the Berkshire Natural Resources Council website; Yokun Ridge Map & Guide

**This enjoyable loop takes you through diverse woodland to a pleasing lookout on the southern slope of Lenox Mountain. Historic homesites and an estate's reservoir add interest.**

## DIRECTIONS

From Exit 2 (Lee) off the Mass Pike (I-90), turn right and follow Route 20 (which just after Cranwell Resort becomes Route 7/20) for 4.1 miles to Route 183 South (Walker Street) on the left at a traffic light. Drive for 1.1 miles to the center of Lenox (at the monument) and continue straight on Route 183 south for another 1.5 miles (past the entrance to Tanglewood Music Center) to where Richmond-Lenox Road bears away from Route 183 to the right. Follow it uphill for 1.4 miles to a circular gravel parking area on the left (where a sign marks Olivia's Overlook). The lot is bounded on the left by an elegant stone wall.

# BURBANK TRAIL

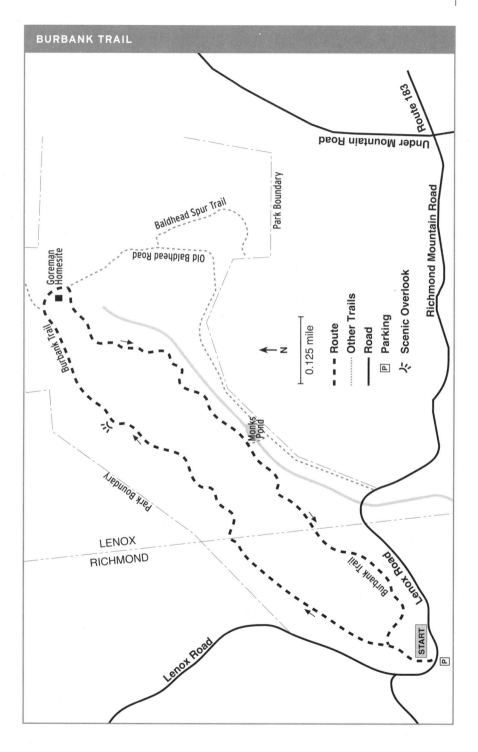

Route 183

Under Mountain Road

Park Boundary

Baldhead Spur Trail

Old Baldhead Road

Goreman
Homesite

Burbank Trail

Richmond Mountain Road

N

0.125 mile

- - - Route
......... Other Trails
——— Road
Ⓟ Parking
☀ Scenic Overlook

Monks
Pond

Park Boundary

LENOX
RICHMOND

Lenox Road

Burbank Trail

Lenox Road

START

Ⓟ

## TRAIL DESCRIPTION

The best view of the route is from the parking area and takes in Stockbridge Bowl (a.k.a. Lake Mahkeenac) and the verdant ridges beyond. This fine parking area is named for Olivia Stokes Hatch, whose family donated the land to Berkshire County Land Trust and Conservation Fund. A plaque atop an elegant stone wall explains that Tennessee Gas Pipeline Company constructed the parking area in 1992.

To reach the trailhead, however, you must cross Lenox Road; use caution! A kiosk complete with large trail map is situated about 50 feet into the forest. Walk up into the diverse woodland of eastern hemlock, oak, ash and red maple. Note the gray schist outcrops veined with milky quartz. This erosion-resistant rock type forms the spine of the Lenox-Stockbridge mountain ridge. Soon you'll enter a darker forest in which hemlock predominates. Yellow, black, and gray birches, as well as shade-tolerant American beech and sun-loving oak, join in. In spring a wet depression to the right is filled with a profusion of purple violets.

Follow the fine red-blazed path to arrive at an intersection and money pipe. Choose the left path to proceed toward the ridge top. Begin a moderate climb past schist outcrops, and emerge into sunlight as you reach a power-line cut. A thick mat of wintergreen on the left bears coral red fruits that catch the eye. This sunny, dry ribbon across the landscape also provides suitable growing conditions for pale corydalis, characterized by tubular pink-and-yellow flowers in May. Eastern towhees are among the species that nest in such artificial shrublands. Listen for their *chewink* calls and *drink-your-tea* songs.

Back in the moister forest the trail undulates under oaks, hemlocks, and mountain laurel shrubs. Woodland wildflowers here include clintonia (a.k.a. blue-bead lily), Indian cucumber-root, and sessile-leaved bellwort (a.k.a. wild oats). All produce yellow flowers. In time the pathway climbs, gently at first and then more steeply, paved in spots with bedrock. It bears left, parting a dense growth of skunk currant. As you might surmise, when crushed, the shiny, maple-like leaves of this low shrub emit a fetid odor. Striped maple is the small tree with tight greenish bark. Even its flowers, produced in May, are green.

After a few more undulations, you'll arrive at a very short side trail that leads left to a vista point. The view to the northwest through a gap in the forest is limited but very nice. A plaque behind you indicates that the trail was named for Kelton Burbank, a local attorney and supporter of Berkshire Natural Resources Council. Lowbush blueberries thrive in the acidic soils beneath the pines and oaks. Return to the main trail and turn left. Hazel, striped maple,

**Monks Pond provided water for the estate assembled by Anson Phelps Stokes and later owned by Andrew Carnegie.**

red maple, and especially witch hazel are numerous beneath the oaks. Gaudy scarlet tanager males sing their burry refrains from high in the oaks in late spring and early summer. In contrast, their yellow-green mates blend in with the foliage. When you reach a wider wood road, turn right onto Old Baldhead Road and descend. The left branch leads to Reservoir Road.

The treadway, somewhat rutted and rocky, descends through a forest of white ash, big-tooth aspen, black and gray birches, red maple, and red oak. A remnant stone wall parallels the roadway on your left. Opposite is a cellar hole—all that remains of the Gorman homesite, occupied by that family from 1852 to 1892, although dates on a cement marker just beyond indicate occupation from 1838 to 1898. The Gormans farmed this 44-acre hardscrabble lot until they sold it to Wall Street financier Anson Phelps Stokes to become part of his Shadowbrook estate. Philanthropist Andrew Carnegie later owned it.

Here Burbank Trail turns right, while Old Baldhead Road continues straight. Another cellar hole (the Broderick homesite) lies just right of the roadside a short distance farther. Follow Burbank Trail, which is more pleasant than walking the old roadway. Morrow's honeysuckle, an introduced exotic ornamental, crowds the path and outcompetes native vegetation. Soon saplings of pioneering black cherry trees become numerous, indicating this was once open ground. During the eighteenth century, virtually the entire ridge was denuded of timber. Much of it was reduced to charcoal to feed the local iron furnaces.

After treading across a series of bog bridges, continue a very gradual descent to a stone wall composed of small pieces of schist. Sheep fences are seldom built of such small material. Reach a hemlock stand and head into a shallow gorge through which a small brook spills. Some stately specimens of the evergreen border the stream. Very little sunlight reaches the forest floor and as a result, little can flourish beneath the hemlocks. The corpses of sun-loving gray birches, which preceded the conifers, have succumbed to their shade. The wide path makes its way through woodland dotted with sofa-sized boulders. Numerous log-and-stone water bars shunt water off the trail.

A green pond in a serene setting soon greets you on the left. This was the estate's reservoir. On a May outing, I saw a lone drake mallard that seemed oddly out of place here. During the twentieth century the reservoir took on the name Monks Pond. A Jesuit order owned the property at the time. The Kripalu Center for Yoga and Health, below Olivia's Overlook, now occupies the former monastery. Follow the path straight, past the tumbling waters of the earthen dam's spillway. Burbank Trail follows fairly high above the flow, and ledge outcrops make the scene picturesque. Listen for the calls of the 21-inch-tall barred owl—*who cooks for you, who cooks for you all*. This hillside is quite steep, and the downslope side of the treadway was reinforced with rock during construction, making for excellent footing. Cross the power-line cut in a different location where tall mountain laurel shrubs bloom profusely in the late June sunshine.

Continue the gradual descent under hemlocks and then through deciduous woodland of birch, beech, maple, and oak before reentering evergreens. A huge hemlock snag stands on the right, giving the forest a primeval feel. Before long, you are back at the first intersection and money pipe. Turn left and retrace your steps across Lenox Road (again, use caution) and your vehicle.

## MORE INFORMATION

Open during daylight hours, year-round. Hiking, mountain biking, and horseback riding are permitted. Motorized vehicles, fires, camping, littering, cutting or removing trees or plants is prohibited. Berkshire Natural Resources Council, Inc., 20 Bank Row, Pittsfield, MA 01201; 413-499-0596; http://www.bnrc.net.

## FEEDING THE FIRES OF INDUSTRY

In the mid-nineteenth century Massachusetts was only 25 percent shaded by a forest canopy. Fully 75 percent of the land was devoid of tree cover. Beginning in earnest during the 18th century, the ancient forests that greeted the first white settlers were systematically cut. Colonists used timber for house construction and firewood, and they cleared the land for agricultural use, to be sure, but not until the Industrial Revolution did the wholesale clear-cutting of Massachusetts woodlands move into high gear.

Early in the life of our young nation, this area was the center of a booming iron industry. In his book *Exploring the Berkshire Hills: A Guide to Geology and Early Industry in the Upper Housatonic Watershed*, historian and geologist Ed Kirby chronicles this little-known period in the area's past, a period when the nation's industrial epicenter was right here. Iron was discovered here in 1731, and eventually 43 blast furnaces were built to process locally mined ore. The iron was used to manufacture cannons and cannon balls for the American Revolution and, later on, wheels for railroad trains. Not until large quantities of a higher-grade ore was discovered in the upper Midwest did the prominence of the Berkshire industry diminish.

The fuel that fired the blast furnaces was not coal, but the more abundant and therefore cheaper locally produced charcoal. Thousands upon thousands of forested acres were cleared to make charcoal to feed the insatiable blast furnaces. Charcoal making was a laborious proposition. Men called colliers cut up to 30 cords of wood that required seasoning for a year in order to dry it. The collier constructed a mound from the 30 cords of wood in the shape of a wigwam, which was covered with ferns and sod to slow the combustion process, while airflow was controlled by vents at the base of the mound. The smoldering mound was tended for four weeks as the wood was slowly transformed into charcoal.

Of course at first, the furnaces burned charcoal from the abundant woodlands so close at hand, but as those were exhausted, sources radiating farther and farther out from the furnace were required. Eventually, with local forests decimated, charcoal had to be imported from elsewhere, making it too expensive as a fuel when compared with coal. But by then the landscape had virtually been laid bare. Today's woodlands are only now recovering from the far-reaching effects of the iron industry.

## TRIP 29
## SCHERMERHORN GORGE TRAIL

**Location:** Lenox, Lee, Washington
**Rating:** Difficult
**Distance:** 3.7 miles
**Elevation Gain:** 620 feet
**Estimated Time:** 2.5 hours
**Maps:** USGS East Lee; trail map available online at the October Mountain State Forest website

**From the still waters of the wildlife-rich Woods Pond to the cascading flow of Schermerhorn Brook, flanked by massive trees, this hike provides dramatic contrasts.**

### DIRECTIONS
From Exit 2 (Lee) off the Mass Pike (I-90), turn right after the tollbooths and follow Route 20 (which just after Cranwell Resort becomes Route 7/20) for 4.6 miles to Housatonic Street in Lenox. Turn right onto Housatonic Street and drive 1.3 miles to where the pavement makes a sharp turn to the right. Leave the pavement by continuing straight ahead on gravel, parking on the right between the railroad tracks and the pedestrian bridge. Be sure not to block the driveway to the private residence on the left. Also, be careful not to obstruct access to the informal but frequently used canoe landing on the pond edge to the right. There is space here for approximately four vehicles. You may also park outside the tracks, on the right. Be aware that this is an active rail line.

### TRAIL DESCRIPTION
Cross the arched steel-and-wood pedestrian bridge over a constriction at the south end of Woods Pond and admire the splendid scene of October Mountain reflected in the usually still waters. The scene is especially eye-catching during fall foliage season in early to mid-October. The Housatonic River plunges over Woods Pond Dam—which backs up the river's flow to create the 100-acre pond—about 200 yards to the right (south). A profusion of exotic Morrow's honeysuckle lines the gravel roadway beyond the bridge.

Bear left upon reaching a gravel road and pass under high transmission lines. If you visit from May to early July, you'll be impressed by the exuberance of bird life. Lemon-yellow sprites—yellow warblers—sing enthusiasti-

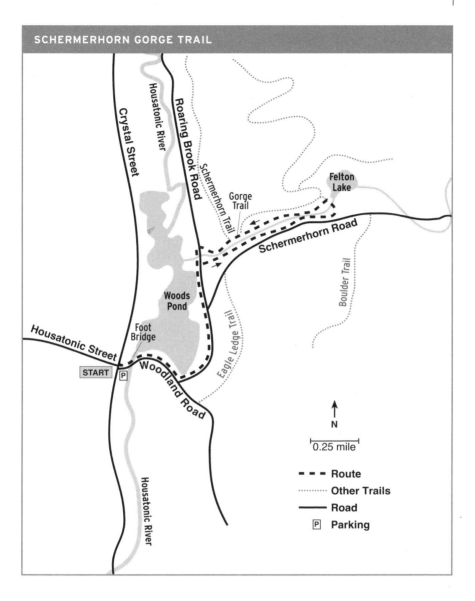

SCHERMERHORN GORGE TRAIL

Housatonic River

Crystal Street

Roaring Brook Road

Schermerhorn Trail

Gorge
Trail

Felton
Lake

Schermerhorn Road

Boulder Trail

Woods
Pond

Eagle Ledge Trail

Foot
Bridge

Housatonic Street

START  P  Woodland Road

Housatonic River

N

0.25 mile

- - -  Route
.........  Other Trails
———  Road
P  Parking

cally from the tops of shrubs, and myriad avian life forms abound in and
around the pond—belted kingfisher, Canada goose, wood duck, mallard, and
warbling vireo, to name a few.

The roadway hugs the pond shore, affording lovely views of pond and hills.
The bucolic scene belies the fact that Woods Pond holds the highest concen-
trations of carcinogenic polychlorinated biphenyls (PCBs) in this river system.
Bear left at another gravel road to continue around the pond. Primarily young
white ash, black birch, sugar maple, and gray and yellow birch trees stand

**A handsome keystone arch spans Schermerhorn Brook soon after it leaves October Mountain State Forest's Felton Lake.**

above the water body. A few massive white pines tower in stark contrast to the young deciduous growth—the body of one multitrunked giant lies where it crashed to earth. Walk past a huge red oak on the right and you'll encounter more impressive trees along the roadway.

Pass a wooded swamp on the left that is luxuriant in spring with skunk cabbage and, on somewhat drier ground, wild leek—an aromatic relative of the onion. Pass two wood roads on the right separated by a modest high-gradient stream flowing soothingly down the hillside over rocks into the pond. Blue diamond blazes mark the state forest boundary to your right not long before the intersection with paved Schermerhorn Road on the right. Continue straight and note the sign designating the boundary of the George L. Darey Wildlife Management Area along the Housatonic. Appreciate the age of more giant oak trees that escaped the ax long ago.

The sound of rushing water heralds your arrival at the trailhead steps before the bridge over Schermerhorn Brook. Enter the forest to the right on a footpath and begin a moderate climb under sugar maples, ashes, and oaks. Blue blazes mark the route. The brook gushes to your left, catapulting over and around boulders of gneiss and quartzite—a magical sight. A low evergreen shrub—

American yew—thrives in the shade near the cascade. This scene, primeval and majestic as it is, might have been captured on canvas by an artist of the Hudson River School.

The trail turns right, continues to climb, and then bears left to ascend above the flow under oaks and hemlocks to a point at which you can gaze down on the brook—but watch your footing. A lovely little two-step waterfall is soon visible below. The rugged slopes of the gorge hold some impressive oaks and hemlocks. One hemlock trunk is fully 3 feet across. The trail moves farther from the stream as the incline eases. Eventually it levels out and rejoins the brook, perhaps 30 feet above it. Mountain maple—a small understory tree similar in size to striped maple but with brown bark and smaller, toothier leaves—grows in the gorge along the flowage.

Walk over stone steps and past a jumble of gneiss boulders as the streambed continues very rocky. Note the characteristic alternating dark and light bands of the gneiss. A delightful trail! In spring and early summer the loud, ringing notes of the bobbing, striped Louisiana waterthrush can be heard even above the roar of the water. These warblers winter in the tropics and nest along fast-flowing upland streams. On the right, a hemlock is growing into a rock crevice, inexorably splitting the rock apart. The brook soon splits in two, forming a narrow floodplain. You'll reach the partial stone foundation of what might have been a millhouse long ago.

You'll emerge briefly into a sunny patch of young maples; Schermerhorn Road is very near. After reentering the shady hemlock forest, you'll pass a fallen tree that was cut years ago to accommodate the trail. This section was 100 years old when it fell, judging by a tree ring count. Some impressive white pines and a mammoth oak stand on the left. The steep aspect of these slopes made timber harvesting here less economical, resulting in some truly impressive specimen trees today. The deep, reverberating drumming of the crow-sized pileated woodpecker is an increasingly common percussion in such mature woodlands of the Berkshires. Even if you don't hear or see one of these memorable birds, you will happen across their deep, rectangular excavations. These aren't nest cavities, but rather spots where dead tissue was removed by the bird so as to reach carpenter ant colonies.

In places the stream is a frothy white ribbon darting among the rocks. The gorge deepens again, and soon the path approaches the brook closely. After the brook negotiates a 90-degree bend to the left, the well-blazed trail follows it up to a gravel roadway. A handsome keystone arch bridge built of native stone lies ahead, and beneath it flows Schermerhorn Brook, the outlet stream from Felton Lake—now close at hand. Turn to cross the bridge. An earthen dam up to your right impounds the water body. You may want to gaze upon the lake before returning along the opposite side of the gorge. Three-inch-long bullfrog tadpoles swim about in the concrete spillway.

The return trail begins just beyond the bridge on the left, under planted Norway spruces, and is marked by a sign; it continues blue blazed. The path follows the rim quite closely and passes a small derelict shack to your right. The gorge seems deeper from this side, and the descent is moderately steep on a good trail. Light gaps are filled with hobblebush, maple-leaved viburnum, and fly honeysuckle. There are patches of young American beech as the path closely approaches the brook. Canada mayflower fills one light gap. The ruins of the possible mill are more easily observed from this side now. You will walk under some very large oaks just before you cross a tributary stream on large, flat stones and continue downward along Schermerhorn Brook.

Blooming hobblebush shrubs in early May add beauty to an already lovely scene. The woodland is more predominantly deciduous in this area—especially rich in oaks. Both Solomon's seal (with greenish flowers hanging down from each leaf node) and false Solomon's seal (with a froth of tiny white blossoms at the tip of the stalk) thrive on the forest floor. This trail appears less traveled than the other. The brook tumbles over moss-cushioned boulders. If you are like me, you'll want to capture the scene with a camera. The roaring of the brook intensifies with the gradient. Stone steps take you down to brook level again. The gorge is shallower here.

The yellow trumpets of fly honeysuckle are more numerous. Blue cohosh, which has oddly purple-green leaves, blooms in spring in a sunny canopy gap. Your descent steepens as the gorge narrows markedly and the brook drops precipitously. The trail is characterized by steep sections and, concomitantly, the cascades become ever more dramatic as you proceed downward. Finally bear right away from the brook, amble down more excellent stone steps, and then negotiate a series of switchbacks down the slope. Reach the brook, pass a huge oak on the right, and arrive back at Woodland Road. Turn left and retrace your steps to Woods Pond, the pedestrian bridge, and your vehicle.

## MORE INFORMATION

Open sunrise to half an hour after sunset year-round. Access is free. Alcoholic beverages are prohibited. Pets are permitted but must be on a 10-foot-maximum leash and attended at all times; proof of rabies vaccination required. Vehicles are not permitted on the Schermerhorn Gorge Trail. October Mountain State Forest, 256 Woodland Road, Lee, MA 01238; 413-243-1778; http://www.mass.gov/dcr/parks/western/octm.htm.

## TRIP 30
## OCTOBER MOUNTAIN STATE FOREST–
## FINERTY POND

**Location:** Becket, Washington
**Rating:** Moderate
**Distance:** 6.0 miles
**Elevation Gain:** 870 feet
**Estimated Time:** 4.0 hours
**Maps:** USGS East Lee

**From a busy highway, the route follows the Appalachian Trail over wooded promontories, under a northern hardwood canopy, to a serene pond ringed by mountain laurel.**

## DIRECTIONS

From the west: Take Exit 2 (Lee) off the Mass Pike (I-90), turn left after the tollbooths, and follow Route 20 (Jacob's Ladder Scenic Byway) east for 4.2 miles to a paved pullout on the right and the AT parking area at the Lee/Becket border. The gravel lot accommodates some seven cars.

From the east: From Route 8 north/Route 20 in Becket, follow Route 20 west for 7.9 miles to the paved pullout and AT parking area on the left.

From the south: From the intersection of Route 8 south/Route 20 in Becket, drive west for 2.7 miles to the pullout and parking lot on the left.

## TRAIL DESCRIPTION

From the kiosk, complete with large display maps of the Appalachian Trail (AT) route, walk east a short distance to the Pedestrian Crossing sign on the left. *Do not walk along Route 20, as this is very hazardous—no shoulder in spots.* Use caution crossing the highway. A narrow blue-blazed access trail leads into a forest of American beech, eastern hemlock, and white pine. Tiny and fuzzy, the paired white blossoms of partridgeberry bloom in ground-hugging mats here in early summer.

The path parallels Route 20 for about 100 yards. Bits of rusty barbed wire are imbedded in tree trunks on the left—evidence of former livestock pasturing. You'll soon reach the AT at a Y intersection. Turn left and follow the white-blazed trail uphill under red and sugar maples, bearing left at an especially large sugar maple. Cross a wet area filled with light-green sensitive fern,

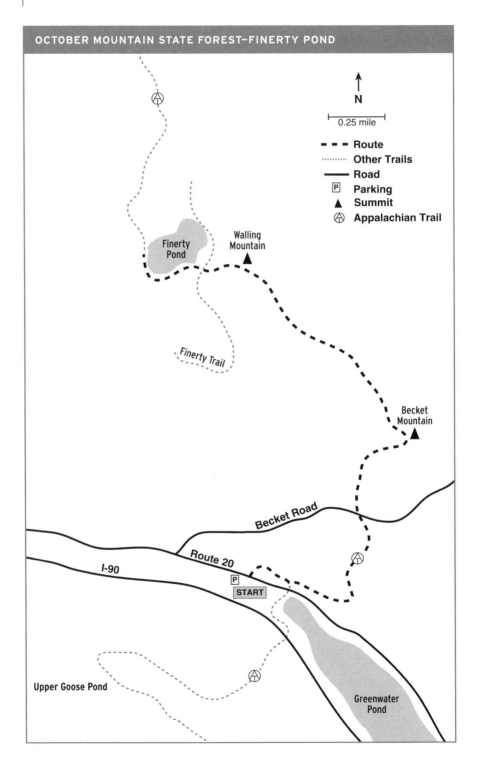

## OCTOBER MOUNTAIN STATE FOREST–FINERTY POND

N

0.25 mile

- - - Route
........... Other Trails
——— Road
P Parking
▲ Summit
Ⓐ Appalachian Trail

Finerty
Pond

Walling
Mountain
▲

Finerty Trail

Becket
Mountain
▲

Becket Road

Route 20

I-90

P
START

Upper Goose Pond

Greenwater
Pond

a species used to delineate wetlands. A sign attached to a tree gives distances to various landmarks along the route. A probable vernal pool lies in a depression a bit farther on the right. Turn and climb stone, then log steps up a slope of maple, hemlock, birch, and oak. A mammoth twin white pine commands attention on the left. Canada mayflowers bloom in spring in the acidic soil beneath the pines. Abundant beech saplings, often sprouting in clones from the same rootstock, populate the understory.

Cross the first of several boulder fields. The hard gneiss rocks are alternately banded light and dark. A moderate climb brings you to a level old woods road where the trail turns right. The sound of flowing water should be evident as you reach a four-way intersection with a snowmobile route. Bear left at an adjoining wide track and skirt a dark hemlock ravine cut by a gurgling brook. The AT soon splits away from the wood road and bears left to enter a power-line right of way. Various ferns and yellow loosestrife flourish in the sunny depression. Rejoin the brook under a canopy of hemlocks and cross it on moss-covered stones. The soothing sound of running water replaces—at least for now—the mechanized din of the highway and turnpike.

The trail climbs gradually through mixed rock-strewn woodland. Intermixed with the dominant beeches are large multitrunked oak trees that indicate the species may have been selectively logged here some 90 years ago, since multiple stems sprout from cut stumps. Cross a shallow rushing brook on stones and follow the level path up to paved Becket (Tyne) Road. You could start your hike here by parking on the wide gravel shoulder (space for just a few cars), cutting off 0.7 mile each way. Cross the pavement and climb easily under hardwoods and past a boulder field on the slope to your right.

For a bit you'll join an old skid road over which logs may have been hauled out. A gray gneiss boulder on the left has weathered into tiers. To me it appeared vaguely like the armored hide of a rhinoceros. (OK, it takes some imagination, but you get the idea.) It lies next to a dead beech. The vast majority of the American beech trees in this forest unfortunately are diseased and dying. A minute scale insect makes a tiny incision to get at the tree's sap. A fungus invades the tree through the hole and ends up wreaking havoc with the tree's circulatory system. An outward symptom is rough, broken black bark all over instead of smooth gray bark. Bear right and pass over a knoll with some big non-native Norway spruces. The narrow trail traverses bedrock in spots through young beech woods with an attractive fern growth.

A short climbs takes you to the top of Becket Mountain, at elevation 2,178 feet, where you level out in a pretty glade of hay-scented fern. Concrete footings are all that remain of a tower that stood here when the summit was open.

A female bullfrog, such as the one above, has eardrums that are equal in size to her eyes, whereas a male's eardrums are larger than his eyes.

An AT register hangs from a tree. Turn left and pass a cluster of gneiss boulders to begin an easy descent along the slope's contour. At the end of June here one year I watched a male black-throated blue warbler feeding a begging fledgling. An angular flat-topped boulder on the right is capped by wild oats—a lily (not a grass) that flowers pale yellow in spring.

Begin an easy climb and cross another jumble of rocks. A wet spring and summer tends to produce a bumper crop of fungi along the trail. Watch for yellowish coral fungus protruding from dead logs. Zigzag up another slope and amble through a rather extensive fern glade under broad-leaved trees. Begin another easy descent and level out among hobblebushes in attractive, rocky woods. Soon the character of the forest changes markedly. Scattered maple trees on this flat ridgeline permit enough light to reach the forest floor for a dense layer of raspberry, ferns, elderberry, and climbing false buckwheat to thrive. The area has a disturbed look and was probably logged.

Climb again and level out on top of Walling Mountain. It might be difficult to tell that you're at 2,200 feet above sea level, given the minor elevation change since the last bump along the ridge. You'll pass impressive car-sized hunks of gneiss and the woodland wildflowers clintonia and Indian cucumber-root. The latter has modest but beautiful little flowers with recurved yellow petals hanging from a second tier of whorled leaves. The descent gets a bit rougher.

Luxuriant patches of shining club moss, a nonflowering fern relative, look-ing like a carpet of green bottlebrushes, poke up from the leaf litter. Wood frogs and red efts wander the forest searching for invertebrate prey as the path switchbacks down.

You'll reach Finerty Trail, a wood road used by all-terrain vehicles. Cross it, and Finerty Pond is tantalizingly visible through the trees ahead. The now wider AT leads down to a 10-foot-high laurel bush on the right and turns left to follow near the shore. Occasional glimpses through the vegetation hint at the pond's lovely setting. If you pass this way in late June and early July, you'll be treated to a fantastic laurel flower show. A sizable yellow birch stands on the left just before you tread on a cushioned path beneath hemlocks to a contem-plative spot near the water's edge bordered by abundant laurel shrubs.

The trail continues around the pond, but at about 80 feet distant, to a very large black cherry tree (note the white AT blaze on the black, flaky-barked trunk), where a short side trail leads right to a nice expansive view of peaceful Finerty Pond. What a striking and welcome contrast from the din of speed-ing motor vehicles at the hike's start! In summer, bullfrogs bellow and green frogs announce your arrival with a little scream as they flee. Dragonflies and damselflies alight on logs in the water. They must be alert to the presence of frogs. Twigs stripped of bark by beavers litter the shore. Meadowsweet shrubs crowd the verge, but laurels steal the show. Listen for the dry rattle of the belted kingfisher (about 1 foot long, with a shaggy crest) from somewhere across the pond.

The AT soon swings away from the shore, so this is a fitting destination for the hike. You may well choose to linger and enjoy the serenity. When ready, retrace your steps some 3 miles to the parking area. Near the end of the hike, be sure to turn right, where the AT splits off and goes down to cross Route 20. It's much safer to walk back parallel but above Route 20 than along the pavement.

## MORE INFORMATION

Carry out all litter. No motorized vehicles, mountain bikes, horses, tree cutting, or fires permitted. Camping allowed in designated areas only. The Appalachian Trail Management Committee is responsible for maintenance, management, and protection of the nearly 90 miles of the AT in Massachusetts; volunteers do this work, with assistance from the Massachusetts Department of Conservation and Recreation. Massachusetts AT Committee, Berkshire Chapter AMC, P.O. Box 2281, Pittsfield, MA 01201; 413-528-8003; at@amcberkshire.org; http://www.amcberkshire.org/at.

## TRIP 31
## WASHINGTON MOUNTAIN MEADOW TRAIL

**Location:** Washington
**Rating:** Easy
**Distance:** 2.5 miles
**Elevation Gain:** 30 feet
**Estimated Time:** 2.0 hours
**Maps:** USGS East Lee

**What is now a marsh was originally designed as a drinking-water reservoir in the 1980s. Leakage forced its abandonment, and that serendipitous failure now provides wetland habitat for a variety of creatures from dragonflies to moose.**

### DIRECTIONS

From the intersection of Routes 8 and 20 in Becket (known locally as Bonny Rigg Corners), follow Route 8 north for 4.8 miles to McNerney Road on the left (where the highway curves right). Turn onto McNerny Road and then immediately left again onto County Road. Drive down County Road (which later becomes Lenox Whitney Place Road) for 5.8 miles to an intersection of gravel roads in October Mountain State Forest known locally as Four Corners. Turn left on West Branch Road and travel just over 0.4 mile to a gravel pullout on the right where the road curves left to become Schoolhouse Road. There is space for several vehicles. The trailhead is approximately 60 feet back in the direction you drove in.

### TRAIL DESCRIPTION

A sign marks the start of the Washington Mountain Meadow Interpretive Trail as you enter a dim Depression-era Norway spruce stand on a universal access path of fine crushed stone that runs along a stone wall. A portion of this 800-foot-long path is currently closed at post 9 due to flooding, but sections are still passable and it links to the longer Outer Loop Trail that permits you to circumambulate Washington Mountain Marsh. Interpretive marker 1 is just to your left at a nineteenth-century cellar hole, while marker 2 is located adjacent to a stone wall that marks the boundary of a family cemetery. They are the last reminders of farming here. New York fern now populates a glade under white

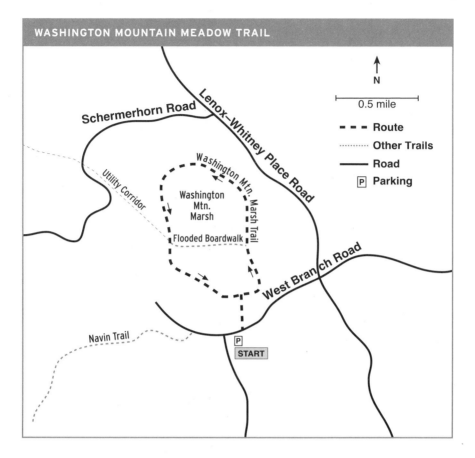

ash, black cherry, and maple as the wall veers away at a 90-degree angle. Fragrant balsam fir intermingles with spruce at interpretive marker 3.

When you reach a Y split, turn right to leave the universal access trail and follow blue blazes over a cushioned treadway with red maples and balsam firs overhead. You'll know you've encountered balsam firs by their delicious fragrance. Continue through an attractive mixed forest. One hemlock has five trunks! A part of the trail becomes narrower and somewhat overgrown in summer, with raspberry canes reaching out to engulf the path, but then widens again. The red eft, the wandering terrestrial stage of the red-spotted newt, is an abundant denizen of the forest floor, especially during wet conditions. These charming little salamanders, which spend years roaming the woods before returning to ponds to breed, are poisonous to would-be predators. They morph from red-orange to yellow-olive when making the change. The trail bears left, passing marker 13. Shining club moss protrudes from the leaf litter like a deep carpet of AstroTurf. The flowering plants wood sorrel, goldthread, and clintonia, along with nonflowering mosses, are indicative of northern forests. The spruces now are native red spruce.

In summer the comical gulps of green frogs alert you to an approaching wetland. Soon you'll arrive at a wooden sign indicating that the Outer Loop (1.4 miles long) turns right, at the interface of forest and marsh. A short path leads to the edge of the aquatic world and your first glimpse of a mile-long vegetated wetland of cattails, sedges like wool grass, leatherleaf clumps, meadowsweet shrubs, and dozens of other plant species. In midsummer, foamy, light pink clusters of meadowsweet crawl with pollinating bumblebees. A series of bog bridges once enabled visitors to cross to the far side of the marsh, but higher water levels have made that impossible. A beaver lodge is visible toward the north end. Follow Outer Loop along the marsh's perimeter past immaculate white birches.

Ground-hugging dewberries form a dense, shiny green groundcover along portions of the trail. These relatives of blackberries and raspberries are also tasty when ripe. Gray-green pixie cups and British soldiers, the latter looking a bit like red-tipped kitchen matches, have colonized patches of otherwise sterile-looking earth. These associations of fungi and alga are true pioneers. Scan the ground too for signs of fairly recent returnees to the Berkshires. Moose, the largest members of the deer family, frequent this area, as evidenced by 6-inch-long tracks sunk deep into the soft earth. Woody vegetation once cut back to create the reservoir has recolonized the perimeter with young growth providing abundant browse for these magnificent creatures.

Prickly blackberry and raspberry canes crowd the trail, while along the horizon sharp-tipped spruces crown the ridgeline. Looking like green velvety antlers, staghorn club moss pokes up along the path. This club moss is perhaps the least encountered of the four common species in the Berkshires. So far, you have traversed a number of damp spots via two-plank bog bridges. Now the bridges lead you through cattails that wave in the breeze, with invasive common reed to the left. Marsh ferns thrive in the saturated soil.

This section is clearly boggy, as affirmed by plants found in acidic wetlands—sweetgale (a shrub with spicy-fragrant leaves), highly absorbent sphagnum moss, and the carnivorous round-leaved sundew. Each leaf of the sundew is appointed with an array of hairlike filaments tipped with sweet, sticky droplets that attract and ensnare unsuspecting insects. In midsummer, sundews put up a wiry red stalk of tiny five-petaled white stars. Spikes of greenish-yellow flowers pushing up through the moss belong to a modest yet

**Bog bridges lead through wetland areas where sphagnum moss and round-leaved sundew thrive in the acidic conditions.**

lovely little orchid—green wood orchis. There are even highbush blueberries that offer ripe fruit to hikers in July and August at a convenient height.

And so the trail continues with areas of higher ground interspersed with wet reaches necessitating bog bridges. Bear left again, past a shrubby area on the right filled with goldenrod, meadowsweet and steeplebush shrubs, and sapling birches. Twining virgin's bower lies atop the shrubs and shows off pretty white blossoms in late July. *Portions of the path may be flooded at certain seasons, so you'll want to wear shoes you don't mind getting wet, or perhaps rubber boots.* If you are like me, you may be content to trade wet feet for a taste of ripe red raspberries. And plentiful they are in July. Meadowsweet favors the drier sections while joe-pye weed, a tall forb crowned by a flat-topped bouquet of magenta-pink blossoms in midsummer, can tolerate wetter conditions. Bumblebees are partial to both.

Pass through a shrub-filled telephone-cable right of way. *The next bog bridges you encounter may have very slick surfaces from algal growth, so tread with caution.* After reentering the maple, yellow birch, and hemlock woods, listen for the clear, whistled *Old Sam Peabody, Peabody, Peabody* of white-throated sparrows here at 1,800 feet above sea level. By now the trail has taken you farther from the marsh through a logged area where young birches and black cherries have pioneered the return of woody growth. Ferns hem in the path and threaten to conceal it as the trail gains height. Hay-scented fern glades hide the forest floor between the red maples, red spruces, balsam firs, and hemlocks. Wood sorrel and goldthread plants each have three leaves, but one looks like clover (wood sorrel), while the other's leaves are dark green and reflective.

Cross the buried cable corridor again, and soon you'll find yourself back at the marsh. A fairly large volume of water flows under the plank bridges, replenishing the wetland after storm events. A small, nondescript olive-green bird of the alder thickets is, appropriately enough, called alder flycatcher. Its plumage won't catch your eye, nor will its song—a raspy and curt *fee-bee-o*— catch your ear. If you missed getting a close look at the sundews and orchids earlier, there are more on this side of the marsh. Continue to tread along an undulating path over hummocks with young deciduous growth and marshy sinks spanned by bog bridges. Finally you'll arrive at a view of open water. The unmistakable gurgle of flowing water turns out to be seepage through a classic arching beaver dam with the top of the span pointing upstream. Clever engineers these rodents.

Bog bridges lead just below and parallel with the branch and mud structure decorated by the white powder-puff globes of buttonbush in midsummer. In contrast, raspy-leaved rice cutgrass tears at your pants (or skin if you're unfortunate enough to be wearing shorts) as you make your way over the bog bridges in summer. Reenter the woods to reach a signpost at interpretive marker 8. The interpretive loop turns left, but it is flooded and impassable at the next marker. Instead, continue straight and gain ground easily through a young forest of maple, beech, and yellow birch. Pass by an oddly shaped conical gneiss boulder and enter mixed woods. Bear right on a wider track where a less-traveled side path enters from the left. Follow along a low slope to your right, and at interpretive marker 6 you'll arrive at a post indicating that Knob Loop (0.4 mile long) leads straight ahead.

Turn left and descend on a woodland path through young woody growth to revisit the marsh. The now very familiar bog bridges span this southern end of the wetland, past cattails, leatherleaf, sweetgale, birch, young red spruce, balsam fir, sphagnum moss, green wood orchis, and marsh fern. A plant that appears to have a tuft of cotton candy at its apex is cotton grass—not a grass at all, but a true sedge. It's also been dubbed bog cotton.

After interpretive marker 5 you'll traverse a fairly lengthy section of plank bridges to upland forest, where you bear right. At marker 4 you reach the end

## CHILLING OUT

Many people believe that so-called cold-blooded aquatic animals like frogs and turtles burrow into the mud each fall and blissfully await the return of spring. That's only partly accurate. In reality, what some of these creatures pull off is nothing short of miraculous. The wood frog, a species totally reliant on vernal pools for procreation, literally freezes solid and lives to croak (or, more accurately, quack) about it! Similarly, the tiny spring peeper and the gray tree frog have the same incredible ability. We of course have no such powers of resurrection. When our tissues freeze, our cells rupture and die. In the miraculous cases of these frogs, however, natural forms of antifreeze prevent the water from crystallizing and bursting the animal's cells.

And amazingly, these frogs can withstand alternating bouts of freezing and thawing without any apparent negative effects. To be sure, some species, such as the locally common green frog, do lie on the bottom of ponds, slowing down their body processes to a point barely sufficient to sustain life. Their breathing and heart rates fall to extremely low levels. Of course, in this state of suspended animation these creatures are totally vulnerable. Lucky for them that beavers are vegetarians.

I once observed a sleek mink emerge from a beaver pond through a jagged opening in the thin ice coating its surface. The ice was barely thick enough to support the animal's weight. It was carrying a frog in its mouth. Upon spying me, it dropped the frog and bounded a short distance away. After a few moments though, the mink retraced its steps, picked up the frog, and made off with it into the safety of an abandoned beaver lodge.

Like frogs, turtles face the same constraints when winter's chill comes calling. Not able to internally regulate their body temperatures at a level necessary to maintain normal activity, turtles also must retreat to a safe place below the ice. There they wait out the season until the spring sun rises high enough each day to melt the ice sheet entrapping them. Biologists refer to this resting state as brumation.

Thus these creatures and their kin spend half of their lives less than fully alert. Perhaps that is one major reason why turtles live so long. Sometimes, it seems, it is better just to lay low.

of the universal access portion of the route. Follow the wide path, once again inhaling deeply the sweet aroma of balsam, to the Y junction near the start of the hike. Bear right and walk approximately 0.1 mile back to your vehicle.

## MORE INFORMATION

Open sunrise to half an hour after sunset year-round. Access is free. There are no restroom facilities along the trail. Alcoholic beverages are prohibited. Pets are permitted but must be on a 10-foot-maximum leash and attended at all times; proof of rabies vaccination required. October Mountain State Forest, 256 Woodland Road, Lee, MA 01238; 413-243-1778; http://www.mass.gov/dcr/parks/western/octm.htm.

## TRIP 32
## BASIN POND

**Location:** Lee
**Rating:** Easy
**Distance:** 2.7 miles
**Elevation Gain:** 290 feet
**Estimated Time:** 1.5 hours
**Maps:** USGS East Lee; online trail map available at the Berkshire Natural Resources Council website

**A walk through a magical mixed broadleaf and evergreen woodland, this partial loop trail is as yet a mostly undiscovered Berkshire gem and a wonderful walk with small children.**

## DIRECTIONS

From Exit 2 (Lee) off the Mass Pike (I-90), turn left after leaving the tollbooths and follow Route 20 east for 4.0 miles to its intersection with Becket Road in Lee. Turn left (north) onto Becket Road and follow it uphill for 0.3 mile to a small gravel parking area (with space for perhaps four vehicles) on the left. Watch for the sign here.

## TRAIL DESCRIPTION

An angular gneiss boulder at the edge of the parking area serves as a rocky portal and a portent of things to come. A few feet beyond, a map kiosk relates

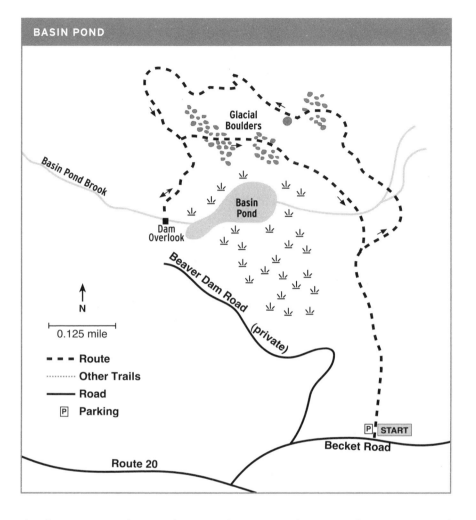

the fascinating and tragic history of Basin Pond. Twice—first in 1886 and again in 1968—the failure of flawed earthen dams led to multiple losses of life downstream. In 1975, Clark-Aiken Company sold the property to conservationist N. Robert Thieriot. Following Thieriot's death in 1998, his estate bequeathed the land to Berkshire Natural Resources Council in 2001.

Follow the red blazes north under a luxurious canopy of sugar maple, red oak, American beech, black birch, and eastern hemlock. Soon you cross the first of numerous rocky brook beds filled with a jumble of gray boulders. Below the deciduous trees grow striped maple, hobblebush shrubs, and ferns, and below them, 6-inch-tall club mosses that resemble a Lilliputian woodland. In contrast, in the deep shade of the hemlocks, virtually nothing grows. The path undulates through scenic woodland, making for easy walking for the first

**Mammoth glacial boulders are a highlight along the expertly constructed paths of the relatively unknown Basin Pond property.**

half mile. Acorn-loving blue jays and white-breasted nuthatches call out from the branches, while hermit thrushes and ovenbirds haunt the forest floor.

At a trail split, turn right and follow the now red-triangle-blazed trail up the slope through predominantly young beech forest. Odd flowering plants called beechdrops are parasitic on the tree's roots. They lack green chlorophyll, but when seen close-up, the brownish purple trumpet-like blossoms are quite attractive. Yellow birch, black cherry, and white ash now appear along with the oaks. You will appreciate the great effort expended by master trail builder Peter Jensen and his crew as you cross another intermittent brook bed on a large, flat capstone bridge. Their handiwork is quite evident throughout this trail network.

The sloping terrain is laced with rocky stream channels, most of which are dry in late summer, and angular boulders jut out everywhere from the forest floor. These are referred to as talus slopes on the map kiosk. They were certainly dropped by a retreating glacier. The hard gneiss rocks are characteristically banded dark and light.

Follow the contours of the slope roughly westward. An eye-catching red oak more than 3 feet in diameter splits into twin trunks some 20 feet above the ground. This sun-dappled woodland, owing to the lack of major soil disturbance, is virtually free of the invasive, exotic plant species found in so many other forests of the Northeast. Beguiling eastern chipmunks chirp and cluck from the forest floor when an intruder approaches.

You'll reach another trail split with both paths marked by painted red rectangles. Turn right beneath an increasing number of red maples—crimson in autumn—to follow the quarter-mile spur trail downhill to the earthen dam and a fine view of Basin Pond. An opening filled with light-loving bracken fern and goldenrod marks the location of the dam. Crest the low rise for scenic views of wetlands and ridge, and beaver-dammed Basin Brook—the viewing platform at the end of the abutment is a nice sunny spot for lunch or a snack. Human attempts to create a lake for a vacation-home development is evidenced by old protruding tree stumps, while beaver handiwork is visible below the earthen dam in the form of a classic U-shaped stick-and-mud dam. The shrubs offer food and cover to birds like the gray catbird.

Retrace your steps to the Y fork and turn right to continue. At another sloping boulder field my wife and I chanced upon a prickly porcupine making haste for its den among the boulders. It soon disappeared into a deep crevice. Sapling-sized mountain maples sprout up through the rocks, some topped by leathery fronds of evergreen wood fern. Farther on, the path wends between two monumental opposing glacial relics. The presence of all these stones, large enough to almost give one the impression that they are animate, imparts a most appealing aspect to this landscape.

Soon the trail morphs into an old roadway along which glistening, deep green Christmas fern flourishes. The woodland is now mostly maple and ash, at least for a while. After you reenter the shady beech woods and pass a 2.5-foot-diameter hemlock, you'll cross a brook bed where in spring water cascades over a layered emerald-green moss-covered ledge. Bog bridges keep your feet dry as you negotiate a seepage area among yellow birches a bit farther on. Soon you'll reach the initial intersection to close the loop. Turn right and follow the needle-cushioned treadway back to your vehicle.

## MORE INFORMATION

Open during daylight hours. Motorized vehicles, fires, camping, littering, and cutting or removing trees or plants are prohibited. The Berkshire Natural Resources Council is a private, nonprofit land conservation organization that holds some 14,000 acres in order to preserve the rural character of the Berkshire landscape. Berkshire Natural Resources Council, 20 Bank Row, Pittsfield, MA 01201; 413-499-0596; http://www.bnrc.net.

## PREDATOR AND PRICKLY PREY

Porcupines are humble creatures. They don't put on a show unless threatened, and they mind their own business unless provoked. Our regenerating woodlands have encouraged the return of a number of former natives. This prickly rodent, while always present, had a much smaller population in the mid-nineteenth century. Today it is common throughout the region.

Porcupines have many detractors. They do, after all, eat the inner bark from tree limbs, which isn't beneficial for the tree, and dog owners are wary of these walking pincushions. But I find them engaging nonetheless. One is most apt to find their lifeless bodies on roadways where they are vulnerable to our high-speed vehicles. At night their essentially black, bristly pelage reflects little light, making them highly vulnerable.

Porcupines are usually silent, but they do make weirdly human wailing sounds. Young porcupines, called porcupets, are outfitted with a set of stiff spines. Legend has it that these creatures can throw their spines, but that is fantasy. Upon close approach porcupines do erect the spines on their backs into a formidable fan-shaped array designed to deter attack.

Porcupines spend the day in trees they have been feeding in or ensconced in dens located in rocky crevices where they are safer from predators. In summer the rodents eat leafy greens instead of the bark rations of winter. Their barbed quills offer a decided edge against many would-be attackers, but one carnivore has their number, so to speak. That predator is the fisher. Sometimes called fisher cats, these are actually large, lithe weasels second in size only to the river otter. Fishers were long absent from the Berkshires but were reintroduced to the region partly in an attempt to control the burgeoning population of porcupines. Fishers are large and powerful, dark brown—almost black—and they climb with aplomb. They leave paired tracks a foot or more apart on the snowy landscape. Red squirrels and porcupines are among their culinary favorites. While red squirrels are fast and agile in the treetops, porcupines are slow and clumsy.

Fishers attack the spiny rodents, which may outweigh them, by striking where the animal is most vulnerable—its soft, unprotected abdomen. Concomitant with an increase in porcupines has been an increase in their chief predator. Telltale signs of porcupines are fairly numerous in our woodlands if you are observant. Watch for sawdust-filled fecal pellets and barkless branches high in trees in addition to tracks, especially in rocky areas.

## TRIP 33
## UPPER GOOSE POND

**Location:** Becket, Lee, Tyringham
**Rating:** Moderate
**Distance:** 3.7 miles (4.7 miles with round-trip to AT cabin)
**Elevation Gain:** 385 feet
**Estimated Time:** 2.0 hours
**Maps:** USGS East Lee

**This out-and-back hike on the AT takes you to one of the Berkshires' most scenic ponds, a serene location reminiscent of northern New England.**

### DIRECTIONS

From the west: Take Exit 2 (Lee) off the Mass Pike (I-90), turn left after the tollbooths, and follow Route 20 east for 4.2 miles to the Appalachian Trail (AT) parking area on the right at the Lee/Becket border. The gravel lot accommodates some seven cars.

From the east: From the intersection of Route 8 north and Route 20 in Becket, follow Route 20/8 west for 7.9 miles to the AT parking area on the left.

From the south: From the intersection of Route 8 south and Route 20 in Becket, follow Route 20 west for 2.7 miles to the parking area on the left.

### TRAIL DESCRIPTION

From the kiosk with large display map, walk east a short distance to the pedestrian crossing sign at Route 20. *Do not walk along Route 20, as this is very hazardous—no shoulder in spots.* Use caution crossing the highway! A narrow, blue-blazed access trail leads into a forest of American beech, eastern hemlock, and white pine. Paralleling Route 20 for about 100 yards, it soon joins the AT. Turn right and follow the white-blazed path down to the highway.

Cross Route 20, pass through a gap in the guardrail, and proceed down wooden steps. Old orchard trees litter the ground with apples in fall. A brown AT directional sign indicates that the side trail to Goose Pond Cabin is 1.6 miles away. Soon you'll cross Greenwater Brook on a wooden bridge at a former mill site and arrive at the earthen dam that holds back the waters of Greenwater Pond. Turn right toward the Mass Pike; bear left under the bridge

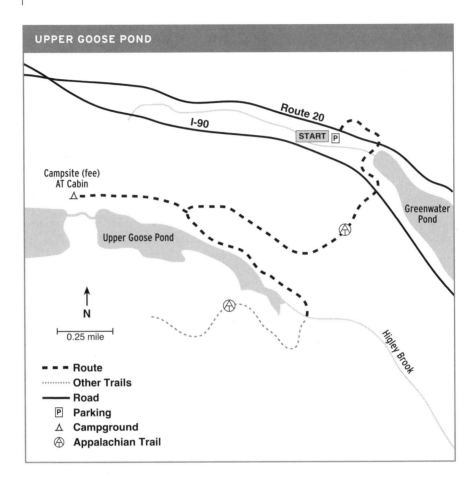

**UPPER GOOSE POND**

Route 20

I-90

START P

Campsite (fee)
AT Cabin

Upper Goose Pond

Greenwater
Pond

N

0.25 mile

Higley Brook

- - - Route
········· Other Trails
——— Road
P Parking
△ Campground
Ⓐ Appalachian Trail

and circle up and around to cross over the westbound lanes, then cross a second bridge over the eastbound lanes. The October Mountain plateau looms behind you.

Reenter the woodland and reach a trail split. Take the white-blazed left fork (the other is a snowmobile corridor) and ascend fairly steeply under a canopy of sugar and red maples, white ash, yellow birch, and red oak. A metamorphic rock ledge (gneiss) pops up on the left. Bear left around the ledge and up over stone steps and past more outcrops amid the steady roar from the interstate. Ferns and green-trunked striped maples shade tiny evergreen club mosses. Higher up, red oak becomes more common. As you level out briefly, watch for an impressive 2.5-foot-diameter white ash on the left bearing an AT blaze. Ashes provide the sturdy lumber required for ax handles and baseball bats.

As you begin climbing once again, notice the young, shade-tolerant beech trees covering the north-facing slope along with birches, maples, and oaks. At

**So close to the Mass Turnpike, yet appearing to belong in northern New England, Upper Goose Pond is a gem.**

the boundary of the Upper Goose Pond Natural Area, on the height of land, you'll find an AT register. You may want to peruse it for interesting insights into the exploits of AT thru-hikers and other trail users. From here, descend gradually through small patches of hobblebush. This shrub is attractive at all seasons. Large clusters of small white flowers in spring give way to red fruits in summer and multihued foliage in autumn. Even the large, straw-colored buds are distinctive in winter. The din of the highway has faded away, and you're now in a different world.

An impressive gray ledge—uptilted at 30 degrees—juts out to your right as you bear in that direction. This attractive woodland now includes stands of low mountain laurel and its tiny relative wintergreen. This sunnier south-facing slope encourages a dominance of oaks, through which a screened view of a ridgeline is possible. Follow the slope contour, then descend and walk along an impressive gneiss ledge exposed for more than 250 feet. Brown and black rock tripe clings to its vertical face, turning green only after absorbing moisture. Descend again and soon you'll reach a junction and sign indicating that the Upper Goose Pond Cabin is 0.5 mile down the side trail. If you have the time, it's worth a visit. The cabin, which offers overnight accommodation, is picturesquely situated on a laurel-studded slope above the lake. Privies are available at the cabin and at the designated camping area.

Continue straight, following the AT on what is now an old wood road through beech, oak, black birch, and mountain laurel. Turn right, off the road, where white blazes lead toward the lake. When you reach Upper Goose Pond, turn left to follow the shoreline toward Higley Brook at the pond's eastern end. Stunning views of the 45-acre pond (elevation 1,465 feet) abound through gaps in the vegetation. You'll soon reach the site of a former sportsman's lodge—Mohhekennuck—constructed in the first decade of the twentieth century. A fallen chimney is all that remains. A short path leads to a tiny gravel beach popular as a canoe landing. Continue on the southbound AT along the shoreline through mountain laurel that is frothy with pinkish-white blossoms in late June.

A thick growth of shining club moss carpets the forest floor at one spot on the right. Ghostly white Indian pipes—parasitic on oak roots—bloom here in summer. The hardwood forest is also home in summer to many species of colorful wood warblers, olive-green vireos, and musical thrushes. The pathway moves away from the water prior to arriving at little Higley Brook, spanned by a modest wooden bridge. Lovely Canada lilies bloom along this permanent water source for the pond in early July. Goose Pond Road is 1.9 miles farther, but this is the end point for our hike. Retrace your steps approximately 0.5 mile to the lodge ruins and 100 yards beyond to where the AT bears right, up the slope. Be alert, as this intersection can be missed.

## MORE INFORMATION

No fires permitted; camping in designated areas only. The Appalachian Trail Management Committee is responsible for maintenance, management, and protection of the nearly 90 miles of the AT in Massachusetts; volunteers do this work, with assistance from the Massachusetts Department of Conservation and Recreation. Massachusetts AT Committee, Berkshire Chapter AMC, P.O. Box 2281, Pittsfield, MA 01202; http://www.amcberkshire.org/at; at@amcberkshire.org; 413-528-6333. Appalachian Mountain Club Regional Trail Coordinator: 413-528-8003.

**Location:** Becket, Chester, Middlefield
**Rating:** Easy–Moderate
**Distance:** 4.3 miles
**Elevation Gain:** 260 feet
**Estimated Time:** 2.0–3.0 hours
**Maps:** USGS Chester, East Lee; map available online

**A fairly easy walk takes you to a deep valley where the utilitarian beauty of three massive standing keystone arches makes for a fascinating and scenic hike back in time.**

## DIRECTIONS

From the intersection of Route 20 and Route 8 north in Becket, drive east on Route 20 for 4.2 miles to Chester Village. Turn left onto Middlefield Road and follow it for approximately 2.5 miles to the gravel Herbert Cross Road on the left, where Middlefield Road curves right. The sign is not easily seen from the south. The parking area at the top of the road has an interpretive kiosk with map and can accommodate approximately six vehicles.

## TRAIL DESCRIPTION

After reviewing the information on the kiosk, amble down the gravel Herbert Cross Road under a canopy of oaks, white birch, big-tooth aspen, and eastern hemlock. Note the CSX railroad tracks below, to your left. Soon you'll level out and reach fast-flowing Babcock Brook, crossing it on a metal bridge. Keystone Arch Bridges (KAB) Trail markers—note the one tacked to a tree on the left—and blue blazes delineate the route. The high-gradient stream has polished the brook's hard quartzite boulders to a smooth finish, making for a picturesque scene. The cascade (identified as "falls" on the map) tumbles over grayish rocks generously dotted with lichens. The hemlock-shaded pools provide habitat for native brook trout, caddis fly larvae, and crayfish.

To your left flows the clear West Branch of the Westfield River, and before you anticipate it, a screened view of the Double Arch Keystone Bridge appears. You'll have to walk down to the bank to obtain a clear view—watch your footing. This rail line is heavily traveled, and a freight train may rumble over

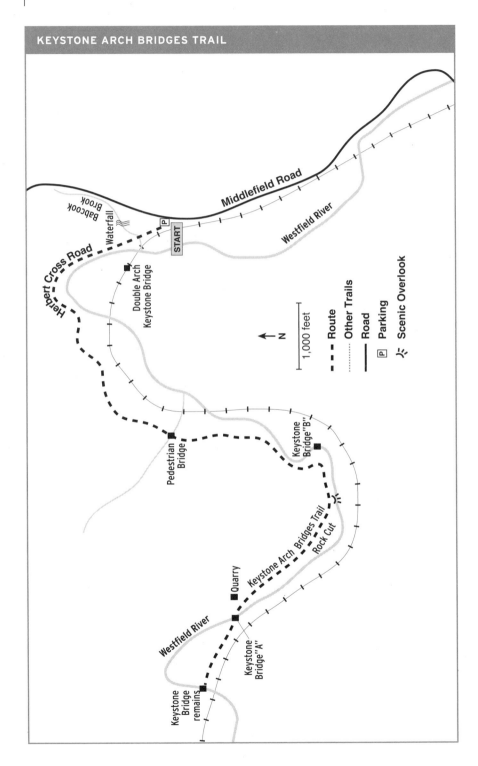

KEYSTONE ARCH BRIDGES TRAIL

Middlefield Road

Babcock Brook

Waterfall

Herbert Cross Road

START

P

Double Arch Keystone Bridge

Westfield River

N

1,000 feet

- - - Route
········ Other Trails
——— Road
P  Parking
ᑐᒧ  Scenic Overlook

Pedestrian Bridge

Keystone Bridge "B"

Keystone Arch Bridges Trail

Rock Cut

Quarry

Westfield River

Keystone Bridge "A"

Keystone Bridge remains

the arches as you maneuver for a photo. Continue down the road, walking upstream just above the swift-flowing river. A monstrous hemlock that must be three centuries old, judging by its girth, but only about 65 feet high, leans toward the stream. It's fascinating to think it must have witnessed the arch's construction.

Hemlocks shade the schist cliff face on the right, where evergreen wood ferns cling. During wet periods, water flows down the outcrop in a sort of drip irrigation system that makes it possible for flat, clingy liverworts to thrive in the spray. An interesting native woody plant—witch hazel—produces straggly yet welcome yellow blossoms in late autumn along the roadway. When its ripe seedpods explode, seeds are hurled up to 20 feet from the parent. This shrub-tree's branches have been used for centuries by "water witches" hoping to divine the presence of subsurface water.

You'll reach a 90-degree bend to the left of both river and roadway where scenic views abound. Cold, utterly clear, oxygen-rich water tumbles over the West Branch's rocky streambed. The river is stocked with coldwater species like trout, and in spring kayak enthusiasts flock to test its class III and IV rapids. It's no wonder that 16 miles of the West Branch were added to the National Wild and Scenic Rivers system by an act of Congress in 1993. Continue paralleling the river, where better views are possible after leaf fall. A polished, water-sculpted, elephant-gray boulder lies near the bank, bearing witness to the scouring effects of eons of flood events. A big sugar maple borders the road on the right. A seemingly out-of-place cement block structure rising 30 feet, 150 feet off to the right, served as a clock tower on property once occupied by an artists' colony.

At a trail split, follow the KAB Trail to the right, away from the Westfield and toward impressive rockwork ruins on the left. Farther on stand four cut granite posts. A thick growth of shining club mosses—ancient, nonflowering plants—carpet the forest floor beyond the stones. Brushing against their candle-like strobules in fall releases a cloud of minute spores. Another species of club moss, prince's pine, populates a miniature evergreen forest after the roadway bears left. The true woodland, however, is composed of deciduous wildlife-food-producing American beech, black cherry, maple, and oak. Highbush blueberry shrubs fill a depression on the right.

You will arrive at a gap in the wall where a blazed woodland path turns right. At a gray boulder, bear left and walk gently uphill. Black birches appear. In fall their foliage is golden. Soon you'll reach a kiosk containing information about local flora and fauna. You will find yourself walking through open woodland near the bottom of a steep hillside with ledge outcrops. A patch of raspberry brambles thrives in a light gap opposite a stone wall that once enclosed a pasture. Gypsy moth caterpillars, capable of stripping a tree of leaves, hatch from fuzzy beige egg masses attached to tree trunks and rock faces. An impressive beech shoulders a big outcrop whose dark surface is cushioned by such masses. The rock is also studded with protruding garnet crystals.

Beneath the leaf litter, short-tailed shrews use their keen sense of smell to hunt worms, insects, snails, and even mice larger than themselves. On one visit, we found a dead 3-inch-long shrew on the path. Larger predators usually reject them as food due to their unpleasant odor and taste. Briefly emerge into a small brushy field and then reenter the forest; a roadway heads uphill on the right, but instead continue straight and descend into a narrow ravine on a single track to a handsome fiberglass-and-wood pedestrian bridge. An unnamed brook plummets over jagged boulders at this spot. Cross and bear left, following the steep hillside's contour. Watch your footing as you clamber along. Beech roots crisscross the treadway.

Cross an old wood road where Christmas ferns grow luxuriantly and remain green all year. On a sunny but brisk November day, we were surprised to spot a live camel (cave) cricket with antennae longer than its body on a layered schist boulder crowding the trail. Walk downhill, easily at first, then more steeply, under beeches and large, platy-barked black birches to the soothing sound of flowing water. The river is visible through the trees. Join a gravel roadway and bear right to follow this old Pontoosic Turnpike—a stage route between Boston and Albany—upstream, above a river terrace. The turnpike followed the route of an American Indian trail called Unkamit's Path. A small stone foundation lies silent on the right as you approach the West Branch at a particularly photogenic location. The river bears left, as does the turnpike. Soon a shielded view of the 65-foot-high Keystone Bridge C emerges.

At a T intersection an information kiosk relates the fascinating history behind the construction of this railroad line. A few more steps to the left, and you're atop the arch. In the twentieth century, the curvature of the route was lessened to reduce track wear by shifting the tracks to the far bank, where you see them now. Return to the kiosk and continue straight along a vertically layered rock cut. A bit farther a massive stone retaining wall on the left hints at the tremendous labor required to complete the project. Steep slopes culminate in a ridgeline high above the river on the far side. Proceed on the level roadway through another rock cut, this one several hundred feet long, with walls 30 to 40 feet high, that is perpetually shaded and cool; shade-tolerant hemlocks crowd the north-facing side. It was dug using only hand tools and black powder.

**Built to support mid-nineteenth century trains, the keystone arch bridges easily handle today's much heavier locomotives.**

Two concrete footings (signal stands) appear as bookends just before you reach another retaining wall on the left. The stone came from quarries like the one on the right, now overgrown. A steep, narrow path on the right leads down to a fine close-up view of the arch. Caution: There is a dangerous drop-off! Drill holes on the blocks are clearly visible, as is the keystone at the peak of the arch that holds it all together. Chester blue granite for the arches was cut and transported to the site. When ready to proceed, walk over the arch. Hanging grapevines appear on the left before you reach an old wood road leading down to the right. Continue straight, through another road cut, where tenacious black birches have taken root in crevices. As the trees grow, their roots inexorably pry apart the stone.

You will reach the remains of the keystone bridge destroyed by flood in 1927. A poured concrete bridge was built to replace it. Be sure to stay off the tracks! This is the end of the route. Retrace your steps, being alert for the narrow ascending trail on the left—off the old Pontoosic Turnpike—that leads up into the forest. A small sign and an arrow on a tree point the way, but it's easy to miss. One other trail split to be aware of upon returning is at the far end of the small brushy field where the KAB Trail bears left, away from a wider wood road.

## MORE INFORMATION

MassWildlife manages the Walnut Hill Wildlife Management Area; Regional headquarters: 400 Hubbard Avenue, Pittsfield, MA 01201; 413-447-9789; masswildlife@state.ma.us. Motorized vehicles, camping, open fires, and alcohol are prohibited along the trail. Hunting is permitted in season. Friends of the Keystone Arches maintains the trail and offers guided hikes for groups of 10 to 25. Trail maps are available at Chester Station. A donation of $10 per person is suggested and used for trail maintenance; P.O. Box 276, Huntington, MA 01050; 413-667-8755; http://www.KeystoneArches.org.

# 3

# SOUTHERN BERKSHIRES

**THE SOUTHERN BERKSHIRES REMAIN THE MOST AGRICULTURAL** part of the Berkshires. Hayfields and dairy barns dot the landscape of the broad Housatonic River valley, while the valley's marble bedrock fosters lime-loving plants. The Southern Berkshires combine quaint towns and villages, pastures dotted with cattle, forests in which mountain laurel puts on a dazzling show, and summits and ridgelines that offer endless views. Some consider this section to be the most scenic in the region.

The sixteen excursions in this section include strenuous summit climbs, easy strolls in pastoral settings, spectacular waterfalls, and even some old-growth giants. For instance, magical Ice Glen (Trip 35) is a cool respite from summer heat; Guilder Pond and Mount Everett (Trip 44) offer a laurel bloom second to none; the section's highest summit, Alander Mountain (Trip 47), boasts one of the most expansive vistas in the Berkshires; while the quartzite summit of Monument Mountain (Trip 36) is a beloved destination for many. Southern Berkshire waterfalls are justly popular with many hikers as well. Bash Bish Falls (Trip 45) is the commonwealth's most spectacular, and Race Brook Falls (Trip 46) is evocative in its own right. For an easier stroll, try the lovely Lime Kiln Farm Wildlife Sanctuary (Trip 48) or the botanically renowned Bartholomew's Cobble Reservation (Trip 49). No matter what your preference of scene or level of difficulty, this section has it all.

## TRIP 35
## ICE GLEN AND LAURA'S TOWER

**Location:** Stockbridge
**Rating:** Moderate
**Distance:** 1.9 miles
**Elevation Gain:** 580 feet (610 feet if climbing tower)
**Estimated Time:** 1.5 hours
**Maps:** USGS Stockbridge

**This primordial rocky cleft, studded with mammoth hemlocks and pines, holds pockets of ice into summer. An intersecting trail leads to a summit with a view.**

### DIRECTIONS
From Exit 2 (Lee) off the Mass Pike (I-90), turn left after the tollbooths and almost immediately turn right onto Route 102. Follow Route 102 for 4.6 miles to the Red Lion Inn in Stockbridge (merging with Route 7 in Stockbridge). Turn left at the Red Lion Inn to follow Route 7 south and drive approximately 0.3 mile to Ice Glen Road on the left (immediately after crossing the Housatonic River). Drive up Ice Glen Road for 0.5 mile to a small pull-off parking area on the left. The lot is adjacent to a gravel driveway marked by a small sign for Ice Glen on a wooden post. Be sure not to block this private driveway! Parking is limited here to three vehicles at most. Alternate parking is available at the end of Park Street (take the first left following the left turn at the Red Lion Inn).

### TRAIL DESCRIPTION
Walk about 200 yards up the private gravel driveway lined by white pines; the driveway soon turns to asphalt as the grade increases. Continue straight on a woodland path toward the mouth of Ice Glen, where the asphalt turns right. If you visit in summer, you'll notice a refreshing drop in temperature as you reach the trail. You are greeted immediately by a jumble of large boulders and the mammoth twin pillars of a white pine on the left and an eastern hemlock on the right that serve as a kind of portal to the glen. The oldest hemlocks here are more than 300 years old. Truck- and cabin-sized boulders are green with moss and topped by ferns. Beneath the towering forest giants are little mountain and striped maples and yellow birches. Mosquitoes are often plentiful in the coolness, so be prepared.

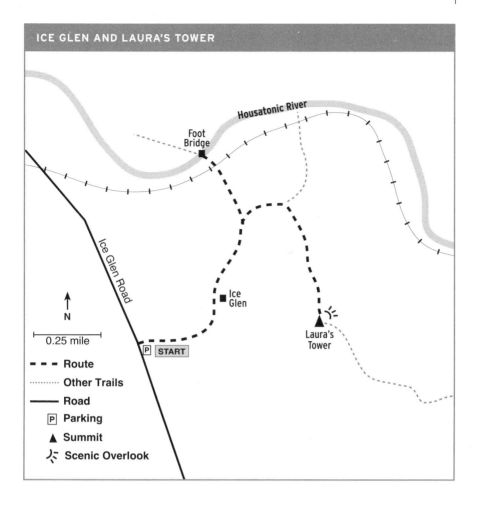

**ICE GLEN AND LAURA'S TOWER**

Housatonic River

Foot
Bridge

Ice Glen Road

Ice
Glen

Laura's
Tower

N

0.25 mile

- - - Route
......... Other Trails
——— Road
P Parking
▲ Summit
⋎ Scenic Overlook

P START

Native stone steps, cleverly placed, lead into the defile as the slopes that create the glen rise abruptly on both sides. The glen inspires a sense of awe. You may feel as though you've stepped back into a time before colonial settlement. Occasional blue blazes on trunks and rocks help guide you, but the best way to stay on the route is to follow the numerous stone steps so expertly arranged that their placement might seem totally natural. The cool microclimate in this north-south-trending cleft, shaded by towering evergreens and insulated by massive quartzite boulders, is really quite amazing. On a sultry summer afternoon I measured the air temperature in two of the glen's cold pockets to be 22–25 degrees Fahrenheit cooler than where I had parked my car in the shade! If you gaze down into the crevices between the boulders, don't be surprised to see remnant ice here, even in summer. In fact, it is so cool that atmospheric moisture condenses to form an eerie ground fog.

**Ancient hemlocks form a towering, dense canopy over the rocky cleft known as Ice Glen.**

Although the glen is less than 0.25 mile long, don't hurry through it. Take your time and watch your footing—the rocks often are wet and a bit slippery in spots. Also, there are some narrow crevices as well as twists and turns, and thus spraining an ankle is always a possibility if you are not careful. Still, this is not a dangerous place to walk if you have the proper footwear and use caution. Besides, it is just too beautiful here to rush through this haven of tranquillity, and you'll want to peer into some of its nooks and crannies.

According to geologists, the final act of the glen's creation began some 15,000 years during the last ice age. The meltwaters from a receding glacier just north of here as well as the effects of freezing and thawing over a multitude of years loosened chunks of quartzite from the opposing hillsides that subsequently tumbled down into the cleft between them.

Listen to the vocalizations of hermit and wood thrushes (characterized by wonderful flutelike phrases), the trill of dark-eyed juncos, the effervescent tune of the tiny winter wren, and a multitude of other songs from warblers and vireos. Birdsong adds to the atmosphere here in late spring and early summer, as do the massive straight trunks that reach for the sky. Four of the state's tallest white pines are located in Ice Glen—one of them is 151 feet high! The oldest are between 170 and 200 years of age. Listen also for the chirping of the gray tree frog (sounding like a purring raccoon) from a tree above you and for the sharp churring of red squirrels.

Some trunks of fallen giants, covered in moss as they are, serve as nursery trees for seedlings that have taken root in their decaying wood. Photographs are hard-pressed to do the scene justice, as this is a majestic place. Low spots collect pools of tannin-stained water. One massive boulder on the left that you'll shoulder past is decorated with rock tripe lichen. It's leafy and green when wet, but platy and brown when dry. The big leaning rock slabs impart a feeling of protection.

The trail levels out and emerges into a bowl. Some 30 feet to the left of the path is an inscription on the moss-covered rock face that commemorates do-nation of the property to Stockbridge in 1891 by David Dudley Field. The for-est is mostly deciduous here, with birches, maples, and ashes. Begin a gradual descent and soon you'll arrive at an intersection with Laura's Tower Trail at a giant triple-stemmed white pine. Turn right onto it. Going straight takes you down to the Housatonic River, which you will do upon your return from the summit.

Years ago a violent windstorm snapped off a number of mature pines, as evidenced by dead snags. One uprooted giant lies on the right. Young decidu-ous trees compete for light under the pines. At the Y intersection, turn right toward Laura's Tower and begin a gradual ascent. Large maples and ashes and a few oaks thrive here too. The grade increases as the trail turns and reaches cabin-sized boulders. Big-tooth aspens, with their straight furrowed trunks, are members of this sunnier woodland, which also includes red oak, birches, red maple, beech, and far more undergrowth (mostly mountain laurel and sapling striped maple) than beneath the shade of pines and hemlocks. Climb the slope by way of a few relatively easy switchbacks. The Laurel Hill Associa-tion's orange diamonds blaze the trail. Recent cutting of young trees indicates an ongoing effort to keep a view shed open.

You'll reach a sturdy 30-foot-high tower, its base 1,465 feet above sea level; climb the steel staircase to a viewing platform just above a low canopy of oaks, red maple, cherry, birch, and ash. While once a 360-degree panorama was possible, tree growth has obscured views to the south. A horizontally mounted brass locator disc is inscribed with the names of promontories, their eleva-tions, and the airline distances to them. It was installed in 1931 and still serves the hiker well today. The most prominent feature to the northwest is West Stockbridge Mountain, 4.5 miles away. Mount Greylock lies 25.5 miles to the north. The namesake of the tower, Laura, was David Dudley Field's daughter-in-law.

A yellow-blazed trail opposite the path you ascended on leads to Beartown State Forest, several miles distant, but retrace your steps to the intersection with the Glen Trail at the three-trunked white pine. Turn right for a brief excursion to the Housatonic River and a handsome footbridge across it for a totally different experience. Descend easily on a trail blazed with both orange and white diamonds through a stand of monolithic white pines. Listen for the cheerful high-pitched whistle of brown creepers, which nest behind slabs of loose bark. Road noise becomes more evident as you reach a power-line right of way filled with raspberry bushes.

Cross the active Housatonic Railroad line (use caution!) to a lovely stone arch and steel suspension bridge built in 1936 by local engineer Joseph Franz. Tread across the wooden decking to obtain a fine view of the Housatonic River. A brass plaque announces that this bridge replaced the original one given to Stockbridge in 1895 by Mary Hopkins Goodrich, the founder of the Laurel Hill Society. The society, founded in 1853, is the oldest village beautification organization in the nation. A trail sign is located on the far side of the river at an accessible trailhead where Park Street terminates. There is space for six to eight vehicles.

During a June excursion, the sight of a tiny female orange-throated Blackburnian warbler gathering spider silk from the bridge railings captivated me. I watched her fly off with the gossamer threads to a tall white pine, where she would use them in nest construction.

A 1.2-mile (round-trip) wheelchair-accessible path—the Mary V. Flynn Trail—was created along the river in 2003. If you are inclined to add mileage to your route, turn right and follow it between the railroad tracks and the Housatonic. Benches are located along the route, and a nice stand of maidenhair fern delights the eye near the looped end.

When ready, retrace your steps through the glen and savor its welcome charms once more before returning to your vehicle and the real world.

## MORE INFORMATION

Trails open sunrise to sunset, daily, year-round. Access is free. There are no restroom facilities at the trailheads. Vehicles, horses, camping, and fires prohibited. Trail maintenance by the Laurel Hill Association, Stockbridge, MA. Ice Glen is owned by Town of Stockbridge; Stockbridge Town Hall, 413-298-4714. Laura's Tower Trail is owned by the Laurel Hill Association.

## TRIP 36
## MONUMENT MOUNTAIN RESERVATION

**Location:** Great Barrington
**Rating:** Moderate–Difficult
**Distance:** 2.7 miles
**Elevation Gain:** 765 feet
**Estimated Time:** 2.0 hours
**Maps:** USGS Great Barrington, USGS Stockbridge; trail map available online

**Some 20,000 hikers annually enjoy a pilgrimage to this fabulously picturesque summit of jagged quartzite boulders capped by pitch pine and mountain laurel; it's one of my favorite hikes.**

## DIRECTIONS
From the east: Take Exit 2 (Lee) off the Mass Pike (I-90), turn left after leaving the tollbooths, and almost immediately bear right onto Route 102. Follow Route 102 for 4.7 miles to its intersection with Route 7 at the Red Lion Inn in Stockbridge. Drive south on Route 7 for 3.1 miles to the reservation entrance on the right. The large gravel parking area has room for many vehicles.

From the south: At the junction of Routes 7 and 23 in Great Barrington, take Route 7 north for 5.9 miles to the reservation on the left.

## TRAIL DESCRIPTION
Begin at the map kiosk shaded by Depression-era red pines, where trail maps are sometimes available. Visitors are encouraged to support the nonprofit Trustees of Reservations with a donation. From the kiosk, turn right and head north on the white-blazed Hickey Trail. White pines, black cherries, red maples, red oaks, and white ashes tower above sapling American beech, witch hazel, and striped maples, the latter of which have smooth greenish trunks. Given that the Monument Mountain Reservation was established in 1899, the forest here has had more that 100 years to regenerate. As a result, many white pines are of impressive proportions. Note the shade-intolerant pioneering gray birches, which are dying out. Initially paralleling the slope contour, the trail passes a twin white oak adjacent to a quartzite boulder. White oaks produce sweet acorns prized by wild turkey and deer.

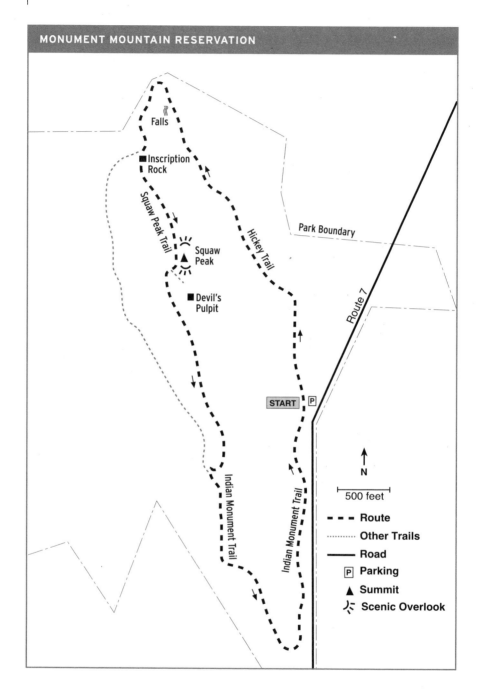

MONUMENT MOUNTAIN RESERVATION

After about 5 minutes of steady walking, take the path as it bears left to begin a moderate climb. Another white-blazed trail turns right and descends, but continue uphill. Note the massive red oak, fully 3 feet in diameter (whose

**Mountain laurel adorns the peak of Squaw Peak, which provides a lofty perch for viewing the countryside, including Mount Greylock.**

acorns in contrast are bitter with tannic acid) on your right. Soon you'll enter the year-round shade cast by eastern hemlocks at the junction with a wider wood road; bear right. The grade for the time being becomes gentler. Gray, angular quartzite boulders become more numerous. A talus slope, created by repeated freezing and thawing over eons, is visible after leaf fall to the left; then a formidable cabin-sized boulder hems in the trail. Crusty lichens and little polypody ferns have colonized its tough, erosion-resistant surface.

To your left, a jumble of massive quartzite boulders reposes at the foot of the mountain. Talus slopes like this are a relative rarity in the region. The hard gray talus (meaning "toe" in Greek) is actually 550-million-year-old beach sand compacted under tremendous heat and pressure deep underground. A verdant mat of ferns caps some slabs.

Bearing left under columnar hemlocks and pines, continue the moderate climb. One white pine is 3 feet in diameter. A mature tree produces thousands of winged seeds relished by birds and small mammals. At a point where the path turns left and ascends more steeply, an attractive hemlock ravine has been carved by flowing water. This is the haunt of the 4-inch-long winter wren, a bird endowed with an amazingly loud and bubbling voice for such a sprite. But listen for it in late spring and early summer. Level out at the top of the ravine and traverse a log bridge over the crystal-clear brook. Soon you'll arrive at a short spur trail on the left that leads to a close-up view of a modest yet lovely waterfall. Mammoth icicles in frozen flow drape the outcrop in winter. The tall and very straight tree reaching skyward to the right is a tulip tree, a southern species near its northern range limit here.

Return to the main trail and walk up more steeply now. One early March, I came upon an unmistakable otter slide in the snow. Clearly the big weasel had engaged in a controlled descent toward the brook. Hemlocks, red maples, and oaks mix as you push up the ravine. The path narrows and ascends in steps to the reservation's northern boundary, marked by red blazes. Switchback left at the big outcrop and level out among mountain laurel shrubs. After negotiating another log bridge, you'll be heading up again through boulders decorated with flaky rock tripe; this lichen greens up after rain.

You will reach the intersection with Indian Monument Trail on the right, but continue straight on what is now Squaw Peak Trail. To the right rests Inscription Rock, whose chiseled prose relates the story of the property's donation in October 1899 by Virginia Butler in memory of her elder sister, Rosalie. From here the path winds up through and over quartzite boulders to the summit at 1,642 feet. Gnarly pitch pines (so prominent on Cape Cod), white pines, and mountain laurel dominate these craggy heights. The laurels put on a dazzling display in late June when their half-inch pink blossoms illuminate the summit.

Watch your footing as you wend your way among the quartzite blocks. Conditions may be extremely hazardous in winter, and travel on the summit is not recommended at all during icy conditions! A number of fine vantage points invite you to relax and enjoy the view. To the north floats the bluish double hump of Mount Greylock, almost 30 miles distant. Much closer, at the foot of Monument Mountain, sprawl the vegetated waters of Agawam Marsh. To the south the Housatonic River valley, lined with erodable marble, is spread out below, and Mount Everett looms to the southwest. Not all these landmarks are visible from the same perch, so move about to get the full effect. From one such spot at the end of a spur trail to the left on Squaw Peak, you'll gaze down on a columnar formation dubbed Devil's Pulpit, a favorite haunt of turkey vultures. And the summit can be a fine place from which to witness the spring hawk migration up the valley in late April.

When ready to resume walking, continue on Squaw Peak Trail as it descends moderately for the most part, cutting across contour lines on the west flank of the mountain. In early summer, listen for the sweet trill of yellow

The barred owl is more often heard than seen. This one, roosting on an oak limb along Indian Monument Trail, was a pleasant surprise.

and olive pine warblers that nest among the pine boughs. The male's song is reminiscent of the dark-eyed junco, another breeder here. You'll level out as you reach Indian Monument Trail. Turn left under big white pines, hemlocks, large oaks, red maples, beech, and black birch. This old wood road has a gentle grade, and many walkers use this longer route in reverse to reach Inscription Rock and on to the summit.

On that early-March hike, I was thrilled to come upon a round-headed 21-inch-tall barred owl basking in the afternoon sunlight on its perch 35 feet up in an oak. It kept an eye on me through slit eyelids. As you advance, the road noise from Route 7 becomes more audible and eventually obtrusive. The trail bears left to parallel the highway. One day the previous June, the incessant calls of nestling yellow-bellied sapsuckers alerted me to the presence of a nest in a dead pine. The parents were soon on scene with beakfuls of insects for their hungry young.

Under hemlocks the path undulates over rocks as it follows along the foot of the mountain's eastern slope. A triple-trunked chestnut oak stands on the left. You can recognize the species by its rough, platy bark and wavy-edged leaves. Evergreen wood fern and the smaller polypody thrive among the boulders.

## WRITTEN IN STONE

The great natural beauty of the Berkshires has for centuries drawn creative minds to these hills and valleys. Look no further than the Tanglewood Music Festival as proof. Whether in music, art, or literature, "the purple hills," as Roderick Peattie called them, have inspired many a poet and novelist. Best-known among them is a triumvirate of contemporary nineteenth-century authors—Hawthorne, Melville, and Thoreau.

No doubt the single most chronicled meeting of literary minds ever to occur in the Berkshires took place on August 5, 1850, when Nathaniel Hawthorne and Herman Melville hiked Monument Mountain. There, it is said, they became fast friends. As the story goes, Hawthorne, who had a home in Lenox, gave Melville material for his most famous work, *Moby-Dick*, while they huddled together in a cave during an electrical storm. Perhaps the bedrock ledge, over which a waterfall drops during the wet months, was the "cave" in question.

Melville wrote his masterpiece while residing at Arrowhead (which now houses the Berkshire Historical Society), his home on Holmes Road in Pittsfield. Literary lore has it that the sight of Mount Greylock, or Saddleback Mountain as it was known then, dusted with snow, inspired the character of the great white sperm whale. Each year on the anniversary of the authors' outing, a group of aficionados re-creates the hike of these literary giants.

Other influential nature writers have tromped Berkshire paths, Henry David Thoreau foremost among them. Thoreau hiked to Greylock's summit via the still extant Bellows Pipe Trail (Trip 8) and wrote about it in *A Week on the Concord and Merrimack Rivers*. William Cullen Bryant, who spent 10 years in Great Barrington, wrote about Monument Mountain in his poem by the same name in 1824. He penned many other works with natural-history themes at his home in nearby Cummington. Closer to our own time, nature writer Hal Borland, a longtime resident of Connecticut's Litchfield Hills, wrote evocatively about the bucolic landscape he so loved. A trail at Bartholomew's Cobble Reservation (Trip 49) is named in memory of the writer, who passed away in 1978.

A quote from Thoreau seems like a fitting motto for the hiker: "An early morning walk is a blessing for the whole day." Perhaps hiking the Berkshires will inspire you as well.

Some slabs have impressive dimensions and rusty faces where oxidation has revealed the iron content of the rock.

Momentarily, you'll arrive back at the picnic area under the red pines where you began. Note the pileated woodpecker excavations (foraging holes) on a young pine left of the path.

## MORE INFORMATION

Open daily, year-round, sunrise to sunset. Admission is free; on-site donations from nonmembers are welcomed. Picnic tables available; no restroom facilities on-site. Dogs must be leashed at all times. Motorized vehicles, mountain bikes, rock climbing, and fires are prohibited. Hunting is allowed in season. The Trustees of Reservations, Western Regional Office, P.O. Box 792, Stockbridge, MA 01262; 413-298-3239; westregion@ttor.org; http://www.thetrustees.org.

## TRIP 37
## BENEDICT POND LOOP AND LEDGES

**Location:** Great Barrington, Monterey
**Rating:** Moderate
**Distance:** 2.5 miles
**Elevation Gain:** 240 feet
**Estimated Time:** 1.5–2.0 hours
**Maps:** USGS Great Barrington; winter and summer trail maps available online at the Beartown State Forest website

**This trip includes circumambulation of one of the Berkshires' most scenic ponds, spiced up with a fine laurel bloom in late June, and splendid views from the AT for good measure.**

## DIRECTIONS

From the intersection of Route 7 and Monument Valley Road (near Monument Mountain High School) in Great Barrington, turn onto Monument Valley Road. Drive for 2.0 miles to Stoney Brook Road on the left. Turn onto Stoney Brook Road and follow it 2.7 miles to Benedict Pond Road on the left. It is 0.5 mile to the day-use area on the right. The first and larger lot is at the boat ramp, the second at the beach.

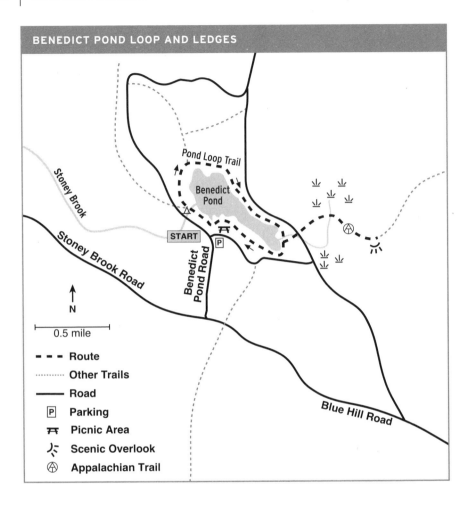

**BENEDICT POND LOOP AND LEDGES**

Pond Loop Trail

Benedict Pond

Stoney Brook

Stoney Brook Road

Benedict Pond Road

START

Blue Hill Road

N

0.5 mile

**- - - Route**
**············ Other Trails**
**——— Road**
**P Parking**
**Picnic Area**
**Scenic Overlook**
**Appalachian Trail**

## TRAIL DESCRIPTION

From the small gravel parking area adjacent to the beach, head left past a kiosk and along a concrete retaining wall at the pond shore. Soon you'll cross a short wooden bridge over the pond outflow and turn left onto the blue-blazed Pond Loop Trail. Descend a few wooden steps, walk parallel with the outflow (shaded by eastern hemlocks), and then bear right under a canopy of mixed hardwoods—oak, birch, and American beech. Witch hazel, scattered mountain laurel, and striped maple dot the rocky woodland. At informal trail splits, remain on the main trail as it roughly follows the pond shore past tenting sites with picnic tables.

You will reach a red-blazed wood road (a snowmobile trail in winter) and cross it. Although predominantly oak now, the forest includes red maple, black birch, and a few peely-barked hop hornbeams. At the junction with the Ski

**In winter, water seeps from crevices in a gneiss ledge to create a fabulous icicle display.**

and Bridle Trail, stay straight on the blue-triangle-blazed path and enjoy sporadic glimpses of 35-acre Benedict Pond through gaps. You'll pass through a couple of low, wet areas marked by cinnamon and sensitive ferns—wetland indicators. Sensitive fern has persistent brown beadlike spore capsules. Pointed stumps, recently cut by beaver, are also in evidence. Ten-foot-high arrowwood shrubs, with arrow-straight branches, border the path as you traverse a small wooden bridge.

As you round the northwest end of the pond, red maples become common. They are among the first to offer up bright autumnal foliage. Pass by some white pines and, on the left, a patch of trailing arbutus—the state flower—which blooms delicate pink in May, hence its other moniker, mayflower. A wooden bench at the water's edge invites a pause. In winter ice anglers dot the otherwise-featureless white expanse. The first tilted gray gneiss bedrock outcrops pop into view on the left. Towering straight white pines grew up in woodland crowded by others of their kind. One pine trunk's center is rotted from about 35 feet up—perhaps the result of a lightning strike. White ash, black cherry, and beech join the mix, although oaks still rule. Camouflaged brown creepers hitch their way up the furrowed pine trunks looking for insect eggs and larvae hidden in bark crevices.

At a trail split, take the left fork (the right is blocked by fallen trees, and both join up later). An 18-foot-high gneiss outcrop juts up where the paths rejoin. After another dampish area, hobblebush and beaked hazelnut shrubs lead to a second wooden bench under pines at pondside. A clump of low-growing sheep laurel shrubs is easy to overlook just left of the bench, while highbush blueberries hug the shore. A bit farther along, watch for a beaver lodge only 6 feet out. The trail undulates past taller mountain laurels and enters a shady hemlock stand. Here the path hugs a picturesque gneiss ledge displaying its characteristic dark-and-light banding. Common polypody fern is anchored to the rock, while in winter a fabulous display of icicles inspires poetry. Water dripping from and through crevices in the ledge creates these crystalline stalactites. Watch your footing in winter, as this section can be very icy!

Soon you'll reach a broad roadway that accommodates snowmobiles. Bear right to follow it gently downhill. To your left is another gneiss spine. A few brilliantly white paper birches are to be admired on the left. Black birches meanwhile populate the rising slope beyond. After passing a stand of spruces on the right, you'll arrive at the Appalachian Trail (AT) intersection. Turn left to follow the white-blazed AT north toward the Ledges, about 0.75 mile, or 15 minutes, distant. (Alternately, to continue around the pond, cross the stream and turn right.) Walk uphill under oak, maple, and birch. Level off and observe more ledges—some dotted with leafy brown rock tripe, a lichen that turns green after a rain.

Bear left and ascend rocky steps tight along the rock face. The path wends its way through oaks and laurel above the left slope of a rocky ravine. At the head of the ravine, turn right and cross a wooden bridge over an outflow stream that originates a few feet upstream at a sizable beaver swamp. Clamber over bedrock, and bear right to walk along the opposite side of the 40-foot-deep defile near the verge, amid oaks and pines. After leaf fall, distant blue ridgelines become evident. Lowbush blueberry and tiny, shiny-leaved wintergreen thrive in the acidic soil beneath the trees—of shorter stature here on the bony ridge top.

Watch for more trailing arbutus just before the vista point. When you reach a benchlike outcrop at a gap in the woody vegetation, you have arrived at the Ledges. A more convenient spot for a relaxing snack with splendid views would be tough to find! Mount Everett, at 2,624 feet high, is visible as the high point along the third ridgeline to the southwest. In winter, two downhill ski runs are also apparent.

When ready, retrace your steps to the wide roadway and turn left, cross the brook over a wooden bridge set on handsome mortared stone abutments, and turn right to follow the blue-and-white-blazed trail around the southeast end of the pond. After a small spruce stand, negotiate the soggy ground safely via a series of bog bridges. Unusual for this area is a collection of white cedar trees, or arborvitae, between the treadway and the pond. These flat-needled evergreens are generally bog denizens. After a minor brook the trail bears right to hug the shore. But shortly the AT veers left and up to the wood road; stay straight to continue on the Pond Loop Trail. The Benedict Pond shoreline is here bordered by a dense growth of evergreen mountain laurel that blooms luxuriantly in late June.

Although not as showy as laurel, the abundant hobblebush shrubs have conspicuous ocher buds in winter and white flower doilies in spring. The flower heads include both tiny fertile flowers and larger infertile ones that attract the attention of pollinators. Pass through a hemlock grove and by picnic tables—a sure sign that you are back at the boat ramp. A kiosk is also situated at this end of the loop. At the paved road, turn right toward the beach parking area and your vehicle.

## MORE INFORMATION

Open daily, year-round, sunrise to sunset. A $5-per-vehicle charge applies mid-May through mid-October. Restrooms and drinking water—at the day-use area—are available seasonally. Pets must be on 10-foot-maximum leash at all times and owners must have proof of current rabies vaccination. Camping is available in designated areas mid-May through mid-October; reservations are required. All-terrain vehicles are permitted on designated trails May through November only. Snowmobiles are permitted with 4 inches minimum of hard-packed snowbase. Alcoholic beverages are prohibited. Beartown State Forest, 69 Blue Hill Road, P.O. Box 97, Monterey, MA 01245; 413-528-0904; http://www.mass.gov/dcr/parks/western/bear.htm.

## PINE CONE JOHNNIES

As you hike Berkshire trails, you can't help but be impressed by the work of the Great Depression-era Civilian Conservation Corps (CCC). In my opinion, the CCC is one of President Franklin Delano Roosevelt's enduring legacies. Created during a time of national economic calamity, the CCC gave meaningful employment to thousands of young men. They built roads, countless trails, ponds and dams, various park facilities, and even such noteworthy structures as Bascom Lodge atop Mount Greylock (constructed between 1933 and 1937). What amazes me is that so much of their handiwork is still serviceable today. Certainly our public lands had never before (or, for that matter, have never since) seen such an infusion of peoplepower directed at creating and improving recreational facilities.

At the height of the CCC's involvement in Massachusetts, 68 camps employed up to 10,000 men. Of these camps, 14 operated in the Berkshires. Monuments to their work are everywhere, which is especially amazing since it has been 70 years after the CCC workers left the woods.

At the Sperry Road Campground in Mount Greylock State Reservation and at the Benedict Pond dam in Beartown State Forest, wayside exhibits relate some of the fascinating history made by the recruits. We owe these "Pine Cone Johnnies," as they were known, a debt of gratitude.

In his fascinating book *Berkshire Forests Shade the Past*, local historian Bernard A. Drew relates the tale of two CCC companies that operated in Beartown State Forest on one site from June 1937 until October 1941. According to Drew, each camp was assigned some 200 men, most in their early 20s and all from Massachusetts. Fort Devens, northeast of Worcester, served as their boot camp. The U.S. Army was responsible for the operation of the camps, while the U.S. Forest Service was charged with overseeing the work. Local men were hired to act as foremen. At Beartown their accomplishments included building and fortifying roads, adding 6 miles of trails, and constructing two dams—one of which expanded the size of Benedict Pond to 35 acres. In fact, the Beartown companies were among the most active in all of New England.

## TRIP 38
## BECKET LAND TRUST HISTORIC
## QUARRY AND FOREST

**Location:** Becket
**Rating:** Moderate
**Distance:** 3.0 miles
**Elevation Gain:** 400 feet
**Estimated Time:** 1.5–2.0 hours
**Maps:** USGS Otis, East Lee; trail map available online

**The Becket Quarry is a place frozen in time. Trails wind through
northern hardwood forest, among granite boulders, over small
brooks, and to a panoramic vista.**

## DIRECTIONS

From the west: From Exit 2 (Lee) off the Mass Pike (I-90), turn left after the
tollbooths onto Route 20 and follow it east for 12.1 miles to Bonnie Rigg Hill
Road on the right. Follow it uphill for 1.3 miles to an intersection with Quarry
and Algerie roads. Turn left onto Quarry Road and drive 0.9 mile to the gravel
parking area on the right.

From the east: From Exit 3 off the Mass Pike (I-90) in Westfield, turn right
after the tollbooths onto Route 20 and follow it west for 12.2 miles through
Westfield, Russell, Huntington, and Chester and into Becket to the intersection
of Bonnie Rigg Hill Road on the left. From this point, see directions above.

## TRAIL DESCRIPTION

A kiosk with trail maps and trail register is situated at the far end of the circular gravel parking area. Visitors are asked to sign in and out. Your education
begins at interpretive panel 1 on the parking-lot island where a Sullivan drill
rests. This device was used to drill the holes into which explosive charges were
placed. And this is the site where granite blocks were loaded for final processing in the neighboring town of Chester.

To begin, walk past the cable and up the old roadway beneath a canopy of
oaks, maples, American beech, yellow birch, and eastern hemlock. In spring
a stunning wildflower display includes trout lily and red trillium. You'll soon
reach the large grout pile, a tall heap of granite chunks, on the right. Interpretive

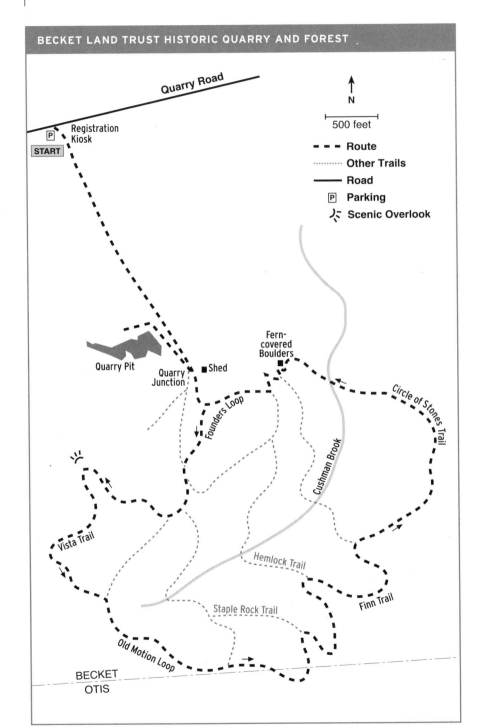

BECKET LAND TRUST HISTORIC QUARRY AND FOREST

Quarry Road

N

500 feet

- - - Route
.......... Other Trails
——— Road
P Parking
人 Scenic Overlook

P Registration
Kiosk

START

Quarry Pit

Quarry
Junction

Shed

Founders Loop

Fern-
covered
Boulders

Circle of Stones Trail

Cushman Brook

Vista Trail

Hemlock Trail

Staple Rock Trail

Finn Trail

Old Motion Loop

BECKET

OTIS

**This substantial pit, now water-filled and potentially hazardous, is just one of many reminders of the quarry's 100-year history.**

panel 2 explains that this is the waste material resulting from decades of quarrying. Do not climb the pile. In summer, when warm moist air comes in contact with the cold air flowing from the bottom of the pile, it condenses to form fog. A bit farther, on the left, is a small grout pile at interpretive panel 4. Soon you'll reach Quarry Junction.

Several old roadways radiate from here. The skeleton of an electrical generator shed and the rusting hulks of two trucks, one used to haul the granite to Chester for processing, and the other used to hold the compressed air that powered the drills, are visible (see panels 5 and 7). When you return here later, you'll have the opportunity to gaze upon the impressive water-filled quarry pit, a short distance to the right. After studying the interpretive panels, follow the leftmost road past the shed, and immediately you'll reach an intersection at the stiff leg derrick site (panel 8). Opposite the derrick is the rail grade to the motion (panel 9). A "motion" is a small quarrying site where granite blocks were cut. Stay left and proceed past the rusting artifacts of a bygone era—the quarry operated for about 100 years, until 1950.

Turn right onto Founders Loop, blazed with blue paint and plastic diamonds, and head gently uphill among granite boulders. Rocks seem more abundant than trees here! You'll reach a junction with the old roadway again at a wall built of massive granite blocks; turn left. The rock is the same hue as the beech trunks. On the right is a rusty section of rail. Soon you'll reach a Y intersection where Founders Loop Trail bears left. Continue straight, however, on the red-diamond-blazed Old Motion Loop Trail. Unfortunately, after leaf fall, the din of the Mass Pike is audible. At another fork in the trail, follow the right path gently uphill approximately 100 feet to the green-diamond-blazed Vista Trail on the right. Turn onto Vista Trail.

The hillside is clothed in oak and beech. One summer I found a well-concealed ovenbird nest with five creamy, brown-flecked eggs under the concealing leaves of a beech sprout. A fungal disease that blackens their bark disfigures many of the beech trees here. Although mostly young, one larger specimen displays the scars left by a black bear that climbed this tree for its tasty nuts. You'll arrive at the vista point and granite bench—a nice spot to linger. Tree clearing has opened up a fine view of Round Top Hill to the east.

Bear left around the bench to continue. A few young red maples show scars where a moose tore off strips of the outer bark with its incisors to get at the nutritious inner bark. The fact that the bark was torn off to a height of 7 feet is a telltale sign. A gentle descent leads past a battleship gray granite outcrop on the right. A few red spruce and hemlock appear, but American beech still rules this woodland. Beech sprouts prolifically from cut stumps and by means of runners. Rejoin the Old Motion Loop Trail (blazed with red plastic diamonds in both directions). Across from you, perhaps 50 feet away, stands a massive, leaning red oak. The giant—more than 4.5 feet in diameter—is pocked with den cavities where branches have rotted out.

Turn right on the Old Motion Loop Trail, and soon you'll pass a very large, multitrunked white pine on the left some 3.5 feet in diameter. A thick accumulation of needles cushions the treadway. Amble along easily through beech and hemlock woodland. Granite appears to have been quarried at what is now a depression on the right where big angular blocks are piled. Sullivan drill marks are evident on some. The depression, rimmed by winterberry shrubs whose coral-red berries dazzle the eye in fall, fills with water and may well serve mating salamanders as a vernal pool in spring.

You'll reach an intersection on the right with Staple Rock Trail, which is blazed with purple and yellow plastic diamonds; follow it. You'll descend gradually. Watch for a 2-foot-long piece of rail that juts out of the ground to your left. At a junction with the Finn Trail, blazed with pink plastic diamonds, turn right. It is currently marked by green blazes. Walk down on the wide old road past pockets of hay-scented fern, which yellows and dies after frost. Turn

**Porcupines dine on leafy greens in summer and den in rocky crevices.**

left onto a single track just before a tree that has fallen across the road. Note hobblebush shrubs with their large, paired heart-shaped leaves. Shining club moss and ferns carpet the ground. Follow along the rocky contour of the hill and reach an intersection with the Hemlock Trail blazed with white and light green plastic diamonds, at a jumble of boulders. Turn right to continue on the Finn Trail. A slope drops off on the left to a flat terrace. Large rotting stumps are testimony to logging decades ago. Young beech trees and red maples are now dominant.

After an old roadway joins your path on the left, you'll reach a three-way intersection with Laurel Knob Trail (blazed with yellow plastic diamonds) on the left and Circle of Stones Trail on the right. Turn right onto the Circle of Stones Trail, blazed with orange plastic diamonds. You'll soon cross a small gurgling brook on short wooden bridge sections. Watch your step, as the slippery-when-wet boards may shift underfoot! Pools are patrolled by predatory skating water striders. The shady woodland is home to lovely singing hermit thrushes spring through fall and tiny spring peepers year-round. These little tree frogs blend in marvelously with the leaf litter.

Descend through more hemlocks on a soft treadway. Tall common reed stalks in the distance hint at a wetland off to the right. A cabin-sized granite boulder protrudes from the forest floor. You'll reach flowing Cushman Brook and cross it on wooden bridge sections. Hemlock and red maple thrive in the damp soil. I observed a tiny winter wren preening its feathers after taking a bath in the brook.

The path then leads up through a fairyland of granite boulders—many capped by a luxuriant growth of polypody fern, spinulose wood fern, and club moss. This spot has the feel of a temperate rainforest. Porcupines may well den in the rock crevices. Now walk more steeply uphill to reach a wider roadway without signage. The trail bears left and then away from the faint road. The path widens again and reaches an intersection with Laurel Knob Trail. Continue to the right, and head uphill on Circle of Stones Trail. Note the large twin-trunked gray birch anchored on a rock to your left. Soon you'll reach a more obvious, signed intersection; this is Founders Loop, blazed with blue diamonds. Turn right and follow the blue-diamond markers to the plaque erected to recognize the many donors who made acquisition of this land possible. Turn right to retrace your steps to Quarry Junction.

Just past the generator shed, turn left and walk past the guy derrick site (interpretive panel 6) gently up to the edge of a quarry pit with 65-foot-high granite walls. Watch your footing and stay back from the edge. Granite steps lead up to a terrace where you'll see granite blocks into which quarry workers cut their initials and the years 1868 and 1894.

## MORE INFORMATION

Owned and maintained by the Becket Land Trust, which invites public participation and support. Open during daylight hours. Visitors enter at their own risk. Pets must be kept under control. Collecting and motorized vehicles are prohibited. Becket Land Trust, Inc. P.O. Box 44, Becket, MA 01223; becketlandtrust@ becketlandtrust.org; http://www.becketlandtrust.org.

## TRIP 39
## TYRINGHAM COBBLE RESERVATION

**Location:** Tyringham
**Rating:** Moderate, with some steep sections
**Distance:** 2.0 miles
**Elevation Gain:** 380 feet
**Estimated Time:** 1.5 hours
**Map:** USGS Otis

**This wonderful loop trail takes you through bucolic pastures to a pair of ancient resistant bedrock promontories with splendid views of the lovely Tyringham Valley.**

### DIRECTIONS

From Exit 2 (Lee) off the Mass Pike (I-90), turn left after the tollbooths and then immediately right onto Route 102. After only 0.1 mile, turn left onto Main Road and follow it through the valley for 4.1 miles into the village of Tyringham. Turn right onto Jerusalem Road and drive 0.2 mile to the gravel parking lot on the right, which has space for about fifteen vehicles.

### TRAIL DESCRIPTION

After reviewing the information posted on the map kiosk, walk through a wooden gate to your right toward a small red cattle barn and turn left to follow along the edge of an expansive hayfield, where eastern bluebirds raise their young in nest boxes provided for them. After passing through another gate at the foot of the cobble, turn right and follow along a row of venerable sugar maples. Barbed wire indicates livestock grazing that continues to this day. The trail is marked with circular white blazes on wooden posts, although the mowed trail is easy to follow.

The lower slopes of Cobble Hill, first cleared for pasturage by colonial farmers in the late eighteenth century, are now clothed in grasses and goldenrods, with scattered multiflora rose shrubs, crab apple trees, and white pine seedlings. Prickly exotic Japanese barberry shrubs, once omnipresent here, have largely been eliminated. Enjoy the commanding view of colonial-era homes in the valley. Upon reaching a fork in the trail, turn left to walk uphill (continuing straight leads to a metal footbridge over tumbling Hop Brook and Main Road). One hundred yards beyond, at another intersection just before a

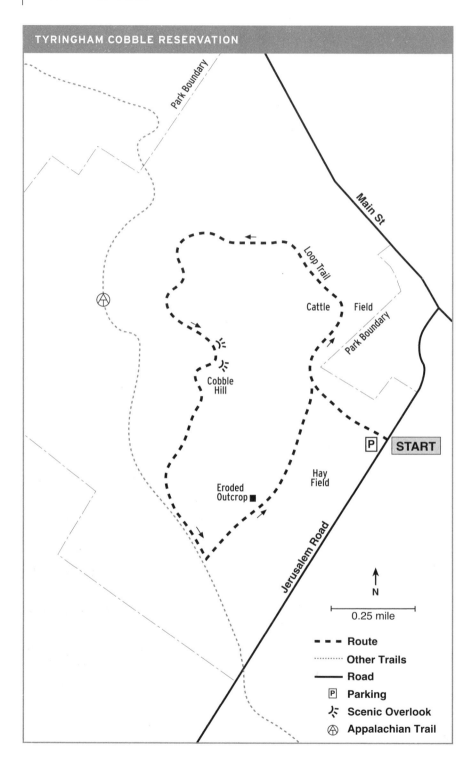

**TYRINGHAM COBBLE RESERVATION**

Park Boundary

Main St

Loop Trail

Cattle    Field

Park Boundary

Cobble
Hill

START

P

Hay
Field

Eroded
Outcrop ■

Jerusalem Road

N

0.25 mile

- - - Route

.......... Other Trails

——— Road

P  Parking

光  Scenic Overlook

Ⓐ  Appalachian Trail

stone wall and fence, take the left path and push steeply upward. Swing right and enter a white pine stand at a barbed-wire fence. Pass through a wooden gate, turn left, and walk uphill following white blazes on trees that include white ash, sugar maple, and black birch.

You'll level out after a short climb, on a wide treadway among an all-too-thick growth of winged euonymus, also known as burning bush (another invasive exotic shrub), and the aforementioned barberry. Several species of woodpeckers frequent these woods, including the hairy woodpecker, the red-bellied woodpecker, and the yellow-bellied sapsucker. Sapsuckers forsake the north in autumn. Chatty and omnivorous red squirrels collect and store pine seeds, gather mushrooms, and relish the occasional meal of bird eggs or nestlings. The trail climbs moderately under good-sized white ash trees where invasive oriental bittersweet vines rope around trunks, eventually strangling them. Sun-loving oaks appear near the summit. After you pass through a stone-wall gap and a wooden gate, you'll reach the top of the first cobble. Although it is slightly lower than the second promontory, some of the best vistas are to be had from this more open vantage point.

Wonderful views of the valley, nearly 500 feet below, and the wooded hills beyond greet you from the grassy summit, also graced by a few eastern junipers (a.k.a. red cedar). Loop briefly over the top, walk through another wooden gate and reenter the woodland. An attractive, layered gneiss (pronounced "nice") ledge on the left may catch your eye before you enter a hemlock stand and turn left to continue along the hill's contour. It was the gneiss rock's stubborn resistance to erosion that created the cobble. The path crosses ledges that sport a growth of small ferns called common polypody—a species almost always anchored to rock. The scant soils atop this second, slightly higher cobble (elevation 1,340 feet) restrict the growth of trees, making for the low stature of the windswept woodland of oak, hemlock, and a prickly field form of juniper.

Excellent views of the valley are to be had from a short side trail on the left. Soon the ledge trail begins to descend, reaching a brushy field at a bedrock outcrop that under sunny skies sparkles with mica crystals. Idyllic views of the valley may convince you to linger here for a bit. Follow the worn path through the field where lowbush blueberry thrives to reach an intersection with the Appalachian Trail (AT), the 2,000-plus-mile-long footpath from Maine to Georgia. Turn left (south), heading gently downhill past staghorn sumac (with its fuzzy stems), juniper, crab apple, and goldenrod.

After about 150 yards, you'll leave the AT and rejoin the Cobble Trail on the left, cutting across the shrubby field being invaded by trees to reenter the woodland at a barbed-wire fence lined by crab apples. Negotiate another swinging

A pock-marked block of marble—disconnected from the underlying bedrock—has been weathered into a fantastic form.

wooden gate designed to keep livestock out, turn right, and amble downhill. Note the impressive sugar maple on the right. After leaf fall, the rabbit-like visage of an intriguing block of marble appears ahead. Over eons, the forces of wind and water have pockmarked the soft rock. Like the White Rabbit in *Alice's Adventures in Wonderland*, this rabbit seems oddly out of place.

At the outcrop, turn left and follow the base of Cobble Hill past another formidable sugar maple. Enjoy fine views of the hayfield through gaps in the foliage. Black birch—young trees have tight blackish bark—is numerous, along with ash and maple. In late fall the parking area comes into view as you reach a fence line and parallel the upper edge of the field. More barberry and bittersweet indicate human disturbance as you pass through another wooden gate at a barbed-wire fence and continue down a short distance to close the loop. Turn right and retrace your steps back to your vehicle.

## MORE INFORMATION

Open year-round, daily, sunrise to sunset. Free admission; on-site donations from nonmembers are welcome. Dogs must be kept on a leash at all times; mountain biking not permitted. Seasonal hunting is permitted. Owned and managed by The Trustees of Reservations. westregion@ttor.org; www.thetrustees.org; 413-298-3239, ext. 3000.

## TRIP 40
## QUESTING RESERVATION

**Location:** New Marlborough
**Rating:** Easy
**Distance:** 2.6 miles
**Elevation Gain:** 330 feet
**Estimated Time:** 1.5 hours
**Maps:** USGS Tolland Center, USGS Ashley Falls, USGS Great
Barrington

**A loop trail takes you back into a forgotten history of early colonial
settlement where the first non–American Indian children born in
Berkshire County came into the world.**

### DIRECTIONS
From the intersection of Routes 57 and 23 in Monterey, take Route 57 east
for 2.4 miles to the village of Hartsville; continue on Route 57 for another 2.5
miles to New Marlborough Hill Road on the right. Follow New Marlborough
Hill Road for 0.6 mile to a hillside gravel parking lot on the left with room for
eight to ten vehicles.

### TRAIL DESCRIPTION
Walk past a metal gate and head gradually and steadily uphill on a wide grassy
roadway. An intermittent brook has carved a shaded ravine to the right. In
fall, the predominant sugar maples produce a shower of orange and yellow
leaves. Bordering the roadway, you will find quartzite boulders and a variety
of ferns, including interrupted, sensitive, Christmas, bracken, long beech, and
the delicate maidenhair.

Beneath the larger trees—white ash and red maple—the spindly, spreading
form of witch hazel puts forth modest yellow flowers when you would least expect it—autumn. Indian cucumber-root and false Solomon's seal bloom here
in early summer. After the road levels off, a layer-cake schist outcrop peers out
from trees on the left. Another ledge shows off a 6- to 10-inch-thick milky-
white quartz vein. At an intersection with a one-track road on the left that
has a chain across it, continue on the wide roadway and soon you'll emerge
into a wildflower-filled meadow after about 10 minutes of walking from your
vehicle.

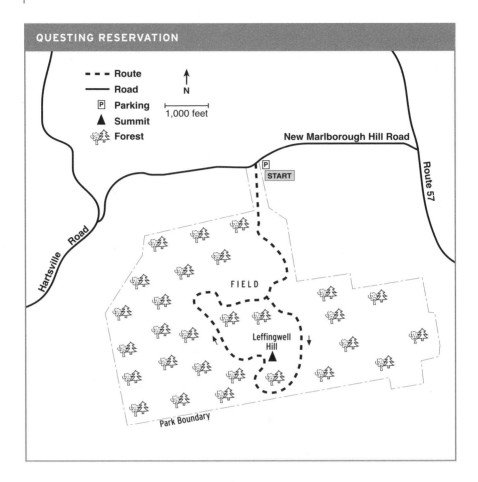

Follow the wide mown path left along the field edge; in summer enjoy watching some of the many colorful butterfly species recorded from this 17-acre meadow, including monarch, tiger swallowtail, red admiral, and pearl crescent. Showy New England asters and goldenrods refuel southbound migrant monarchs with fat-rich nectar, while fuzzy bumblebees clamber over flowers heavy with pollen in late summer. Reach a fork in the trail. A sign marks the start of the loop trail. Bear left and enter woodland of red maple, white ash, black cherry, and scattered large white pines. Hay-scented and New York ferns carpet the forest floor. The trail soon turns sharply right and passes through a gap in the stone wall—the first of many you'll pass through. Raspberry canes abound. A few spicebush shrubs thrive in the moist, rich soil and offer bright red berries to migrant thrushes in late summer. A bit farther on, a massive multitrunked red oak some 4 feet in diameter rears up behind a stone wall composed of relatively small schist rocks. The well-built wall stands 4.5

**Stone walls delineate former pastures within the colonial Leffingwell Settlement abandoned in the late 1800s.**

feet high in places. More woodland lies beyond the wall on the gentle slope of Leffingwell Hill, but with decidedly less underbrush.

Turn left and follow along the wall through dense shrubs under a canopy of red maple, black cherry (the one with the flaky black bark), and white pine. After a jog in the trail, the woodland shows signs of recent disturbance—relatively young woodland and the presence of invasive exotic oriental bittersweet vines. A few gnarled apple trees also attest to former human presence. In late summer tall white snakeroot hems in the path.

Turn right again onto another former roadway bordered on the right by a stone wall. Here the woods have an open appearance. A bit farther, stone foundations appear on the left. Japanese barberry—also an invasive exotic—is another clue to former human habitation. This disturbed woodland has an "unruly" look about it, unlike the forest you passed through earlier. Soon bear right at another chained gateway along a posted private property line. Pass by a rock pile on the right. Settlers piled stones too small for stone-wall construction in field corners. Leffingwell was abandoned in the late nineteenth century.

Soon white pine (note the five slender needles) becomes predominant. The seeds of this species require bright sunlight to germinate, indicating that this pine woodland was once an open field. Light green hay-scented fern (or boulder fern, as it is sometimes called), is abundant here. Soon you'll enter a shaded hemlock grove and then arrive at a magnificent red oak of more than 4 feet in diameter—larger than I have seen just about anywhere else in Berkshire County! It has a massive columnar trunk with a burl near its base. It must have started life at the inception of the Leffingwell Settlement. Oddly, it is almost the only oak within view. Far smaller and younger red maple, gray birch, white ash, and black cherry are far more numerous.

Soon after you enter a shaded woodland of eastern hemlock (some moderately large), walk downslope and then under white pines to enter a sun-dappled fern glade. As you continue downhill, white ash (with tight crosshatched bark) becomes the most common tree; ash seedlings are abundant below their parent trees. The white blazes that have been few and faint previously become more prominent. Soon you'll reach the southeast corner of the field that you happened upon earlier. Follow the wide mown path to the right along the woodland edge. Young gray birches with long-pointed leaves line the path. At the end of summer, I flushed a ruffed grouse here. A bit later, a regal red-tailed hawk sailed overhead. Close the loop at the trail intersection and turn left, then right to retrace your steps about 0.6 mile back to the parking area.

## MORE INFORMATION

Questing Reservation is owned and managed by The Trustees of Reservations, a private, nonprofit conservation organization. Open daily, sunrise to sunset. Admission is free. Open to hunting in season by written permission. Mountain biking not permitted. Questing Reservation, 413-298-3239, ext. 3000; www.thetrustees.org.

## MONARCHS OF THE MEADOW

With burnt-orange-and-black wings and an ebony body flecked with white, the monarch butterfly is among our most well-known insects. Each summer it graces our meadows and roadsides. In fall, schoolchildren bring its multihued caterpillars indoors in jars stuffed with milkweed, its obligatory food supply, in hopes of witnessing a miraculous transformation. The larvae—full-grown when the size of an adult's pinkie finger—consume only plants of the milkweed family. The aptly named milkweeds contain sticky white latex loaded with cardiac glycosides. These toxins do not harm the caterpillar, the pupa in its gold-studded chrysalis, or the winged adult—but woe to the predatory bird that dines on it. An immediate gastric reaction causes the bird to wretch until the offending meal has been ejected. Thus the bold colors of the larva and adult warn creatures with color vision, like birds, of the toxin—an effective means of protection for the species as a whole, if not the individual butterfly unlucky enough to provide an object lesson for an errant blue jay.

Although monarchs are so conspicuous in summer, the winter whereabouts of monarchs residing east of the Rocky Mountains were still strangely unknown until the 1970s. For centuries the southward movement of these big, showy butterflies had been observed as they headed steadily toward an unknown destination. In the late 1960s, scientists at the Royal Ontario Museum and University of Toronto began wing-tagging the butterflies in an effort to track them to their wintering grounds. One day in January 1975, a couple searching for the location came across tagged insects among clusters of tens of thousands high in the fir-clad transvolcanic mountains of central Mexico. One mystery had been solved.

Each year these monarchs spend approximately four months in a resting state, at a high, cool elevation that enables them to subsist on the stored fats they imbibe through uncoiled feeding tubes during the sunny days of late summer and early autumn. Lipid-rich goldenrods and asters of northeastern and midwestern meadows provide the fuel they need to complete a 2,000-mile journey to a place they have never been. Yet these overwintering butterflies do not return to New England the following summer. Rather, it is the offspring of their offspring that arrive here in June. They feast and reproduce, and it is only the last generation—five generations removed from the overwintering brood—that follow their urge to migrate toward an unknown land. Truly one of nature's miracles!

## TRIP 41
## DRY HILL RESERVATION

**Location:** New Marlborough
**Rating:** Easy
**Distance:** 1.5 miles
**Elevation Gain:** 35 feet
**Estimated Time:** 1.0 hour
**Maps:** USGS Otis; trail map available online

**Frothy pink-and-white displays of mountain laurel transform the peaceful forest into a botanical garden in late June, making this a pleasant walk with young children.**

### DIRECTIONS
From the intersection of Routes 57 and 23 in Monterey, follow Route 57 east for 5.7 miles to New Marlborough Center. Turn left onto New Marlborough–Monterey Road and drive 0.7 mile, bearing left on Old North Road. Follow it for almost 0.2 mile to a gravel parking lot on the left with space for eight to ten vehicles.

### TRAIL DESCRIPTION
Walk through a gap in the split-rail fence at the right end of the lot, passing a money pipe and a sign delineating reservation regulations. Note that hunting is permitted on the 206-acre property in season. Initially, the forest is composed largely of sugar and red maples, black cherry, and red oak. Pass through the first of several fallen stone walls. Some specimen sugar maples stand monumentally along the wall to your right; you'll appreciate a closer look at the end of the walk. Soon you'll reach a stand of spreading oldfield white pines. Oval white blazes on tree trunks mark the path. Even in late fall, the round, leathery leaves of pyrola grace the trail; their nodding whitish flower spikes appear in summer.

The next wall you pass through is noteworthy in that it is some 10 feet wide! Most of the wall's stones are quartzite, the same tough metamorphosed 550-million-year-old beach sand that Monument Mountain (Trip 36) and Pine Cobble (Trip 5) are made of. Broken rocks look like old-fashioned sugar candy. A few prickly Japanese barberry shrubs, with oblong red fruits, are another indicator of soil disturbance. American beech saplings—whose tan,

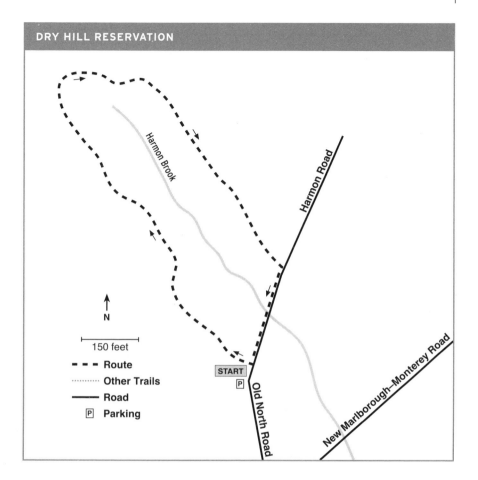

**DRY HILL RESERVATION**

Harmon Brook

Harmon Road

New Marlborough–Monterey Road

Old North Road

N

150 feet

- - - Route

·········· Other Trails

——— Road

P  Parking

START

P

papery leaves flutter in the slightest breeze right into winter—are numerous, while cherry trees exhibit bulging cankers or burls caused by fungal infection. In May, the delicate white bells of Canada mayflower enliven the woodland as you tread the essentially level and wide old wood road. The shiny, dark green leaves of wintergreen are attractive year-round.

As you amble along the hillside contour, an interesting mix of tree species—yellow birch (a northern hardwood), white pine, and white oak (whose leaves have rounded lobes) appears. Many mammals, including familiar gray squirrels, and birds, wild turkeys preeminent among them, covet the sweet acorns. A ridgeline to the right is visible after leaf fall. At your feet, prince's pine, seedling white pines, lowbush blueberry, and staghorn club mosses (note their miniature, fuzzy green "antlers") populate the forest floor, as do scattered quartzite boulders. The old road veers off to the left, but stay right on the blazed path. Young black (sweet) birch trees become quite common. The

**White or paper birch, which is distinguished by its characteristically orange inner bark, was widely used by indigenous peoples for canoe construction.**

pliable twigs of this handsome tree are rich in oil of wintergreen. Along with balsam, it is one of my favorite natural Berkshire scents.

Suddenly you'll find yourself in the midst of an extensive and vigorous mountain laurel thicket; some shrubs are 15 feet in height. And if you have timed your visit well (mid-June to early July), the laurel boughs will be heavy with nickel-sized blossoms of white and pink—a gorgeous sight! A careful observer might also find a few sheep laurels that are only a couple of feet tall and with smaller, darker pink flowers. The path now becomes lumpier with quartzite. At a T intersection with a cart road, bear right (note sign on tree), and soon you'll reach another sign that points left. Follow this single track, a bit difficult to discern (blazes here are faded), into oak-maple woods. Ghostly white Indian pipes push up through the oak leaf litter and bloom in summer, drawing their nourishment from oak roots.

As you descend very gradually, note the damp bowl on your right where deep green eastern hemlocks thrive. These appear to have been spared an attack by the tiny sap-sucking insect known as the woolly adelgid, at least for now. White (a.k.a. paper), yellow, and black birches are all present. The trail bears left after joining an old roadway and soon reaches gravel Old North Road (Harmon Road). Turn right; the road crosses an intermittent unnamed brook and parallels a stone wall. Three grand sugar maples stand like sentinels along the wall just before the lot. No doubt they yielded countless buckets of sap during their long lives.

## MORE INFORMATION

Open year-round, daily, sunrise to sunset. Free admission, although donations may be placed in the metal money pipe at the trailhead. Seasonal hunting is permitted subject to state and town laws. A Trustees of Reservations hunting permit is required as well. Trail bikes and motorized vehicles and fires are prohibited. Carry in, carry out. The Trustees of Reservations; 413-298-3239; westregion@ttor.org; http://www.thetrustees.org.

## TRIP 42
## JUG END STATE RESERVATION

**Location:** Egremont
**Rating:** Easy
**Distance:** 2.0 miles
**Elevation Gain:** 270 feet
**Estimated Time:** 1.5 hours
**Maps:** AMC Massachusetts Trail Map #2: B2, USGS Great Barrington; trail map available online

**Bucolic meadows with a stunning backdrop of ridges clothed in mixed woodlands beckon hikers to enjoy a landscape reverting to a time before commercial development.**

## DIRECTIONS

From the intersection of Route 7 and Route 23/41 in Great Barrington, turn onto Route 23/41 and drive southwest for 4.0 miles. Turn left onto Route 41 south (at Mill Pond), and in 0.1 mile turn right onto Mount Washington Road. Follow it for 1.7 miles to Jug End Road on the left. Stay on Jug End Road for 0.5 mile and turn right into the large gravel parking area.

## TRAIL DESCRIPTION

The 2-mile Jug End Loop Trail begins at the far left end of the parking area near the concrete footing of the former barn's silo. The massive deluxe cattle barn that once stood here was turned into a hotel in 1935. For 40 years, beginning in the 1930s, this 1,158-acre scenic conservation property was the site of a booming year-round resort and ski area known as Jug End Barn Resort. By the way, the somewhat odd name Jug End is actually derived from the German word *Jugend*, meaning "youth." Certainly many young people of days gone by enjoyed their family visits to the former resort. Today, families can enjoy the natural delights of this place.

A steep but brief climb in two steps leads up a grassy knoll to an old wood road where you turn right to follow triangular blue blazes. Sugar maple, white ash, and black cherry form a canopy over the path. Signs of former habitation include daffodil and yew plantings and sections of rusty barbed wire. A substantial stone wall dissects the meadow below to your right. The resort's swimming pool once lay beyond the wall. Up the slope to your left is an old apple orchard.

Big-tooth aspens rise like columns before an easy rolling descent, while a specimen sugar maple stands on the right. You'll reach a field edge bordered by apple trees. Walk easily along the right field edge, passing trees heavy with pinkish-white blossoms in early May. The flowering apples attract buzzing pollinators and birds that feed on insects attracted to the flowers and foliage. One brilliant May morning I delighted in watching several bright yellow-and-bluish-gray blue-winged warblers dashing about from tree to tree in search of insect prey and uttering their insect-like *beee-bzzz* songs.

Reenter the deciduous woods of maple, cherry, ash, and gray birch that shade the tall shrub witch hazel. Cross a small stream, and soon you'll arrive at a dark wall of planted Norway spruces. The path skirts the spruce plantation, while on your left a brushy tangle of raspberry canes, cherry, Japanese barberry, and multiflora rose have colonized a light gap. Chestnut-sided warblers prefer early successional habitats like this. Listen for the *pleased, pleased, pleased to meetcha* refrain of this yellow-capped, chestnut-flanked sprite. No plant life can exist in the total shade of the spruces, in contrast to the shrubs thriving in the forest opening. Native grape and exotic, invasive oriental bittersweet vines crowd the trail. The grape vines cause no harm to the supporting trees.

Soon you'll find yourself surrounded by deciduous woodland of big-tooth aspen, maple, and ash, with some white pines. At another mowed field, the path hugs the woodland edge where oaks, maples, and white birches—in a row—flourish. Glance up periodically for large soaring red-tailed hawks scanning the meadow for rodents. You are walking in a bowl bordered by ridges. Enjoy the splendid view. From the right, Mount Whitbeck, Mount Sterling, and, beyond the radio towers, Mount Darby are the prominences along the ridge to

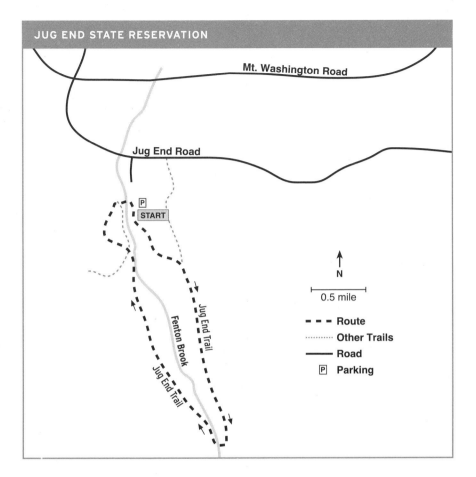

your right (west). A number of ski runs once cut the slopes of Sterling (elevation 1,980 feet). Bear left, reenter the broadleaf woodland with some pine, and jog right onto an old woods road. More old barbed wire remains here.

Back in the forest, notice the copious sugar maple seedlings as you make your way along a sometimes-wet road cut deeply into the earth from years of former use. Reach a mowed hillside meadow. Some New England farmers joked that their cows had longer legs on one side of their bodies in order to graze such hillsides. Shad (juneberry) trees show delicate white-petaled blossoms before they produce leaves in April along the field margins. Pass a marble boulder (plucked and dropped by a glacier?) near a big spreading sugar maple and continue past the end of a treeline separating this meadow from another beyond it. The sound of flowing water soon fills the air.

Head back into the forest and over a series of bog bridges strategically placed on soggy ground. While I was on a May visit, four perfectly camouflaged

American woodcocks suddenly exploded into the air. These chunky "shore-birds" have long bills perfectly suited to extracting earthworms from moist soil. Below to the right is a shaded hemlock gorge from which the sound of flowing water is now unmistakable. As you walk among the hemlocks, feel the cooler microclimate resulting from their deep shade. Hard, gray schist litters the old road. The brook soon comes into view as you start a gentle climb.

Red trilliums bloom in spring around an old cellar hole on the right. At the fork in the road, turn right following blue blazes to cross—on logs and rocks—the clear, cold Fenton Brook. You'll probably be surprised to come upon a stone fireplace and chimney in the midst of a hemlock forest where the trail turns right. Jug End Resort once rented cabins to vacationers. Follow the old roadway under hemlock, ash, black and yellow birches, red maple, and oak. Mountain laurel appears for the first time. Its evergreen leaves glisten brightly when the sun shines. Their waxy surface helps prevent drying in winter. One cut hemlock log displayed nearly 80 growth rings. The rings indicate that growth was rapid during its early years, but slower as competition with other trees for light, water, and nutrients increased.

Descend to cross a rocky, tumbling feeder stream on stones. One chunk of whitish marble in the brook bed has been elegantly polished by the flow. Listen for the enthusiastic bubbling song of the tiny winter wren in spring and early summer here. This open forest of hemlocks—some tall and straight—is evoca-tive. But soon the woodland is once again dominated by sugar maples. Cross a couple of little feeder streams during your gradual downhill ramble and then level out. Two white-tailed does bounded off, their warning flags erect, during my May visit. Violets—yellow, white, and purple—adorn the woods and jack-in-the-pulpit holds forth under his canopy of maroon and green. Likewise, nonflowering plants such as sensitive, Christmas, and even lacy maidenhair ferns grace the forest floor.

A rock wall on the left once kept in sheep. The sound of flowing water in the gorge quite far below to the right provides musical accompaniment—along with the songs of neotropical migrant songbirds back for the nesting season. After a steeper but brief descent, approach the crystal-clear Fenton Brook and its rocky bed, and then bear right at another old roadway. You'll reach a brushy field where the path narrows and turns right, away from the roadway. Note the stake marking the route. A nice view of the ridge again appears as the path continues to follow the brook downstream. Cross a tiny flow on a cut log bridge to a T intersection. Little yellow warblers and gaudy Baltimore orioles pour out their songs from perches here in late spring and early summer.

**Mount Whitbeck, Mount Sterling, and Mount Darby constitute the high points visible from a field patrolled by red-tailed hawks.**

Instead of following the blazed trail to the right, turn left and follow along the field edge before bearing right to reach a grassy track. I must admit a bias in favor of fields and other open areas where views are likely and wildlife may be more plentiful along the boundary between field and forest. And besides, this is a just a short detour. Bear right at the grassy track. Soon the track turns left, but continue on the narrow trail toward the right along the woodland edge. You'll join the path you shunned earlier in a few more steps and follow it downstream along the brook past mature Norway and seedling spruces as well as other ornamentals—forsythia, arborvitae, and rhododendron. Turn right to cross the handsome wooden bridge and amble back to your vehicle.

## MORE INFORMATION

Open sunrise to sunset year-round. Access is free. Day-use-only parking permitted. Pets must be on 10-foot-maximum leash, attended at all times; must have proof of current rabies vaccination. Carry-in, carry-out trash policy. Motorized vehicles and alcoholic beverages prohibited. Hunting permitted in season. Jug End State Reservation & Wildlife Management Area, Jug End Road, Egremont, c/o RD East Street, Mount Washington, MA 01258; 413-528-0330; http://www.mass.gov/dcr/parks/western/juge.htm.

## TRIP 43
## ELBOW TRAIL TO APPALACHIAN TRAIL AND JUG END

**Location:** Sheffield
**Rating:** Difficult
**Distance:** 7.2 miles
**Elevation Gain:** 1,000 feet
**Estimated Time:** 4.5 hours
**Maps:** AMC Massachusetts Trail Map #2: B3, USGS Ashley Falls

**A little-known woodland path provides access to the Appalachian Trail, Jug End, and some of the most spectacular views in the southern Taconics.**

### DIRECTIONS

From the intersection of Route 7 and Route 23/41 in Great Barrington, turn onto Route 23/41 and drive southwest for 4.0 miles. Turn left onto Route 41 south (at Mill Pond), and follow it for 3.1 miles to the entrance road for Berkshire School on the right. Follow the entrance road to your first right, and shortly to a T intersection, at which point you follow the sign to Berkshire Hall, a large building with three front doors. Then bear left just before a tan brick building, Stanley Dorm, and follow the road up a steep hill, passing a wooden house on your right and eventually to a gravel road and a kiosk for a total of 0.6 mile from Route 41. Park along the edge of the gravel on the right under a leafy canopy.

### TRAIL DESCRIPTION

Examine the kiosk with its large schematic map of the Berkshire School's extensive trail system. Note that the Elbow Trail is blazed in blue. Start up Elbow Trail, an old road between the towns of Sheffield and Mount Washington, and cross, via a wooden bridge, a small intermittent brook that courses among hardwoods and hemlocks. Soon you'll pass the yellow-blazed Cross Trail and then a mysterious deep channel that may have been linked with the old road. Initially this is an easy walk on a rocky old road, but more exertion is soon required. Deep green Christmas fern—green all year—is abundant. It is said that it derives its name from the fact that its leaflets resemble Christmas stockings.

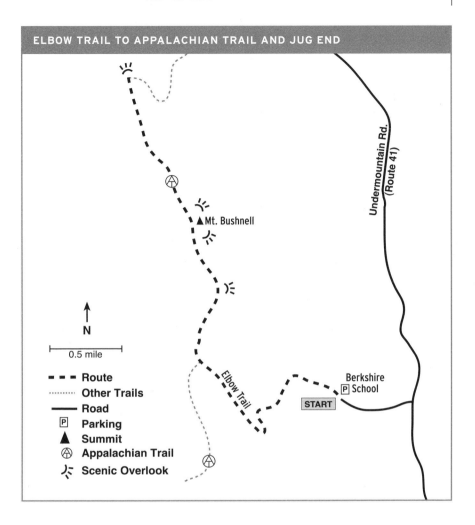

But the most delicately beautiful of ferns in my opinion—maidenhair—grows nearby.

A ramrod-straight three-boled tulip tree stands on the right. After being logged years ago, the stump sprouted to make three trunks. This, the tallest tree in our eastern woodlands, is at the northern edge of its range in the southern Berkshires. Both its impressive cup-shaped orange-and-green blossoms and its leaves invoke the tulip. Pass through a gap in a stone wall that is now out of place under maturing maples, birches, oaks, ashes, white pines, and hemlocks. Where the grade eases, note the juvenile yellow birch whose octopus-like network of surface roots grips the ground. Reach the red-blazed West Run Trail on the left and continue straight under some impressive hemlock trees. The

From the pitch pine-clothed Taconic ridgeline, vistas abound as one gazes northeast-ward toward promontories beyond the Housatonic Valley.

old road you're treading was cut into the steep hillside, and the downslope side built up with rock.

You'll reach a saddle where gneiss bedrock is exposed like the upturned hull of a ship; turn right to switchback along it. You have just passed the elbow! The old road was cut into the slope contour. As you proceed, you'll pass a number of seeps and springs where water bleeds out from the cut bank. Two dripping springs are lined with moss. Oaks increase in number and, under them, mountain laurel. A few sapling-sized chestnut root sprouts are sad reminders of once-magnificent American chestnut groves that the blight wiped out here by World War I. Skirt the head of a ravine that cleaves the slope to the right, and soon after you'll reach the Appalachian Trail (AT) in a small, level clearing, 1.5 miles from the trailhead.

Turn right (north) in the direction of Jug End, and pass by attractive rock outcrops—some vertical planes are blistered with rock tripe, a lichen that becomes grayish-green when wet but brittle and brown when dry. The layer-cake bedrock, standing on end, exhibits obvious contortion from tremendous heat and pressure—the result of tectonic plates colliding, giving rise (literally) to the Taconic Range. The growth of this forest of oak, red maple, birch, hemlock, and white pine has been stunted by shallow soils and harsh climatic conditions, but laurels are extravagant along the footpath in late June. The acidic soil of these pine-oak woods is advantageous for lowbush blueberries too. Much of the trail traverses bedrock that warms in the summer sun, volatilizing the sweet perfume of pine pitch.

After reaching the first viewpoint, which is screened by vegetation, a little more walking rewards you with an open vista at about 1,900 feet elevation and fabulous long-range views to the northeast, east, and southeast. The ragged ridgeline of Monument Mountain (Trip 36) is visible some 10 miles to the north-northeast. Descend from this promontory, steeply in places, brushing by a good-sized mountain ash, with compound leaves, to your left. A bit farther, a sunny outcrop hugging the path is adorned with reindeer lichen, red-capped British soldiers, pixie cups, and rock tripe. All are associations between a fungus and an alga. White blazes decorate bedrock mounds rather than tree trunks here.

Level out among low scrub (bear) oaks, pitch pines, and blueberries (the delicious fruits ripen in July) and stride into a clearing with a view to the east; but more expansive views are yours from Mount Bushnell (elevation 1,834 feet), just a bit farther. From here, a portion of the Berkshire School campus is visible to the southeast. The ridge that juts out in front of it, capped by white pines, is Black Rock. Continue heading northward on an undulating, needle-cushioned path between outcrops under pitch pines and past bear oak, huckleberry, and blueberry shrubs. Mount Greylock (Trips 4, 8, 9, and 10) is visible through gaps in the pines. The branches of pitch pine were once used as torches due to their high resin content. Another peculiar trait of this tree is that its needles characteristically sprout right from the trunk.

Soils deepen and trees respond by growing taller as you continue down more earnestly into a col. Heat-tolerant oaks increase in number and, beneath them, sun-loving bracken fern. In June, pink lady's slipper orchids produce large moccasin-like flowers. After blooming, the flower and stalk wither, leaving two large, veined leaves on the forest floor. The Massachusetts state flower, the modest trailing arbutus, tolerates poor soils; look for its rough-textured, 2-inch-long, tongue-shaped leaves creeping along the path. Other wildflowers in this forest are Canada mayflower (a.k.a. wild lily of the valley), cow-wheat, and starflower.

Level out again on a ledge clearing, pass a minor viewpoint, and arrive at a rock cairn—the Jug End summit (see Trip 42 to learn about the origin of the name). Several communications towers are visible on top of Mount Darby to your left. Stride down from the bedrock and soon you'll be peering out over a gorgeous view of valley, ridgelines, and more distant high points, including Mount Greylock and Monument Mountain. The latter is much closer and to the right of the state's highest peak. You could stop here, but there are three or four spectacular vistas within the next 0.4 mile. You will descend steeply over bedrock to reach the last two and climb back sharply upon your return, but if the rock is dry and your energy and water are holding out, they are worth the additional effort. Mill Pond, at the intersections of Routes 23 and 41, lies serenely below. A dense growth of short polypody fern caps some outcrops.

The gnarled skeleton of a pitch pine stands ahead of you at a point where the AT turns sharply right to descend on rock—an angled two-headed arrow painted on the outcrop points the way. But first, take in the wonderful views from the top of the outcrop. Mill Pond and Monument Mountain line up neatly from this vantage point. There is one more vista point to experience, if you wish. It requires a fairly steep but short descent off the rock promontory via the AT, so watch your footing. This most spacious view is to be had from a terraced outcropping, where you can sit comfortably and enjoy the whole valley laid out before you. The ethereal songs of a hermit thrush, one of our most accomplished songsters, may well drift up to serenade your revelry. The AT makes another sharp turn here to drop down to Jug End Road, but it's finally time to turn back. Be careful working your way back up the ledges, and be sure to turn left at the Elbow Trail junction.

## MORE INFORMATION

Elbow Trail is maintained by the Berkshire School, 245 North Undermountain Road, Sheffield, MA 01257; 413-229-8511; http://www.berkshireschool.org. The Appalachian Trail Management Committee is responsible for maintenance, management, and protection of the nearly 90 miles of the AT in Massachusetts; volunteers do this work, with assistance from the Massachusetts Department of Conservation and Recreation. Massachusetts AT Committee, Berkshire Chapter AMC, P.O. Box 2281, Pittsfield, MA 01202; at@amcberkshire.org; http://www.amcberkshire.org/at; 413-528-6333. Appalachian Mountain Club Regional Trail Coordinator: 413-528-8003.

## TRIP 44
# GUILDER POND AND MOUNT EVERETT

**Location:** Mount Washington
**Rating:** Moderate
**Distance:** 4.2 miles
**Elevation Gain:** 825 feet
**Estimated Time:** 2.5–3.0 hours
**Maps:** AMC Massachusetts Trail Map #2: C3, USGS Ashley Falls

**Guilder Pond is locally renowned for its profuse mountain laurel bloom, while ancient pitch-pine-topped Mount Everett, the highest point in southern Berkshire County, offers sublime vistas.**

## DIRECTIONS
From the intersection of Route 7 and Route 23/41 in Great Barrington, turn onto Route 23/41 and drive southwest for 4.0 miles. Turn left onto Route 41 south (at Mill Pond), and in 0.1 mile turn right onto Mount Washington Road. Drive for 7.6 miles (the road becomes East Street in Mount Washington) and turn left at the sign for Mount Everett State Reservation. Follow the gravel entrance road for just over 0.1 mile to an iron gate. Park along the right side of the gravel turnout. It is possible to drive all the way to the Guilder Pond Picnic Area in summer (gates are open 8 A.M. to 8 P.M.), but this hike begins at the lower gate.

## TRAIL DESCRIPTION
From the metal gate at the bottom of the gravel access road, where a donation pipe is located, stroll steadily uphill on the roadway through a mixed forest of oak, maple, birch, beech, white pine, and hemlocks. Mountain laurel is in evidence almost immediately, especially from late June to early July when it flowers. Some bushes are over 12 feet tall. The roadway winds under a canopy of shading eastern hemlocks, as does the soothing flow of Guilder Brook on the left.

After about 0.9 mile, pass one end of the Guilder Pond Trail on the left and arrive at its namesake water body. At 2,042 feet above sea level, Guilder is either the second- or third-highest natural water body in the commonwealth. Nearly everything you read labels it second highest, but Tilden Swamp in

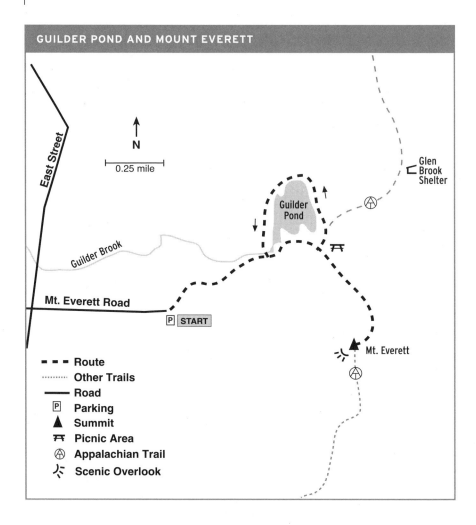

**GUILDER POND AND MOUNT EVERETT**

N

0.25 mile

East Street

Glen
Brook
Shelter

Guilder
Pond

Guilder Brook

Mt. Everett Road

P START

Mt. Everett

- - - Route
......... Other Trails
——— Road
P Parking
▲ Summit
🛏 Picnic Area
Ⓐ Appalachian Trail
🔆 Scenic Overlook

Pittsfield State Forest, flooded by beavers in the mid-1990s, may be a few feet higher. In any event it is a beautiful sight, fringed with pink-and-white laurels as it is. Patches of sweetgale, leatherleaf, and sphagnum moss have colonized the shore. Black whirligig beetles gyrate about on the surface in summer. Later you'll walk completely around it; for now, continue on the roadway another 0.2 mile to Guilder Pond Picnic Area, where toilet facilities are located.

In summer it is possible to drive to this lower parking area for the climb up Mount Everett. The gravel summit road on the right is gated. At the far left end of the picnic area is the other access for Guilder Pond Trail, which you'll use upon your return. But first, follow the white-blazed Appalachian Trail (maps may be available at the large AT sign on the right) up into beech, maple, yellow birch, and oak woodland on a steady incline. After just 0.1 mile, you'll meet the gravel summit road and turn left. Walk a mere 100 feet and turn right to continue on the AT. It leads up on a rocky path. Striped or goosefoot maple is an abundant small tree here, while wood sorrel (with clover-like leaves and white, pink-veined summer blossoms) and clintonia (a.k.a. blue-bead lily) grow in the rich soil.

The summit road parallels the footpath on the left. The AT bears right, climbs a short distance, and turns left to ascend a stone "stairway" adjacent to rocky outcrops. Blue-green spinulose wood ferns soften the sharp angles below yellow birch and mountain ash. A sign on the left reads "Summit 0.1 Mile," but you'll see another just like it a bit farther on. As you make your way up, peek through the vegetation on your left for tantalizing glimpses of the double-humped form of Mount Greylock, 37 miles to the north. It's easy to imagine how its other name, Saddleback Mountain, came to be.

In late June and early July, laurel bushes festooned with clusters of pentagonal flowers crowd the path. I'll admit to an inordinate fondness for their showy blossoms. The modest leaves of trailing arbutus beneath the laurel are thus easy to overlook. Hiking so close to the Connecticut border here, it's fitting that the two state flowers are in such close proximity as well. And mountain azaleas put on quite a show here about a month earlier. Adding much to the overall ambience are shrubby red maple, mountain ash, wild raisin, huckleberry, and lowbush blueberry. The latter two offer tasty treats as well.

After the second 0.1 mile to the summit sign, tread over the schist bedrock that stands on end due to the collision of continental plates hundreds of millions of years ago when these mountains were formed. The thin soil atop the bedrock provides nourishment to bear or scrub oak, also found on Cape Cod. Feel the tough leathery leaves that limit water loss in this harsh environment, and note its tiny acorns. At a blue plastic blaze on the right marked "View," step up onto a ledge outcrop and a vista point gazing eastward to the Housatonic River valley, the Berkshire plateau beyond, and the Twin Lakes just over the Connecticut line. You might even be able to pick out the sloping meadow on Hurlburt's Hill in the Bartholomew's Cobble Reservation (Trip 49).

Soon you'll reach the site of the former summit fire tower, surrounded by little stiff-needled pitch pines, at 2,624 feet. Only the concrete footings remain. The tower, which had fallen into disrepair, was removed by helicopter in 2003. Studies of the summit vegetation had revealed an amazing fact: the gnarled dwarf pitch pines were upward of 200 years old—an old-growth forest in miniature, as it were. The summit is an unusual and fragile environment, so

**Mountain laurel blossoms create an attention-getting floral display along the Appalachian Trail en route to the summit.**

remain on the trail and bedrock so as not to trample the vegetation. Views of the bluish ridgeline of New York's Catskill Mountains—50 miles to the west-southwest—are yours to enjoy.

After taking in the panoramic vistas, retrace your steps down to the Guilder Pond Picnic Area, but turn right to follow the joint AT/Guilder Pond Trail (blazed with blue triangles) through northern hardwoods blended with hemlock, oaks, and laurel, for a short distance. At the Y intersection, the AT goes right. Turn left instead to continue on Guilder Pond Trail. The laurel shrubs are especially lovely beneath another evergreen—eastern hemlock. Some hemlocks have attained a seemingly advanced age, judging by their girth. Together with the needles dropped by white pines, they create a cushioned treadway. The path undulates through and around laurel bushes that tower over your head. This woodland in summer is filled with the birdsong of vireo, warbler, and thrush.

After passing through a fern glade dominated by New York fern (the fronds taper to a point at the bottom as well as the top), ascend the rocky ledge on stone steps that bring you to a point from which a nice view across the pond of the rounded "Dome of the Taconics," as Everett is known, is possible. You may be surprised to see stumps cut by industrious beavers quite high up the slope. Even hemlocks and oaks, not among their preferred foods, have fallen to their sharp incisors. Their lodge is visible on an island in the pond. A ledge runs parallel with the trail. Walk across bedrock again close to the shore. The rock is laced with the white veins of milky quartz.

To your left are a concrete water control structure, wooden decking, and a black plastic culvert that transports water under an old vegetated beaver dam to the pond's outlet stream—Guilder Brook. Water from this side of the mountain eventually finds its way into the Hudson. Although not marked by a blaze, bear right and enter a narrow path ahead to cross a single log span over the outlet stream. A few feet more and you are back on the gravel entry road. Turn right and walk about 1 mile back to your vehicle.

## MORE INFORMATION

Open sunrise to sunset, daily, year-round. Access is free. Toilet facilities are located at Guilder Pond Picnic Area. Pets are permitted but must be on a 10-foot-maximum leash; proof of rabies vaccination required. Motorized off-road vehicles and alcoholic beverages prohibited. Mount Everett State Reservation, East Street, Mount Washington, c/o RD 3 East Street, Mount Washington, MA 01258; 413-528-0330; http://www.mass.gov/dcr/parks/western/meve.htm. The Appalachian Trail Management Committee is responsible for maintenance, management, and protection of the nearly 90 miles of the AT in Massachusetts. Massachusetts AT Committee, Berkshire Chapter AMC, P.O. Box 2281, Pittsfield, MA 01202; at@amcberkshire.org; 413-528-6333; Appalachian Mountain Club Regional Trail Coordinator: 413-528-8003; http://www.amcberkshire.org/at.

## PRETTY IN PINK (AND WHITE)

One of the showiest shrubs to grace the area's woodlands in early summer is mountain laurel, a member of the heath family. Heaths are generally known by their thick, leathery evergreen leaves. Other local members of the group include such familiar woody shrubs as azaleas, blueberries, wintergreen, and trailing arbutus (the Massachusetts state flower). Our neighboring state Connecticut designated mountain laurel as its state flower because it is common in this region.

Mountain laurel sometimes attains heights locally of 12 feet and tends to grow in gnarly thickets that are difficult for a person to penetrate. In the Appalachians to our south, such dense stands are less than lovingly referred to as "laurel hells." But the exuberant floral display this shrub produces in our region from late June to early July is unrivaled. Laurels, especially those in open, sunny locations, show off clusters of nickel-sized blossoms varying in hue from white to pink. In some years the display is especially lavish, and 2008 was such a year. I'm sure I took hundreds of photos of bushes in their full glory that year.

The pentagonal blossoms are decorated with a deep pink central ring and have evolved to cleverly ambush pollinators by whacking them with stamens released by a hair trigger as they crawl over each flower. The tips of the ten stamens dab pollen on the body of the visiting bee, facilitating the transfer of genetic material when it subsequently arrives at another flower. Each bush unfurls thousands of blossoms that en masse thrill the eye. And even when mountain laurel is not in bloom, its shiny green foliage is very attractive, and a welcome sight during the dreary days of winter.

The waxy leaves, said to be poisonous to deer, retard moisture loss during the virtual drought conditions of winter, a necessity for a plant that retains its leaves. In late spring and early summer its foliage shields the nests of exquisitely plumaged black-throated blue warblers, although females are attired in muted tones to avoid detection by predators. The 5.25-inch-long warblers return to their Caribbean winter homes after the brief breeding season in New England. They place their cup nests quite low to the ground in laurels and hobblebushes, where they are sometimes victimized by brown-headed cowbirds. The larger cowbirds deposit their eggs in the nests of smaller hosts. The clueless warblers raise the larger, more aggressive cowbird chick at the expense of their own. Another example of successful deception in nature!

## TRIP 45
## BASH BISH FALLS STATE PARK

**Location:** Mount Washington; Copake Falls, NY
**Rating:** Moderate
**Distance:** 2.0 miles
**Elevation Gain:** 470 feet
**Estimated Time:** 1.5 hours
**Maps:** AMC Massachusetts Trail Map #2: C1, USGS Copake Falls, Bash Bish Falls

**An easy stroll to Massachusetts's most spectacular waterfall, and a short, steep climb for a fine view of Bash Bish Gorge, New York's Harlem Valley, and the distant Catskills.**

## DIRECTIONS

From the intersection of Route 7 and Route 23/41 in Great Barrington, turn onto Route 23/41 and drive southwest for 4.0 miles. Turn left onto Route 41 south (at Mill Pond), and in 0.1 mile turn right onto Mount Washington Road. Drive for 7.7 miles (the road becomes East Street in Mount Washington), following signs, to the intersection with Cross Road. Turn right (a Church of Christ chapel is located on the opposite corner). Cross Road intersects West Street. Bear right on West Street, which becomes fairly steep and winding for the next 0.5 mile. At a stop sign, turn left to cross Wright Brook and left again immediately on Bash Bish Falls Road. Follow it for 2.5 miles into New York State, where it becomes Route 344 (passing the upper parking area in Massachusetts along the way), to the paved large lower parking area at Taconic State Park on the left. The total distance from Route 7 in Great Barrington to Taconic State Park is 16.0 miles.

## TRAIL DESCRIPTION

Check the kiosk on the right at the far end of the lot edged by tall Norway spruces. Examine the detailed map of the route, and at the other kiosk learn about the locale's fascinating tourism and iron industry history. Walk down the old gravel roadway bordered by eastern hemlocks and some chestnut oaks as it follows Bash Bish Brook closely upstream. The translucent, frothy green water flows with a thunderous roar after rains or snowmelt. Shiny, platy schist protrudes from the roadway and lines the stream as you amble gently down to

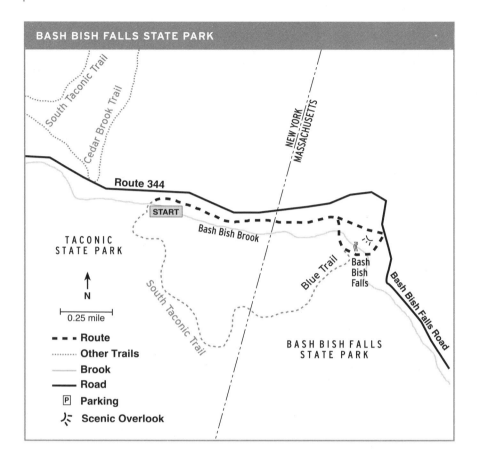

**BASH BISH FALLS STATE PARK**

Route 344

START

Bash Bish Brook

TACONIC
STATE PARK

NEW YORK
MASSACHUSETTS

South Taconic Trail

Cedar Brook Trail

South Taconic Trail

Blue Trail

Bash
Bish
Falls

Bash Bish Falls Road

BASH BISH FALLS
STATE PARK

N

0.25 mile

- - - Route
........... Other Trails
Brook
Road
P  Parking
Scenic Overlook

brook level for a closer look. Large red and black oaks and white ash dot the deciduous hillside on your left, while the right slope is shaded and clothed in hemlocks.

Other hardwoods include maple, and both black and yellow birches. Witch hazel shrubs poke up near the brook. Eastern phoebes build moss-covered nests on little shelves like those offered by the jutting schist boulder on the left. But the roar of the flow makes it almost impossible to discern birdsong. As you begin climbing gently to a bench, big-tooth aspens intermix with hemlocks. The precipitous slope of Bash Bish Mountain, loden green in hemlock attire, forms the far side of the gorge. The treadway becomes a little rougher as it rises some 60 feet above the surging flow. Some mature red oaks on the sunny left slope invite notice. In winter, black-capped chickadees and golden-crowned kinglets hanging from the hemlock branches in search of insects may be among the few birds you'll find. After about 15 minutes of walking, you'll reach the state line and Bash Bish Falls State Park, marked by a brown sign.

**A thunderous roar alerts you to the proximity of the falls' impressive 60-foot split drop into a clear pool.**

Continue a gentle ascent, skirting thicker hemlock growth. Soon you'll reach an intersection with a short gravel roadway that leads left up to a metal gate and the paved road. Stay right, guided by the roar of the falls. A kiosk with a donation pipe is on the left at a falls viewing area bordered by metal railings. Walk down the native stone steps to get a closer look at the spectacle. Be extremely careful when conditions are icy or wet! Massachusetts's most impressive single plunge falls about 60 feet, gushing down in twin streams around a jutting granite outcrop into an icy green pool. No Swimming signs alert visitors to the potential danger.

Legend has it that the falls takes its name from a beautiful Indian princess who was sent over the falls in a canoe to her death as punishment for suspected adultery. Whether true or fanciful, the legend adds a romantic appeal to an already evocative sight.

Angular slabs of schist surround the pool. A feeder brook tumbles down the high gradient slope from the left, adding water to the plunge pool. Water tumbling over the falls originates from springs in the uplands of Mount Washington State Forest. In winter, wind-blown mist coats tree branches with ice.

You'll want to have your camera handy. To continue, climb back up the steps and turn left, walking back down the way you came about 60 feet before turning right on a path that angles up a slope over railroad ties and then bears right onto a wider former wood road. Follow the triangular blue blazes.

Cross a couple of flowages under hemlocks, sugar maples, and ashes, ascending fairly steeply toward the head of the ravine past schist boulders with blue arrows to a twin log bridge across the upper reaches of the feeder brook. The path levels out and continues under towering hemlocks that impart a primeval forest aspect. Some are nearly 3 feet in diameter. Cross a small stream on rocks and cover the remaining short distance through a small stand of white birch to the paved upper parking lot and another kiosk that informs hikers about the presence of the endangered eastern timber rattlesnake.

Head right, along the edge of the lot, and turn right at metal fencing to semi-scramble up schist bedrock to a vista point above the gorge. Atop the crag are white pines, shrub-sized scrub oak, and a lone pitch pine. Common polypody ferns fill the crevices of the upturned schist, which also contains milky quartz veins. From the vantage points along the metal railing (exercise caution), enjoy splendid views west down the gorge to the Harlem Valley and the distant Catskill Mountains. The falls are audible but not visible from here. The green mound of Bash Bish Mountain (1,925 feet) looms up to the left, while oak-clothed Cedar Mountain (1,883 feet) forms the opposite wall of the gorge. Be alert for the guttural croaks of jet-black ravens as they soar overhead. When ready to return, retrace your steps about 1 mile to the lower parking area.

## MORE INFORMATION

Taconic State Park, in New York, is open daily, year-round, sunrise to sunset, weather and conditions permitting. Free access. Campground is open from the first Friday in May through the first weekend in December. Dogs permitted on a 10-foot-maximum leash. Motor and wheeled vehicles prohibited. Taconic State Park, Route 344, P.O. Box 100, Copake Falls, NY 12517; 518-329-3993 (800-456-2267 for camping/cabin reservations); http://www.nysparks.state.ny.us/parks/info.

Bash Bish Falls State Park, in Massachusetts, is open daily, year-round, sunrise to half an hour after sunset. Free access. Pets permitted on a 10-foot-maximum leash; must have proof of current rabies vaccination. Swimming, diving, rock climbing, and alcoholic beverages prohibited. Bash Bish Falls State Park, Falls Road, c/o RD 3 East Street, Mount Washington, MA 01258; 413-528-0330; http://www.mass.gov/dcr/parks/western/bash.htm.

## TRIP 46
## RACE BROOK FALLS AND MOUNT RACE

**Location:** Sheffield, Mount Washington
**Rating:** Difficult
**Distance:** 6.6 miles
**Elevation Gain:** 1,625 feet
**Estimated Time:** 4.0 hours
**Maps:** AMC Massachusetts Trail Map #2: C3, USGS Ashley Falls; trail map available online at the Mount Washington State Forest website

**Spectacular waterfalls, stupendous laurel blooms, and exhilarating views from the southern Taconic ridgeline on Mount Race make this one of the most picturesque hikes in the Berkshires.**

### DIRECTIONS
From the junction of Route 7 and Route 23/41 in Great Barrington, turn onto Route 23/41 and drive southwest for 4.0 miles to where Route 41 splits off from Route 23 in Egremont. Turn left and follow along the Mill Pond shore for 0.1 mile and bear left on Route 41 (Mount Washington Road bears right). Drive for 4.9 additional miles (passing Berkshire School on the right en route at 3.1 miles) and park in a paved pull-off area on the right adjacent to the trailhead.

### TRAIL DESCRIPTION
Sign in at the kiosk trail register. A large topographic map of the route and other information is posted here. Trail maps may be available as well. Black bears and occasionally endangered timber rattlesnakes are encountered. A nonnative mulberry tree near the kiosk produces sweet fruit relished by birds and mammals. Turn left and follow triangular blue blazes down an initially eroded path and cross a shallow brook on stepping-stones. The path bears left and is built up in a wet area under white ashes and sugar maples. Cross a rill and skirt the edge of a field on a narrow path through grasses, bedstraw, red clover, and daisies in summer. A few red cedars are scattered about.

Enter a shaded hemlock forest. As the path widens you'll also note white pines (some large), maples, and oaks—red, white, and chestnut. Chestnut oak sports wavy-edged leaves. Climb very gradually and then level out. At a signed intersection bear left toward the Appalachian Trail (AT) 2.0 miles distant via

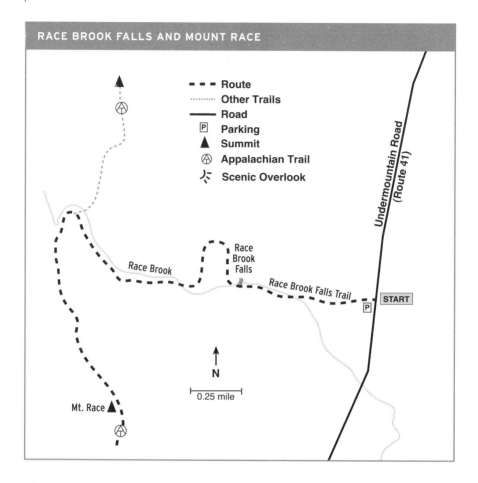

**RACE BROOK FALLS AND MOUNT RACE**

- - - Route
·········· Other Trails
——— Road
P Parking
▲ Summit
Ⓐ Appalachian Trail
⅄ Scenic Overlook

Undermountain Road (Route 41)

Race Brook

Race Brook Falls

Race Brook Falls Trail

P   START

N

0.25 mile

Mt. Race ▲

Ⓐ

Race Brook Falls. Continuing on the essentially unblazed trail soon leads you to the bottom of the Race Brook Lower Falls. During dry seasons it is possible to cross Race Brook below the falls and continue up a steep slope to rejoin the Race Brook Trail. Slippery rocks, high water, and downed trees may make the crossing tricky, however, if you are not sure-footed.

For this hike, bear left to continue on Race Brook Trail through attractive hardwood-hemlock woods. Mountain laurel shrubs make their first appearance, but the best is yet to come. Admire the moss-coated gneiss boulder along cascading Race Brook guarded by sizable hemlocks. The trail bears right, through the shallow gorge. Descend to the brook, cross on stones, and turn left, then right to begin the ascent. Hemlock roots crisscross the pathway. The route climbs higher and higher above the brook on a wide, well-blazed trail. Then begin a steeper climb. Race Brook rushes along perhaps 60 feet below. American chestnut continues to root sprout decades after the blight effectively removed this magnificent species from southern New England's woodlands. As you move farther and farther from the stream, red maple, black birch, and oaks form a leafy canopy over laurel thickets.

You'll reach a signed intersection for Lower Falls Loop Trail on the right, but stay left on the rocky path toward the campsite. The grade increases again, highlighted by ledge outcrops. Switch back to climb the slope. Note the good-sized hemlock perched on a rock on the right. Here in the mixed deciduous-evergreen forest, the summer songs of scarlet tanager (a denizen of oak woods) and hermit thrush (a bird of hardwood and mixed forest) intermingle. Reach an intersection, but turn left as indicated by arrows on a rock to continue the ascent. The path follows the hillside contour. Logs and rockwork ensure the path's integrity on this steep slope.

The rough-barked trunks of chestnut oaks are numerous as you catch a glimpse of a falls through the trees on the right. The slope above you is boulder-strewn. An informal path on the right approaches the base of the falls, but footing is potentially hazardous, so use caution. The falls cascade down layered gneiss bedrock into a clear, green pool. The air is damp and cool. Back on the main trail above, you'll pass below a large hemlock on the left and cross Race Brook—shallow here—on stones. Partway across, marvel at the fantastic view of the high falls from a large, flat rock. Use caution, as rocks are often slippery when wet.

Pass through a narrow gap between gneiss boulders and continue moderately upward under a leafy canopy. Listen for the loud, effervescent refrain of the tiny winter wren during the nesting season. Twenty-foot-high ledge outcrops on the left are bedecked with leafy rock tripe, a lichen that in time turns green and photosynthesizes when wet. There is additional steep climbing followed by a few switchbacks through abundant laurel. From mid-June to early July, the fist-sized masses of nickel-sized laurel blossoms will dazzle you! You will want to have a camera. But just after you've taken numerous shots, you'll find an even more amazing display. Even without the blossoms, this is a very pretty route.

Level out and walk past lowbush blueberry "bushes." Screened views of the Housatonic River valley peek through the trees occasionally. The sound of flowing water presages your return to Race Brook, where cooling breezes prevail. Turn right to follow the crystal-clear mountain stream closely. Rocks jostled by the flow rumble like thunder. Turn left and cross it on a double-log bridge. Water striders skate across the glassy surface of pools. Emerald-green mosses coat the damp stones. One late June, I chanced upon a wood frog far from its vernal-pool breeding site. Its tan coloration made it nearly invisible

**The second falls along the hike fans over gneiss bedrock into a clear pool.**

against the oak-leaf litter. Walk under a pair of wind-thrown trees. Their shallow roots easily separated from the tilted bedrock on which they grew.

At a sign for Race Brook Falls Campsite, bear left and climb toward a long, low, wall-like outcrop, turning right before reaching it. Shortly bear left and then right past wooden tent platforms to a map board and campsite register. A privy stands nearby. You have walked 1.8 miles, and the AT is but 0.2 mile farther. Walk up under maple, beech, oak, and hemlock trees. Bear left, switch back, and ascend the nice stone steps. Level out and enter an even more amazing laurel extravaganza, assuming you're here at the right time. Junction with the AT on the level and turn left (south) toward Mount Race, 1.1 miles distant on a sometimes-steep trail. Cross a wet spot bordered by a bit of highly absorbent sphagnum moss on stones and climb again. A tad of scrambling is required, but nothing major. The wheezy *drink-your-tea* refrain of the robin-sized black, white, and rufous eastern towhee indicates you've entered a shrubbier habitat.

The path follows bedrock outcrops—some showing the polished gouges formed by the abrasive force of thick glacial ice. In sunny openings, watch for the white flowers of tiny three-toothed cinquefoil in early summer. This ridge-top woodland is much shorter, owing to thin soils and a shorter growing season. Soon the first pitch pines appear, and then patches of huckleberry. The pines soon take on a bonsai appearance. Add the luxuriant laurel blossoms, lowbush blueberry, and shrubby bear oak, and the look is somewhat reminiscent of a Japanese garden. The going is fairly level amid laurel and more laurel—the state flower of nearby southern neighbor Connecticut.

You'll reach an outcrop some 20 feet high that you'll have to climb via natural rock steps. On top, note how the gneiss appears to have been melted and recrystallized under tremendous heat and pressure. These rock layers now stand on end. The Taconic Mountains are among the oldest in North America and resulted from the collision of tectonic plates hundreds of millions of years ago. Enjoy the first panoramic views from atop the rock promontory of Mount Race at an elevation of 2,365 feet. Behind you, the rounded form of Mount Everett is only about 2 miles north along the AT. Ahead to the left lie the Twin Lakes across the state line. Short-needled pitch pines no more than 5 or 6 feet tall make for a pleasing dwarf forest on this bony spine.

Continue south another 0.2 mile, which brings you to a large rock cairn where the trail literally begins a breathtaking run along the Mount Race escarpment, offering some of most outstanding unobstructed views of the Housatonic River valley and Berkshire plateau to the east. When you retrace your steps along Race Brook Trail, be sure to watch carefully for the blue triangle blazes, as some turns can be easily missed walking in the opposing direction.

## MORE INFORMATION

Open sunrise to sunset, daily, year-round. Free access. Pets must be on a 10-foot-maximum leash and attended at all times; must have proof of current rabies vaccination. Motorized vehicles, mountain bikes, horses, and alcoholic beverages prohibited. Hunting allowed in season, except along AT corridor and near campsites. Fires allowed in designated areas only. Mount Washington State Forest, RD 3 East Street, Mount Washington, MA 01258; 413-528-0330; http://www.mass.gov/dcr/parks/western/nmas.htm. The Appalachian Trail Management Committee is responsible for maintenance, management, and protection of the nearly 90 miles of the AT in Massachusetts; volunteers do this work, with assistance from the Massachusetts Department of Conservation and Recreation. Massachusetts AT Committee, Berkshire Chapter AMC, P.O. Box 2281, Pittsfield, MA 01202; http://www.amcberkshire.org/at; at@amcberkshire.org; 413-528-6333. Appalachian Mountain Club Regional Trail Coordinator: 413-528-8003.

## TRIP 47
## ALANDER MOUNTAIN

**Location:** Mount Washington
**Rating:** Moderate–Difficult
**Distance:** 5.0 miles
**Elevation Gain:** 790 feet
**Estimated Time:** 3.0–3.5 hours
**Maps:** AMC Massachusetts Trail Map #2: D2, USGS Bash Bish Falls; trail map available online at the Mount Washington State Forest website

**Alander is one of the most scenic summits in the Berkshires. Throw in a roaring mountain brook and attractive mixed woodland alive with birds, and you have a real winner!**

### DIRECTIONS
From the intersection of Route 7 and Route 23/41 in Great Barrington, turn onto Route 23/41 and drive southwest for 4.0 miles. Turn left onto Route 41 south (at Mill Pond), and in 0.1 mile turn right onto Mount Washington Road. Follow it for 9.1 miles (the road becomes East Street in Mount Washington) to the Mount Washington State Forest headquarters on the right. Follow the drive around to the right and the large gravel parking area. Vault toilets are located at the lot's far end.

### TRAIL DESCRIPTION
Trail maps are available at the trailhead kiosk, and hikers are asked to sign in and out. A money pipe for donations is located to the left. Stride across the mowed field where lowbush blueberry plants and tiny four-petaled bluets attract pollinators in spring. Hunts Pond, with its resident Canada geese, lies serenely in a bowl to the left. Soon you'll enter woods of eastern hemlock, beneath which Canada lilies bloom in May. The route is blazed in blue. Listen for the whistled *weeta-weeta-weeteo* song of the black, yellow, and white magnolia warbler, and the buzzy notes of the black-throated green warbler in spring and early summer. After strolling through mixed woods, amble gently down through a second field, where fiery wood lilies brighten the brushy meadow in July. Your destination is visible 2 miles to the west.

At the far end of the meadow, cross babbling Lee Pond Brook on a split-log bridge and turn right onto an old roadway. A stone foundation lies across the

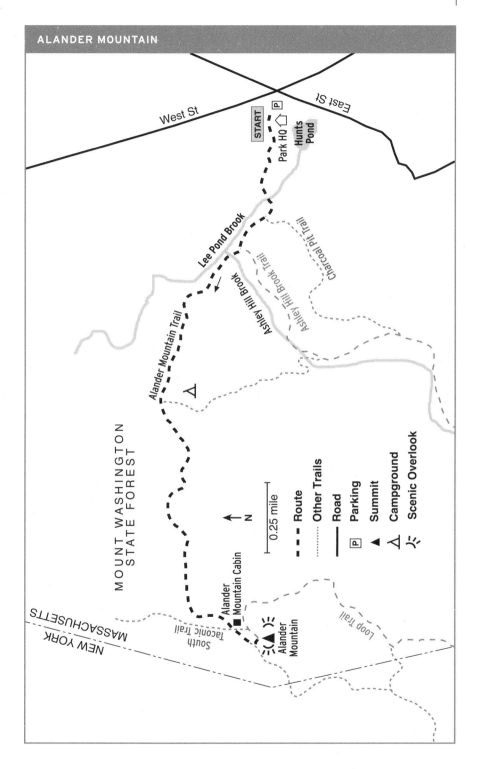

ALANDER MOUNTAIN

West St

East St

START

Park HQ

Hunts Pond

Lee Pond Brook

Ashley Hill Brook Trail

Charcoal Pit Trail

Ashley Hill Brook

Alander Mountain Trail

MOUNT WASHINGTON STATE FOREST

N

0.25 mile

- - - Route
......... Other Trails
——— Road
P Parking
▲ Summit
△ Campground
☀ Scenic Overlook

Alander Mountain Cabin

South Taconic Trail

Alander Mountain

Loop Trail

NEW YORK

MASSACHUSETTS

stream. Charcoal Pit Trail soon leads uphill to the left, but stay straight on the Alander Mountain Trail. This forest was clear-cut between the late 1700s and mid-1800s to make charcoal—fuel for the many area iron furnaces. Note the significant yellow birch on the left, perhaps one of the first to grow back after the last clear-cut. The bark of young trees is much more brassy. At a bench, the Ashley Hill Brook Trail junction is on the left; that trail leads south to Connecticut.

A short descent through hemlocks brings you to cascading Ashley Hill Brook (first audible from some distance) just above its confluence with another high-gradient stream. At the little intersection, turn left to cross the fine split-log bridge over the roaring flow. The scouring, crystal-clear water has polished the schist bedrock to a silvery patina.

Soon you'll arrive at the stone remnants of a possible millrace, where the diverted flow turned a wooden waterwheel. Across the stream, water cascades down picturesque small falls to join the main flow. Climb moderately on the old wood road under the dense shade of deep green hemlocks as the slope drops off sharply to the right. Shade-tolerant American beech (readily identified by its smooth gray bark), yellow birch, and red oak join the conifers. A sign on the right proclaims that the distance to the primitive campground is half a mile. Striped maple is an attractive small understory tree identified by its greenish bark; it, black birch, and black cherry also grow here. The cherry has scaly bark, while that of young black birch is tight.

The roadway continues on level ground through mixed woodland. Little spring beauty delights the eye in May with five delicate white petals veined with pink. This flower thrives in the moist, rich soil adjacent to the treadway. Former heavy use and flowing water have eroded the rocky road that levels out and then steepens as you bear left. The rocks are schist, the tough material that makes up the Taconics. A side trail soon runs left uphill toward the primitive campground. Continue straight, and soon you'll find yourself among mountain laurel shrubs. Laurel boughs support the small cup nests of lovely black-throated blue warblers in spring and summer. Listen for their *beer, beer, bee* songs during the breeding season. After crossing a generally dry stony streambed, the path follows along a pretty little stretch of brook through a shallow hemlock gorge.

More evergreen laurel and a small stream crossing on rocks takes you into maple and oak forest, with a small stream keeping you company on the left. You'll reach a landing that may be a former charcoal-making site. A clue is that the earth is still black from years of use. This is a good spot to pause for a sip of water, as the trail turns right and climbs sharply from here. Head uphill and

**A group of hikers enjoys the expansive three-state views from the open summit of Alander Mountain.**

bear left under hemlocks. This is especially attractive woodland. A tiny metal sign made with a sharp pointed instrument and affixed to a hemlock warns that this is the last source of water during the dry season. Should you use it, be sure to purify it first!

Walk up through lush laurel growth and along a ledge outcrop that parallels the trail on the right. Ahead sits a cabin where hikers may spend the night. A wood-smoke aroma permeates the structure, and a rock tied to a rope serves as a clever counterweight that closes the door behind you. A few feet beyond the cabin, Alander Mountain Trail joins South Taconic Trail. Turn right to follow both up over steplike schist outcrops. Shortly you'll reach an intersection with a small rock cairn and sign. Turn left through brushy scrub (a.k.a. bear) oak and bend right toward the splendid open rock summit of Alander Mountain. The footings of a former fire tower are still obvious on the banded schist.

Lowbush blueberries and glossy-leaved mat-forming bearberry both produce delicate whitish bell-like blossoms in May. In late summer the blueberry flowers transform into copious sweet berries much sought after by bear and hiker alike. Be attuned to the hoarse *chewink* call and the sweet whistled *drink-*

## WARBLER NECKING

Being a birder, I hike with a pair of binoculars slung around my neck. But most hikers do not. And who can blame them? Adding optics to the already considerable weight of pack, water bottles, and trekking poles can dampen your enthusiasm. But having a pair of lightweight, close-focus binoculars can add immensely to your enjoyment of the great outdoors. I'm not just talking about birds; binoculars are great for getting vicariously close to any number of things, from identifying trees by their leaves 60 feet above the ground to observing brook trout in a clear stream to watching colorful butterflies nectaring in a flower-studded meadow. But when it comes to fully appreciating the wealth of bird life around you, a pair of binoculars is almost essential. By the way, birders have a name for the avocational hazard caused by hours of gazing into the tree tops—"warbler neck."

Many of "our" avian summer residents would actually better be described as tropical species that journey northward in spring to take advantage of the bountiful smorgasbord of insect life in our awakening forests. They court, breed, raise young, and then return to the tropics long before cold weather intrudes here. Among these so-called neotropical (New World topical) migrants are a whole host of flycatchers, thrushes, vireos, and wood warblers.

That last group has collectively been dubbed the butterflies of the bird world due to their exquisite plumages and animated movements. Seldom exceeding 5.5 inches in length, about twenty species breed in Berkshire forests, shrublands, and wetland habitats, with the majority being restricted to woodlands. Warblers (none of which actually "warble") often spend their time high in the canopy searching out moth caterpillars and other insects injurious to those forests. Most nest at various levels within or below the canopy, and some, like ovenbirds, nest on the ground. Ovenbirds build domed nests with side entrances that look like the ovens of old. Many warblers, including chestnut-sided warblers, construct neat cups in low shrubby vegetation. Others seldom venture down to where we can get a good look at them—fiery-throated Blackburnian warblers typify that scenario.

Much has been written about the plight of neotropical migrants, as their wintering ranges in the tropics shrink due to land clearing. Here at home, some species are under threat due to loss of breeding habitats. Then too, global climate change will have far-reaching effects, especially for those that require upper-elevation evergreen woodlands for nesting.

*your-tea* song of the eastern towhee, a large black, rusty, and white member of the sparrow family. Gaze skyward for migrant hawks in spring and fall, and vultures all year except winter.

This is the most open and arguably the most spectacular summit in the region; it offers wonderful views of the Catskill Mountains, some 45 miles to the west (right). Nearby, but behind you, is the rounded form of Mount Everett (Trip 44). To your left is an undulating wooded ridge with three bumps. Mount Ashley is the leftmost, Mount Frissell sits in the middle, and Mount Brace (in Connecticut) stands farthest right. Note the rock cairn on the latter's open summit. Ahead and below you lies the verdant Hudson River valley. New York's Route 22 is the ribbon of blacktop that runs south and north along the western side of the Taconics, one of this country's oldest mountain ranges, at approximately 400 million years. You'll want to linger here. When ready to return, retrace your steps, but be sure to turn right at the small cairn in the trail.

## MORE INFORMATION

Open sunrise to sunset, year-round. Free access. Pets must be on a 10-foot-maximum leash and attended at all times; must have proof of current rabies vaccination. Motorized vehicles and alcoholic beverages prohibited. Mount Washington State Forest, RD 3 East Street, Mount Washington, MA 01258; 413-528-0330; http://www.mass.gov/dcr/parks/western/mwas.htm.

## TRIP 48
## LIME KILN FARM WILDLIFE SANCTUARY

**Location:** Sheffield
**Rating:** Easy
**Distance:** 1.75 miles
**Elevation Gain:** 135 feet
**Estimated Time:** 1.5 hours
**Maps:** USGS Ashley Falls; trail map available online

**This excursion offers rolling hayfields with magnificent vistas of Mount Everett, wetlands, meadows, and forests alive with song-birds, and a towering reminder of a forgotten industry.**

## DIRECTIONS

From the north: From the center of Sheffield, at the U.S. Post Office, travel south on Route 7 for 1.1 miles to Silver Street on the right (note the tourist-oriented directional sign) and follow it for 1.1 miles to the sanctuary entrance and crushed stone parking lot (suitable for twelve vehicles) on the right.

From the south: From Route 7 at the Connecticut border, drive north on Route 7 for 3.6 miles to Silver Street on the left (note the sign) and follow directions above.

## TRAIL DESCRIPTION

From the parking lot, where you'll see a wonderful view of Mount Everett (elevation 2,624 feet, 3 miles distant), approach the colorful orientation panel with large map, trail information, and adjacent admission box among apple trees. Trail maps are available here. Blue plastic discs indicating outbound travel mark the route, with yellow ones indicating return travel.

Amble under a canopy of apple trees down the former dairy farm lane—hayfield to the right and marsh to the left—where sweetflag thrives; actually a relative of jack-in-the-pulpit, it has greenish-yellow flower spikes the size and shape of your pinkie and cattail-like leaves. Pink-flowering hairy willow herb borders the wetland edge in summer. You'll reach a small farm pond on the left just before a trail junction. In summer the pond is alive with gulping green frogs and bellowing bullfrogs.

Here Lime Kiln Loop splits. Continue straight up into another hayfield, passing weathering marble outcrops on the right. Marked by a signpost, the path soon bears right and briefly enters regenerating woody vegetation that includes columnar eastern red cedars (junipers) and invasive exotic autumn olive trees that sport silvery red fruits. Emerge into the field again briefly, turn right, and then bear left at another post. Follow the broad path over soggy ground and pass a small quarry area on the left largely hidden by woody growth.

The trail leads gently uphill and passes several corky-barked hackberry trees unusual in these parts. Two species of butterfly caterpillar—hackberry emperor and tawny emperor—feed exclusively on their leaves. After bearing left, you'll notice the cement footings of a former trestle on the right over which marble rock was conveyed to the top of the limekiln (not visible from here). A few feet farther, a wooden bench represents a fine spot for a snack as you survey a larger sloping hayfield and its Taconic backdrop. Sanctuary hayfields are cut annually by a neighboring dairy farmer—but not until late summer—to give grassland-nesting birds time to bring forth their broods.

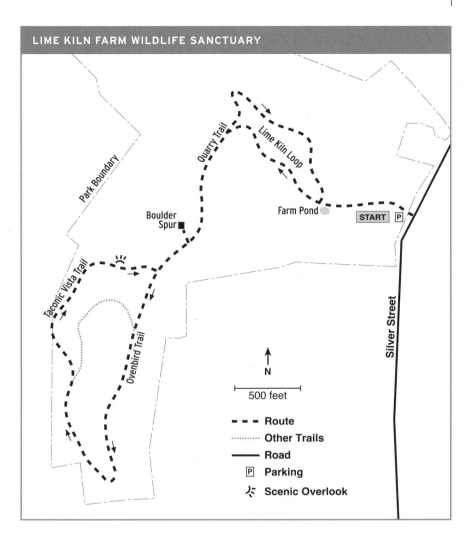

LIME KILN FARM WILDLIFE SANCTUARY

Park Boundary

Quarry Trail

Lime Kiln Loop

Boulder Spur

Farm Pond

START   P

Taconic Vista Trail

Ovenbird Trail

Silver Street

N

500 feet

- - - Route
.......... Other Trails
——— Road
P   Parking
  Scenic Overlook

At this point, Lime Kiln Loop turns right and follows the field edge down past the limekiln, and back to the parking lot, but turn left instead to follow Quarry Trail. You pass a monument to the three women who formerly lived on the property and are responsible for its designation as conservation land in 1990. Reenter the woodland edge and shortly bear left. Soon you'll reach several former marble quarry pits. The first is often filled with water and may serve as a vernal pool. The lovely red-and-yellow blossoms of wild columbine grace the path's borders in June.

Continue over the wide grassy treadway where oriental bittersweet vines drape the trees. This invasive exotic is a real curse as it strangles native trees and robs them of sunlight. In fall the yellow fruit husks split open, revealing bright red-orange fruits consumed and spread by birds such as cedar wax-wings and robins. Before long, you'll enter deciduous woodland and arrive at Boulder Spur on the right. Walk a short distance down this side path for a close look at an imposing angular glacial erratic.

Back at the Quarry Trail, turn right to continue. You'll soon pass a junction with the Taconic Vista Trail on the right, but continue straight. The old farm road—now designated as Ovenbird Trail—passes through mixed woodland that includes hemlock and white pine (some large). Another junction with Ovenbird Trail comes up on the right, but continue straight. Interestingly, yellow-rumped warblers nest among the pines a bit farther on the left, although they are much more apt to choose high-elevation nest sites in the Berkshires.

Ovenbird Trail eventually turns right along the property line. This pleasant path through woodland of oak, black birch, big-tooth aspen, hemlock, and witch hazel, parallels a linear ledge outcrop rising on the right. At a junction on the right, Ovenbird Trail climbs up a very modest slope and returns to Quarry Trail, but continue straight on Taconic Vista Trail. Later it bears right, then left, to pass over and around the end of the ledge, which is softened by an emerald mat of moss. Even after heavy snowfall, the ground is relatively bare below the hemlocks as their dense foliage intercepts and holds much of the fluffy white stuff. So far at least, the hemlocks appear to be unaffected by the hemlock woolly adelgid, which is advancing northward from Connecticut.

After passing a large fallen hemlock trunk cut to make way for the trail, you'll walk through a luxuriant patch of evergreen Christmas fern before turning right to follow an old barbed-wire fence line up into mixed woodland that includes yellow birch. At a signpost marked "Vista," turn left and walk a few feet to the upper edge of a hayfield that affords a stunning view north and west of blue rolling ridges. These fields are loaded with colorful butterflies and darting dragonflies in summer.

After enjoying the view, continue on the main path gently uphill. One fall day, I was amazed to spot a pair of mating stick insects on the trunk of a sapling hickory where they were nearly invisible. The path jogs a bit and soon rejoins the wide former roadway known as Quarry Trail. Turn left and follow the yellow blazes back to the monument to the property donors and the junction with Lime Kiln Loop on the right.

Instead of turning right, however, stay straight and walk along the large field edge down to a signpost. After leaf fall the 40-foot-high limekiln is visible to your right. At the post, turn right and approach the cement cylinder that

**White-tailed deer, like this eight-point buck, usually remain within a several-square-mile area.**

is the former kiln. Built in 1909, this enterprise lasted only three years before it was abandoned. The marble rock was dumped in the top and cooked at temperatures of 1,400 degrees until the moisture was driven off and the rock reduced to powdery lime used in agriculture and many industrial applications. Be sure to stay clear of the kiln and adjacent structures.

Past the kiln on the left stand two enormous hemlocks that must be several hundred years old. Continue down the wide former roadway lined by prickly ash shrubs. While not an ash at all, the branches are certainly prickly and you'll want to avoid contact with them. Walk along the left margin of another field and turn right where a couple of lacy deciduous conifers—American larches—stand. Their needle tufts become a lovely yellow in fall before dropping off. As you continue, note the vegetated wetland on your left. Here alder flycatchers nest in summer. Their diagnostic breeding "song" is a hiccupping *fee-bee-o*.

In summer and fall, plump American woodcocks sometimes flush from beneath the shrubby growth right of the path just before you close the Lime Kiln Loop near the farm pond. Waxwings and robins gobble up the hard bluish berries of cedars in fall and winter. Turn left to stroll back to your vehicle.

## MORE INFORMATION

Open daily, year-round, dawn to dusk. Admission fee: $3 for adults, $2 for children (3–12) and seniors, free for children under 3, Mass Audubon members, and Sheffield residents. No toilet facilities. Dogs, vehicles, hunting, fishing, trapping, and collecting prohibited. Owned and managed by Mass Audubon, 472 West Mountain Road, Lenox, MA 01240; 413-637-0320; berkshires@massaudubon.org; http://www.massaudubon.org.

## TRIP 49
## BARTHOLOMEW'S COBBLE RESERVATION

$ 🚶 📍

**Location:** Sheffield
**Rating:** Moderate
**Distance:** 4.0 miles
**Elevation Gain:** 310 feet
**Estimated Time:** 2.0–2.5 hours
**Maps:** USGS Ashley Falls; trail map available online

**Long beloved by botanists and fern enthusiasts, the Cobble offers terrific birding and wildflower-viewing opportunities, interesting geology, and fabulous panoramic views from Hurlburt's Hill.**

### DIRECTIONS

From the center of Sheffield (at the U.S. Post Office), follow Route 7 south 1.7 miles to the Route 7 and Route 7A intersection. Turn right onto Route 7A and follow it 0.4 mile to Rannapo Road on the right. Cross the railroad tracks and drive 1.5 miles to Weatogue Road on the right. Follow Weatogue Road 0.1 mile and turn left into the reservation's gravel parking area with space for more than twenty vehicles.

### TRAIL DESCRIPTION

Check in at the visitor center or, if visiting when the center is closed, examine the map kiosk at the trailhead to the left. Trail maps are available at the visitor center (both inside and out). Trail intersections are signed. Much of the route is blazed in white.

From the kiosk, walk left and follow Eaton Trail up the rocky slope under junipers (a.k.a. eastern red cedars). You are ascending the smaller of two cobbles ("cobble" is a New England word for hill), composed primarily of erosion-resistant quartzite rock and softer marble. The amalgamation of these two rock types and the soils they produce gives rise to great botanical diversity here. Note the large outcrops, capped by polypody ferns, on both sides of the trail. Delicate maidenhair spleenwort, just one of 50 ferns and allied species to be found in this botanist's wonderland, thrive at the base of the rocks. You'll soon reach the top, where a bucolic view of the Housatonic River valley is yours from a well-placed wooden bench.

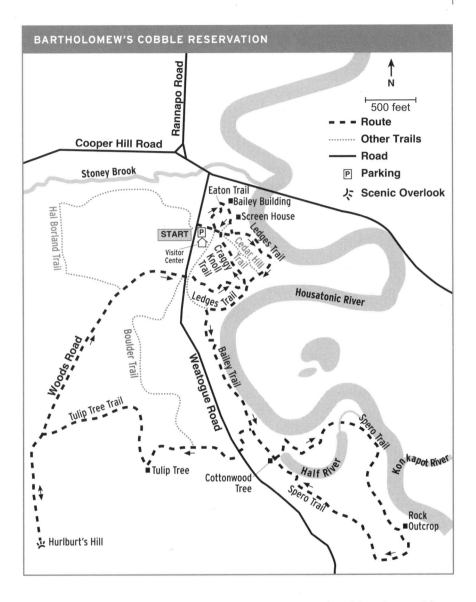

Bear left and proceed downhill under junipers to the old Bailey Building, a former museum. Bear right under white pines on a wide path, and soon you'll arrive at a three-way split. Take the middle branch where invasive garlic mustard dominates in spring. Eastern hemlocks and white pines shade the intersection with Ledges Trail that leads left toward the river. The larger of two moss-and-fern-covered quartzite cobbles hems in the path on the right. Soon steps lead down to the edge of the Housatonic floodplain, where spring's rising

**From the Eaton Trail a bucolic panorama of the Housatonic River valley presents itself.**

waters deposit silt. This flat pasture, nearly encircled by the river, is known as Corbin's Neck. One day it may be cut off by the flow and become an oxbow pond. Watch for bald eagles year-round and fish-hunting ospreys during their spring and fall migrations.

In early spring watch for the attractive pleated leaves of false hellebore rising from the silt and the dainty pantaloons of dutchman's breeches closer to the cliff face. The latter are among "spring ephemerals" that flower before unfurling tree leaves shade the ground. White ashes predominate, but maples are present too. You'll climb a bit to the Cedar Hill Trail intersection under large oaks; continue left on Ledges Trail, which skirts the cobble. After a few steps up, note the massive white ash, more than 3 feet in diameter, on the right. The path continues above and adjacent to the Housatonic and along a marble and quartzite cliff face topped by junipers. Sinewy ironwood, hop hornbeam (both have very hard wood), and birch clothe the slope down to the water's edge.

At a small clearing, turn left onto Bailey Trail and cross a small brook. Skunk cabbage and red osier dogwood thrive in the moist soil. Watch for the "hairy" poison ivy vine snaking up the black cherry on the right. A bit farther, large wild grape vines hang from the trees. After a number of small feeder stream crossings, and being dwarfed by some sizable white pines, reach the Bailey Trail/Tulip Tree Trail junction as you enter a conifer stand. Continue straight under more towering pines. Listen for the sweet trill of pine warblers during spring and early summer. Shallow pools dot the floodplain in spring.

You'll arrive at Half River, an oxbow pond that was once part of the river's main stem. Here Spero Loop turns left. A cottonwood of truly monumental proportions dominates the intersection. This giant, hollow at its base, is more than 6 feet in diameter. It is easily the largest tree I've seen anywhere in the county! Turn left and tread through a floodplain dominated by silver maples tolerant of periodic inundation, and then along the edge of a wet meadow that may not always be passable. The view of the cornfields and hills beyond the undulating river is lovely. The Konkapot River enters the Housatonic on the opposite bank.

Climb out of the floodplain and turn left at the fork to remain on Spero Loop. An interesting schist outcrop juts out of the oak woodland on the left. Schist is also considerably harder than the eroded marble bedrock that underlies the river valley. Enjoy a wonderful view south into Connecticut upon reaching another meadow before beginning another gradual climb into a forest of pines and black birch. A fluffy barred owl feather suspended from a twig alerted me to the presence of this nocturnal mouser during an April outing. The cooling effect of deep evergreen shade is readily apparent under hemlocks as you close the loop and arrive back at Half River. Check the protruding logs for basking painted turtles, and watch for cavity-nesting wood ducks, which may take flight upon your approach.

After crossing a boardwalk spanning a trickle that is nonetheless carving a small ravine, you'll find yourself once more among quartzite boulders. Striking emerald-green mosses pad the face of one low vertical rock face on the left. A big American beech leans out over the water a bit farther. An owl pellet— perhaps from a barred owl and containing the bones of meadow voles—lay at its base on my April hike. Maidenhair fern and round-lobed hepatica do well in the nutrient-rich soil at the bottom of the slope. When you reach the giant cottonwood, continue straight for a short distance to Tulip Tree Trail on the left.

Climb moderately through pines and hemlocks; soon you'll reach the gravel Weatogue Road. Cross it and follow the trail up into mixed and rocky woodland of oak, ash, hemlock, and pine. Continue past the intersection with Boulder Trail. A massive, columnar tulip tree more than 3 feet in diameter and with a spreading crown awaits you. This imposing species, near its northern range limits in the southern Berkshires, is the largest tree of our eastern forests. The treadway may be a bit muddy here during wet weather, but white blazing denotes the trail. Bits of rusty barbed wire and a luxuriant growth of invasive Japanese barberry and multiflora rose indicates former disturbance by humans and livestock.

As you enter a small field, be on the lookout for wild turkey and ruffed grouse, two game species that thrive in a mosaic of habitats. Bear left and walk up to meet Woods Road. Turn left to follow it steadily uphill on a mowed path toward the summit of Hurlburt's Hill. Bluebird nest boxes on wooden posts flank the trail. You might want to catch your breath and look back over your shoulder at the splendid view unfolding, but it only gets better as you continue up the hillside hayfield. From two wooden benches facing north near the crest, a magnificent 180-degree vista offers unobstructed views of Mount Everett and the southern Taconics to the northwest and East Mountain to the northeast. Wow! This is also a fine spot from which to spot southward migrating hawks in the fall.

Retrace your steps down the hill, past the intersection with Tulip Tree Trail, and enter pine, hickory, ash, and cherry woods with barberry and another invasive exotic—winged euonymus. Both escaped from cultivation long ago. A few old apple trees produce fruit for deer and other wildlife. Continue steadily downslope and bear right at the edge of the last field to Weatogue Road. Cross over to Craggy Knoll Trail (crossing Ledges Trail) and walk under junipers—some dead—up to the top of the larger cobble.

Ledges heavily padded with mosses and ferns rise on the left. The marble has been intriguingly eroded over the eons. Listen for the scolding chatter of red squirrels among the pines as you make your way through the cobble outcrops. In late spring the delicate pink blossoms of herb Robert are ubiquitous. Finally, descend rather steeply from the promontory around a quartzite boulder with vertical layering, reaching the Cedar Hill Trail/Ledges Trail intersection. Bear left to the visitor center.

## MORE INFORMATION

Trails open daily year-round, sunrise to sunset. Museum and visitor center open year-round, daily, 9 A.M. to 4:30 P.M. (closed Sundays and Mondays, December to March). Nonmember adult entrance fee $5, child (6–12) $1. Trustees members free. Pets and mountain biking are not permitted. Public programs presented on a regular basis. Bartholomew's Cobble, P.O. Box 128, Ashley Falls, MA 01222; 413-229-8600; westregion@ttor.org; http://www.thetrustees.org.

## FANCIFUL FERNS

Ferns are doubtless the most recognized nonflowering plants throughout the Berkshires. Nearly 65 forms are native. And there is no better place in the entire region to find a diverse array than Bartholomew's Cobble Reservation. Some 50 species of ferns and fern allies (includes club mosses) thrive there. This is due in part to the sweet alkaline soils resulting from the breakdown of marble bedrock. Some species, like maidenhair spleenwort, require such a limey base. Others need the high-organic content of moist, rich woodlands, for example maidenhair fern. A few, like bracken, do just fine on sandy, almost sterile sites. Some thrive on rocky outcrops, common polypody among them. And still others, like royal fern, must have their toes in the saturated soils of wetlands.

All trace their ancestry back several hundreds of millions of years. Like dragonflies and horsetails, two ancient groups still with us today, the tree ferns of the Carboniferous era some 300 to 350 million years ago were giants that would have towered over today's varieties. But the basic fern blueprint remains unchanged. To be blunt, fern reproduction boggles the mind. Spores are their means of propagation rather than seeds. The spores are formed in tiny bodies on the undersides of the leaves (fronds), or on so-called fertile fronds separate from the sterile (green, leafy) ones. The familiar Christmas fern is an example of the former type, while sensitive fern follows the latter design.

And here is where it gets a little weird. Wherever the spores are housed, when ripe, they are released to float on air currents; some land on soil where they grow into tiny heart-shaped plantlets that have both female eggs and male sperm. The sperm swims over to the egg and fertilizes it to produce an embryo that begins to grow. Eventually it forms an independent plant that matures into a full-fledged fern. Amazing!

Some species, like the evergreen wood fern, remain green and alive aboveground year-round, while the majority of local species die back to their rootstocks, only to reemerge in spring as "fiddleheads." Young unfurled fiddleheads of ostrich fern are harvested and sold in the produce departments of upscale supermarkets, but other species are reputed to contain naturally occurring carcinogens. Another fun fact about ferns is that in late spring, female ruby-throated hummingbirds gather billfuls of soft fuzz from cinnamon fern stalks to line their tiny nests.

## TRIP 50
## SAGES RAVINE AND BEAR MOUNTAIN

**Location:** Mount Washington; Salisbury, CT
**Rating:** Difficult
**Distance:** 3.9 miles
**Elevation Gain:** 915 feet
**Estimated Time:** 3.0–3.5 hours
**Maps:** AMC Massachusetts Trail Map #2: E3, USGS Ashley Falls

**This journey takes you into a charming chasm—a veritable mile of delights. Contrasting with that is a short but tough climb to Connecticut's loftiest perch, offering sublime views.**

### DIRECTIONS

From the intersection of Route 7 and Route 23/41 in Great Barrington, turn onto Route 23/41 and drive southwest for 4.0 miles. Turn left onto Route 41 south (at Mill Pond), and in 0.1 mile turn right onto Mount Washington Road. Follow Mount Washington Road (its name changes to East Road in Mount Washington) for 11.4 miles, past the entrances to Mount Everett State Reservation at 7.3 miles and Mount Washington State Forest at 8.8 miles. The last 2.3 miles are on gravel. A small parking area, with space for about five vehicles, is on the left, approximately 100 feet beyond the 1906 granite marker signifying the Massachusetts/Connecticut border. Be sure not to block the metal gate. The road may be closed in winter.

### TRAIL DESCRIPTION

From the parking area, walk around the metal gate on a nice wide, level, grassy track. Showy mountain laurel (the Connecticut state flower) is profligate to the right, while dense ferns—tall interrupted fern and shorter New York and hay-scented ferns—populate a glade on the left. At the trail fork stay left to cross an unnamed brook on stones. The right fork leads to AMC's Northwest Camp, wonderfully situated on a rise under hemlocks. Soon Sages Ravine Brook comes into view to your left and the forest diversifies into multiple shades of green—hemlock and beech—and then virtually pure deciduous growth.

You are walking on an old built-up roadway. It doesn't take long to come upon the first pretty little cascade, but don't get carried away—this is only a teaser. Soon the narrowing path turns rocky and the grade increases through

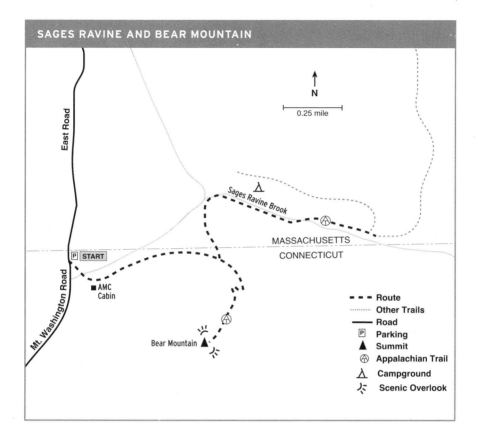

**SAGES RAVINE AND BEAR MOUNTAIN**

laurels. A lush understory of American beech sprouts, striped maple, and laurel fills up the space between big yellow and black birches, then maples, ashes, and oaks. You're now treading on level ground through spacious open woodland along the base of Bear Mountain, which you'll climb later. The oaks—sporting more than one trunk—hint at past logging.

A sign on the left and yellow paint on trees announces that you've entered the 500-foot-wide Appalachian Trail (AT) corridor, and within moments you reach the fabled footpath. Here you have a choice. Turn right to scale Bear Mountain first, or turn left to visit Sages Ravine. If weather is not an issue, turn left and stride downhill under a mixed evergreen-deciduous canopy to arrive at a wooden sign that reads, "You are entering a very fragile environment. Please camp at designated sites only. Help this area to recover from overuse and abuse. Thank you." Here the blue-blazed Paradise Trail takes off to the right, but turn left to continue on the white-blazed AT as it proceeds moderately downhill through a thick stand of striped maple saplings and over stone steps toward the inviting rush of water in motion.

**Looking north, Mount Race and Mount Everett are clearly visible from the massive cairn-like tower atop Bear Mountain.**

The grade eases along Sages Ravine Brook, where the path bears right and runs along steep ledge faces. The next mile or so is without doubt one of the loveliest stream strolls in the region. Each time you think you have gazed upon the most enchanting scene, another presents itself in short order. Spinulose wood fern blankets the lower reaches of the mountain as you arrive at a long double-split-log bridge leading across the stream to Sages Ravine Campsite on a hemlock-shaded bench. But continue straight ahead on the AT, now a rocky, narrow path close to the clear brook. Pools that harbor native brook trout are interspersed with lovely little cascades. Some "brookies" here attain all of 6 inches in length.

At one point a large pool is hemmed in by sheer ledge. Rocks tumble in the current and create a rumbling accompaniment to the birdsong that is difficult to appreciate above the flow. As you proceed downstream, the scene becomes progressively more enchanting. Take your time moving through the ravine. After all, how often do we experience such natural delights? Deep green American yew caps boulders, and wood sorrel (with clover-like leaves) thrives in patches on the forest floor under the impressive light-catching hemlocks. A high-gradient feeder brook empties into Sages Ravine Brook, and a laurel shrub gaily marks the confluence. The AT climbs jauntily above the rock-lined chasm. From above, you can see that boulders have scoured the sides of the vertical walls like a mortar with pestle.

Soon you cross a flow that bounces precipitously down the right slope from one rock ledge to the next in multiple cascades. It's only a sideshow to the main act, but a delight nonetheless. These rocky tributaries cause the main stream to flow with even more gusto. Work your way down through angular boulders. The battlements of a formidable ledge rise above on the right slope. The path leads down to the brook's bank again at a 3-foot-high, yet thundering, falls. The volume of water charging down the ravine is truly impressive. Where the stream makes a serpentine bend under hemlocks, you'll delight to another plunge. This second, actually split into two, is more than 12 feet high. Gazing upstream from an elevated location, the falls align themselves into a truly sublime scene. Note the trough that the torrent gouged into tilted bedrock to the right during flood events.

After reaching a lofty height of about 45 feet above the churning flow, you'll descend again over expertly constructed stone steps into a cool microclimate streamside. What a wonderful relief on a hot summer's day! Here grows long beech fern, a small fern identified by its bottom two leaflets, which point downward. Soon you'll notice a sign affixed to a tree on the right that welcomes hikers to Connecticut. You are actually in Massachusetts here, but only about 1,000 feet north of the state line. The AT crosses the brook on large rocks, but this is the turnaround point for this portion of the hike. The good news is that you'll have a second opportunity to revel in the many delights of Sages Ravine. Retrace your steps to where the initial access trail enters from the right.

Now it's time for a very different hiking experience. If your energy level is low by this point, pass up the ascent of Bear Mountain for another day, as it is very challenging, albeit brief. Otherwise forge on, following the AT as it bears left along the slope contour under a deciduous canopy. But make sure you still have enough drinking water. Descend, and then climb a series of stone staircases over slanting bedrock. The path does zigzag up the steep gradient. You'll negotiate rock ledges where some easy handholds will aid your progress. White blazes are few heading up, and the going can be tricky, so watch your footing; this hike is certainly not recommended during icy or wet conditions.

A few herbaceous dogwoods—bunchberries—have gained a foothold in the scant soil, while mountain azalea, common polypody fern (the little one clinging to rocks), and lowbush blueberries eke out a living in sun-dappled spots. The first pitch pines appear on the right, and more laurel—loaded with blossoms in late June and early July. Ascend more bedrock, but not as steeply. Look carefully at the grooved and polished surface of this stone. Glaciers scoured it some 14,000 years ago. If you have a compass—and you should— note that the grooves line up north-south, the direction of flow of the mile-thick ice sheet.

An evocative pine-resin aroma wafts in the air of sunny gaps as you near the summit. Blueberries and related huckleberry shrubs (note huckleberry's shiny resin dots on the undersides of its leaves) populate the top, as do gray birch, oaks, and cherry. A stone tower appearing as a giant rock cairn sits atop the highest peak entirely within Connecticut's boundaries. The tower has been rebuilt three times. A granite plaque placed in 1885 refers to it as the highest point. More recently it was discovered that the highest point is actually on the south slope of Mount Frissell (2,380 feet in Connecticut), a peak whose summit is across the border in Massachusetts. Given that there are no particularly panoramic views from that slope, Bear Mountain (at 2,316 feet) is to me a much more satisfying high point.

Climb the mound of flat schist flagstones from the backside for sublime views—some stones are loose, so step gingerly. To the near north are Mount Race and Mount Everett along the AT, while the Housatonic River valley and Twin Lakes in Connecticut lie seemingly at arm's length to the east. On a completely clear day, five states may be visible. When ready to start back, retrace your steps to the access trail on the left and follow it back to your vehicle.

## MORE INFORMATION

Camping permitted in designated areas only. Carry in, carry out all trash. Motorized vehicles, horses, hunting, and fires prohibited. Appalachian Mountain Club, Connecticut Chapter, Northwest Camp Committee; nwcamp@ct-amc.org; http://www.ct-amc.org/nwcamp. Appalachian Trail Conference, P.O. Box 807, Harpers Ferry, WV 25425.

# INDEX

# ABOUT THE AUTHOR

**RENÉ LAUBACH** is the director of the Massachusetts Audubon Society's Berkshire Wildlife Sanctuaries. He has been an active birder for many years and is the co-author of *AMC's Best Day Hikes in Connecticut*. He has written seven books on natural history.

# The Appalachian Mountain Club

Founded in 1876, the AMC is the nation's oldest outdoor recreation and conservation organization. The AMC promotes the protection, enjoyment, and wise use of the mountains, rivers, and trails of the Northeast outdoors.

## People
We are nearly 90,000 members in 12 chapters, 16,000 volunteers, and over 450 full time and seasonal staff. Our chapters reach from Maine to Washington, D.C.

## Outdoor Adventure and Fun
We offer more than 8,000 trips each year, from local chapter activities to major excursions worldwide, for every ability level and outdoor interest—from hiking and climbing to paddling, snowshoeing, and skiing.

## Great Places to Stay
We host more than 150,000 guest nights each year at our AMC lodges, huts, camps, shelters, and campgrounds. Each AMC Destination is a model for environmental education and stewardship.

## Opportunities for Learning
We teach people the skills to be safe outdoors and to care for the natural world around us through programs for children, teens, and adults, as well as outdoor leadership training.

## Caring for Trails
We maintain more than 1,700 miles of trails throughout the Northeast, including nearly 350 miles of the Appalachian Trail in five states.

## Protecting Wild Places
We advocate for land and riverway conservation, monitor air quality, and work to protect alpine and forest ecosystems throughout the Northern Forest and Highlands regions.

## Engaging the Public
We seek to educate and inform our own members and an additional 2 million people annually through AMC Books, our website, our White Mountain visitor centers, and AMC Destinations.

## Join Us!
Members support our mission while enjoying great AMC programs, our award-winning *AMC Outdoors* magazine, and special discounts. Visit www.outdoors.org or call 617-523-0636 for more information.

**THE APPALACHIAN MOUNTAIN CLUB**
Recreation • Education • Conservation
www.outdoors.org

# The AMC Berkshire Chapter

The Appalachian Mountain Club's Berkshire Chapter offers a wide range of outdoor activities in western Massachusetts, including hiking, backpacking, paddling, snowshoeing, and skiing, as well as social, family, and young member events. AMC's Berkshire Chapter maintains the Massachusetts sections of the Metacomet-Monadnock and Appalachian trails. You can learn more about this chapter by visiting www.outdoors.org/chapters.

To view a list of AMC activities in Western Massachusetts and other parts of the Northeast, visit: trips.outdoors.org.

# AMC Book Updates

AMC Books strives to keep our guidebooks as up-to-date as possible to help you plan safe and enjoyable adventures. If after publishing a book we learn that trails are relocated or route or contact information has changed, we will post the updated information online. Before you hit the trail, check for updates at www.outdoors.org/publications/books/updates.

While hiking or paddling, if you notice discrepancies with the trail description or map, or if you find any other errors in the book, please let us know by submitting them to amcbookupdates@outdoors.org or in writing to Books Editor, c/o AMC, 5 Joy Street, Boston, MA 02108. We will verify all submissions and post key updates each month.

AMC Books is dedicated to being a recognized leader in outdoor publishing. Thank you for your participation.

AMC BOOKS & MAPS

**EXPLORE THE POSSIBILITIES**

# More Books from the Outdoor Experts

## Massachusetts Trail Guide, 9th Edition

BY JOHN S. BURK

This revised and updated edition provides detailed descriptions of more than 400 trails across the state, including 70 new entries. Find your way easily and accurately with brand new GPS-rendered maps of the state's most popular areas—including the Blue Hills, Mount Wachusett, and Mount Greylock.

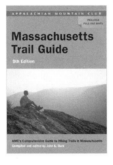

**ISBN: 978-1-934028-25-4**
$24.95

## Catskill Mountain Guide, 2nd Edition

BY PETER W. KICK

This guide offers hikers up-to-date coverage of more than 300 miles of trails in the Catskill Mountains. Inside you'll find detailed descriptions of trails to suit every ability level. This guide features full-color, pull-out, GPS-rendered maps, more than 90 trail descriptions, and guidelines for backcountry hikers.

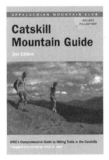

**ISBN: 978-1-934028-19-3**
$23.95

## Southern New Hampshire Trail Guide, 2nd Edition

BY GENE DANIELL AND STEVEN D. SMITH

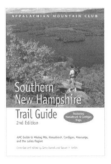

This up-to-date edition describes nearly 200 trails from Monadnock, Cardigan, and Kearsarge to the Lakes Region and the seacoast. You'll also find coverage of the three largest state parks, Pisgah, Bear Brook, and Pawtuckaway.

**ISBN: 978-1929173-60-0**
$18.95

## Quiet Water Massachusetts, Connecticut, and Rhode Island

BY ALEX WILSON AND JOHN HAYES

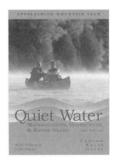

This guide reveals more than 100 spectacular ponds, lakes, and rivers ideally suited for canoeing and kayaking. Each entry includes a detailed tour description, now made even easier to use with the addition of new summaries that detail the distance, habitat type, and natural highlights of each area.

**ISBN: 978-1-929173-49-5**
$16.95